D0425330

SOCIAL PSYCHOLOGY

THE BASES OF BEHAVIOR CALLED SOCIAL

BY

ROBERT H. GAULT, Ph.D.

PROFESSOR OF PSYCHOLOGY IN
NORTHWESTERN UNIVERSITY

Editor of the *Journal of Criminal
Law and Criminology.*

88094

NEW YORK
HENRY HOLT AND COMPANY
1923

COPYRIGHT, 1923

BY

HENRY HOLT AND COMPANY

July, 1923

PRINTED IN THE
UNITED STATES OF AMERICA

Dedicated
TO
ANNE LEE GAULT

PREFACE

In relation to questions of social psychology, it is of utmost importance that readers develop the open, interrogative mind. The scope of the whole subject is so magnificent and the phenomena so many angled that it is particularly difficult to set them in proper array. It is in no spirit of cocksureness that these pages are written.

There are certain fairly well-established facts concerning the original nature of lower animals and men that are shaking our faith in those chapters on the instincts of human kind that found a place in our psychological texts of yesterday. Human nature is seen, not as something eternally fixed and unchangeable, but as altering slowly in response to multiform environing conditions. *Instincts* have been overdone; undifferentiated *instinct* is taking their place, and it is of interest to the student mainly because it is seen as a cornerstone of an infinitely complex web of habits. It is not possible to build a social psychology upon so-called unalterable *instincts* alone as a foundation, nor yet upon *instinct* apart from the habits that are woven with it; and these habits are our sense of social unity; our conventions and customs, the great mass of which are informally passed from person to person and less frequently are crystallized into laws and institutions.

This proposition makes mutual acquaintanceship and understanding the great thing in social psychology. I believe that, rightly developed, the position will ultimately have contributed greatly toward the development of an outlook upon human inter-relations that will meet the needs of peoples whose interests and ambitions clash, but who must work together. These needs will be met and satisfied, not because the peoples will have become mutually *tolerant* of one another, but because they will have grown to *appreciate* each the other. And mutual appreciation will undoubtedly be interpreted as the outstanding need of students and of the general public in our generation.

It is hoped that the book may be useful to teachers and students and to the general reader as well. Problems for discussion are appended here and there. They will be suggestive of others and better ones, that will arise from the experience of those who may make use of the volume.

Acknowledgment is due to many writers. References to their work are collected in Appendix I by chapters and those that have been drawn upon most heavily are mentioned in the text.

In particular, I have great pleasure in this expression of heavy obligation to my colleague, Professor Delton Thomas Howard, who has read both copy and proof and has made useful suggestions for improvement, — suggestions that I have, in the main, adopted and embodied in the text.

I am indebted also to Dr. William Healy, Dr. Robert M. Yerkes and others for tables and charts. Their source, in each instance, is named in the title.

ROBERT H. GAULT

EVANSTON, ILLINOIS
January, 1923

CONTENTS

SOCIAL PSYCHOLOGY

DEFINITION AND SCOPE

SOCIAL PSYCHOLOGY in its widest sense applies to a study of interactions among animals. More specifically, and as the term is usually employed, it applies to the reactions of members of the human race one to another. This is social behavior and the term "behavior" is used here in the sense in which it is employed in the literature of general psychology, to point to an adjustment on the part of an organism to its whole environment, psychic and physical. It may be conscious or unconscious. Not all such adjustments are social, but only those that imply interactions among men, women and children toward one another. They may or may not be accompanied by a consciousness of the social relation.

Non-social behavior is illustrated in the acts of one who has just now suffered a bruised finger from a falling window: he cries aloud, waves his arms in the air; stamps his feet upon the floor and his whole body is thrown into contortion. So soon, however, as he begins to receive encouragement in such behavior from the realization that he is gaining the sympathy of by-standers or from the purpose to gain their sympathy, his behavior becomes social. Likewise it takes on a social character when he realizes that he is making a ridiculous spectacle of himself in the eyes of by-standers, real or imagined, and begins to take himself in hand, to repress himself stoically in order that onlookers may at least not think him a weakling. The same transformation in the psychologic character of his behavior occurs when he realizes that he is, by his undignified resentment of the falling window, traversing his ideal of strong manhood that can " grin and bear it," and accordingly suppresses his external activity at least. We are doing something toward developing social behavior in this respect when we appeal to a suffering and grieving youngster to " brace up now, and be a man." It will, therefore, very often be the developmental history of a given form of behavior that determines whether it is social or not.

It is assumed that the interactions in question were conscious, at least in their origins, excepting in cases in which they may have arisen by accident and have been discovered and made use of consciously at a later time; as for example, when one discovers that one has already unwittingly adopted a mode of speech which elicits favorable response from a neighbor, and therefore deliberately continues to exercise this manner of address until it once more becomes unconscious. A " *purely* instinctive " form of behavior, from this viewpoint, could not be social.

This account of social relations from the psychological angle is a chapter in empirical science. As such, it attempts to derive its data from observation of particular phenomena and to analyze and compare them as to their essential components.

One of the first, if not the very first phenomenon in this connection that comes to the eye of the psychologist is consciousness itself of the reactions of men, one to another. And his next discovery is an anticipatory image of reactions in others, that are seen as inevitable sequences of one's own behavior. These phenomena may be passed over or slightly stressed as the ultra-behaviorist would do. But in doing so the student becomes liable to the charge of arriving at conclusions based upon incomplete induction; for it is a fair hypothesis that forms of consciousness — instable, filmy, and unreliable psychological data though they may be in the eye of the behaviorist — are nevertheless the most patent signs that we have of some inner struggles for adjustment. Besides, as is maintained in this book, by paying no heed whatever to certain forms of conscious life — imagery of others, and anticipatory images of others' reactions — the social psychologist blocks himself at the point of discussing how the individual becomes socialized, and sacrifices the criteria by which he may determine the difference between behavior that is social and behavior that is not social. The observation of one's consciousness at certain angles, we shall see, makes an important contribution to the psychology of social relations.

But the social behavior includes automatic or unconscious adjustments among men — social habits we may call them — and this branch of psychology claims, as one of its functions, the task of accounting for the development of these social automatisms.

So far as social psychology accepts conscious behavior as its object of study it implies those aspects of human consciousness in which one recognizes one's relations to others and *vice versa:* in which one voluntarily seeks to control another's reactions; in which one anticipates one's reaction to the behavior that may possibly be expressed in the life of another at some future time, or the reactions that may occur in the reverse direction; in which one consciously makes adjustments to an ideal that has been developed and expressed by whatever means. Finally, social psychology implies responding to what is " in the air " because " everybody else is doing it " even while, as far as our definite awareness is concerned, we are out of relation to any particular person or persons who are " doing it."

Our consciousness is social when we stop to consider the possible effect of our actions upon others, or when we recognize that effect as having already taken place. The student is socially conscious when he, preparing for an intercollegiate debate, works in the quiet of his study week in and week out, arranging and rearranging his material with a view to getting it into such shape that it will elicit signs of approval from the audience and obtain the decision of the judges in response to his effort. The chess player is socially conscious when he anticipates his next move in case his opponent should make a given play, or contrariwise; the statesman, when he anticipates the needs of the nation and provides for them, as well as when he realizes his error and makes correction. We are conscious in the social sense, furthermore, when we feel constrained to adjust ourselves to an ideal. Whether we associate it with a particular person or not, the ideal is personified, and in adjusting to it, or in responding in any way to its appeal, we are indirectly reacting to its author. Thus when we are reading a book or looking at a picture we may be socially conscious. Indeed, we are so if the book or the picture stimulates the vague or distinct imagery of a recognized ideal. Thus a Millet speaks to us indirectly of the nobility of common labor; a Gilbert Stuart through the face of a Washington, speaks of steadfast patriotism. When we recognize the symbolic language of the artist the predominant aspect of our consciousness is social. Finally, the youths of 1861 and 1917 were socially conscious when they were entertaining a mental imagery of tens of thousands of other youths like themselves all marching eagerly behind the fife and drum, as they were doing on thousands of village greens, and feeling their own patriotic impulses swell in response. Such youths are socially conscious when they realize that they are out because their neighbors are out also. We entertain in our mind's eye either anticipatory or retrospective imagery of responses to behavior, imaged or actual, and this imagery seems to be aimed at the control of our behavior when we are in the social sense conscious. It will be understood that imagery is not necessarily visual; it may be of any other sensory quality, as auditory or motor or what not. Furthermore, it must not be understood as implied in these pages that imagery must be clear cut as it is in the mind's eye of most of us whilst we, in our imagination, are going about through the house in which we visited a week ago or in which we are about to visit. Indeed, imagery, to be effective in the connections in which we are thinking of it here may be vague and undefined to the last degree as when we *image* the population of a state.

But not only are such phenomena as the foregoing meat for the student of social psychology. Such forms of human interaction as great movements of population; the relations of audience and speaker; the formation of a public opinion; the growth of customs, conventionalities and law; invention, progress and social disintegration — all these phenomena and their kind are in the same category. In the last analysis these are reactions of individuals (8), one to another or all to the same situation, but always of individuals who are more or less clearly aware that other elements in the population are moving toward the same ends as they themselves are trying to reach; that other members of the audience are attending to the speaker; that others have joined with them in a public opinion; that their neighbors share the same customs and conventions with themselves and that the invention they are perfecting is needed and is being awaited by many others of their sort.

The social psychologist tries to describe all these reactions from his own angle. He looks into the psychic nature of individuals for the root of all social phenomena. He recognizes this psychic nature as the thing that initiates forms of human interaction and co-operation, and that lays out the course over which they shall run. By psychic nature we mean to suggest not only the conscious aspect of human life but also the unconscious instinct and complexes that form the background of human personality. This nature is conceived as responsible even for those forms of interaction that are characteristic of highly organized and of unorganized human relations alike, and for differences among organizations themselves. Indeed it is conceived of as accounting for the existence of the organization itself.

Preliminary analysis of this psychic nature brings us first to a study of human instinct or inherited disposition which is the native, not acquired, source of impulses toward loosely defined types of behavior. Through the same analysis of human nature we come also upon the natural or inherited capacities of human kind which certainly vary more or less among individuals of the same group and probably among peoples as well. There are also the temperaments of individuals and of groups which are the natural matrix for liability to the emotional reactions that are in varying degree characteristic of individuals and of peoples, and in their way contribute much to the manner in which human interaction will go forward.

Analysis further reveals, whenever it has been projected in any community, a considerable number of defective folk of various sorts — feeble-minded, victims of psychopathic constitution, etc. — each of which implies a stunted or warped basis of instinct or dispositions or capacities, and hence of impulses and motives. As a consequence, there follow anomalies in behavior, failure in social assimilation and interaction, of which the student of social psychology must take notice because all such differences amongst people as those of intelligence level and also of racial character, not to speak of many other factors, such as affiliation with occupational and professional groups and with sectarian orders and castes, affect the unity of a people and their capacity for co-operative activity.

In considerable measure human nature is built up of many acquired traits. The occupation or profession that one follows; the climate and geographic features with which one is surrounded, all these present so many stimuli in a multitude of forms to which the individual every hour of his life is fitting himself. Thus, in response to these situations, dispositions are being formed and deeply rooted in the men and women of successive generations. In important particulars groups of people are, therefore, becoming alike. A tendency toward community customs and conventionalities arises, or a liability to similar responses to similar stimuli. By all these tokens — native and acquired uniformities among groups — mutual understanding within the groups is enhanced and the broader effects of behavior upon one's contemporaries may be perceived in advance. This provides the key to the sense of social unity or of belonging together, or of social solidarity in the community.

This " sense of unity " among a people is in this volume regarded as identical with the main current of social consciousness. It is a part of the consciousness of the individual alone. It is really one's own sense of belonging with a large or small group, which has developed (1) out of one's right or wrong interpretation of many signs as indicating that all are thinking or feeling alike: and (2) out of behavior of others that is recognized or foreseen as a more or less inevitable sequence of one's own action and *vice versa*. However far we may wander and whatever we may be doing, we never quite shake off a feeling of peculiar intimacy and unity with the family in which we have grown up from our infancy; and the sense of wide embracing social unity, that is such a desideratum in the eyes of the social psychologist, is of precisely the same stuff. It is more than the mere consciousness of kind and more than the imitation consciousness. This sense of unity and social consciousness in general is intensified by the appropriate physical reaction. That is, it is intensified in the boy of '61 when he marches with the rest. This is the case, at any rate, until the process of automatization is well on its way. The "sense of unity" is not understood in this volume as implying the existence of a "group mind" (5), and "over soul" (9), or of a "super-consciousness" in the sense of something distinct from the personal consciousness. We believe it is made clear in subsequent chapters that an account of no group of phenomena of social psychology requires such an assumption to be made.

All the backgrounds and reactions that have been suggested above tend toward the establishment of fixed relations among people. They do not point the way by which such changes in social relations as may properly be described by the term "progressive" may be brought about. But this, too, is a problem for the student of social psychology and consideration of it must take us into a study of great leaders who are given credit for having brought to pass changes described as progressive.

Finally, we shall be interested in the reverse of social progress, or in disintegration as it is illustrated in the behavior of criminals and others who destroy without supplementing their destruction by constructive activity.

The means by which investigations in social psychology are made must necessarily be of varied character. Obviously, laboratory experimentation, supplemented by more casual observation of people and their arts, is the method by which most reliable information may be secured relating to native dispositions or instinct and capacities that in considerable measure are the sources of impulses (or motives according to good usage) toward human interaction. It is appropriate, too, that the experimental method as applied either to lower animals or to men be invoked for contribution to the purpose of the social psychologist. If we agree to the assertion of continuity of lower and higher life then the most fundamental characteristics of the lower forms must persist in the higher. Not only so, but since the acquired dispositions are on their part also sources of motive power, similar in this respect to natural dispositions, we should be justified in turning to experimentation as applied to the learning process for additional data in this branch of inquiry. But more important, even if much less satisfactory from the view-point of the student whose ideal of worth finds expression only in what he can say in mathematical formulae, are the interpretations of biography, of statistics, and of affairs; of the symbolism in myths and in art and in many of the case studies of the student of abnormal psychology and the practitioner in the field of mental disease. These studies often lay bare the motives of human social behavior.

CHAPTER II

THE SENSE OF SOCIAL UNITY

THE phrase that is used in the title of this chapter will in some minds suggest " social solidarity," which very frequently carries the meaning of immobility as applied to a stationary portion of the population. Again it may mean that a group of people are on practically the same level as measured by intellectual or other capacities or attainments. It is sometimes used in the sense of a group of animals that behave in a uniform manner instinctively: biological solidarity. The solidarity of convention and custom in the human family is an aspect of this and is treated in another chapter. Once more, the term is used in the sense of a community of interests, ideas, etc., among the members of the group, and this may be the resultant of uniform stimulation of all the members of the group, as all individuals in a class in mathematics acquire a knowledge of a certain set of formulae because they are set forward by the teacher; a solidarity of training.

No one of these applications is of the greatest significance to the student of social psychology. It is conceivable that a population could be the least mobile: that its members could stand upon a given level of attainment and capacity, and that there could be in it a perfect community of ideas and interest (they might cherish the same thoughts and ambitions) without there being at the same time any feeling or sense of belonging together and any enthusiasm for working together arising therefrom (solidarity in a psychological sense). The individuals composing the population are in such cases in the same relation to one another as the trees of a forest: a relation of juxtaposition and no more, save as one interferes with another's movements and food supply, and incidentally affords protection to others, as one tree incidentally protects another in case of storm.

The solidarity that is of greatest interest in our connection is that *sense of unity* or *feeling of belonging-together* that makes every member of a group seem to himself to be kin to every other member: to be moving in co-operation with every other member toward the same goal: a sense that all are animated by the same purposes: that all stand for the same ideals; that somehow all together are making progress, and a sense of confidence in every member of the group that his behavior will bring to pass reactions on the part of others, the general character of which can be foreseen.

The members of the same family, club, profession, city, state, or nation experience a sense of standing together in a peculiar relationship: they feel that they belong together: that they are in reality one body. So vivid is this experience on the part of the member of many a family, club, or profession that he cannot contemplate his actual or projected behavior at any critical juncture of his affairs without taking very earnestly into consideration the attitude or possible attitude of his confreres in reaction to his behavior. Inevitably, he, at such junctures, has a very intense realization of the strength of the bonds by which he is bound to others. At times when a wave of public feeling spreads over the land, too, this same experience comes to the foreground vividly. In the ordinary course of events it is in the margin; but I believe it is a correct statement that within no given period do we have a sense of aloofness from others in *all* our relations. There is, of course, a host of stimulus-response relations which are wholly outside the scope of our subject. The sun shines upon me through my window and I draw toward it with satisfaction; the horse's hoofs clatter loudly upon the brick pavement and I resent the disturbance; the clock strikes eleven and I determine to hasten my writing so that I may be able to complete my task tomorrow. Such psycho-physical processes as these crowd every minute of our lives. They are not social experiences. They have nothing to do in the matter of determining a sense of social unity though they may indirectly suggest it. Thus the clattering hoofs may at once bring into my mind's view my newly arrived neighbor to whom I once described this as a quiet street. I am immediately brought to realize my responsibility for his discomfiture. In other words I realize that he and I stand in a peculiar relation to each other; between us is a social unity or solidarity, as it is sometimes called, and it is a unity in the psychological sense. Illustrations of a similar felt relationship through a large group could be multiplied.

What, for instance, is a nation? It is not a form

of government nor officials nor provinces nor states
centrally controlled excepting in local affairs; it is
not battlements nor constitutions and codes of law;
neither is it men and women. It is not all of these
together. It is, however, a group of people amongst
whom the *feeling of nationalism* holds sway and who,
because they cherish this feeling, have built up a
government and a code of law, etc., and who recognize
some of their number as intrusted with the responsibility of administration.

"But, in the last analysis, nationalism is something
over and above all its constituent elements, which it
works into a new and higher synthesis. There is
really nothing recondite or mysterious about nationalism, despite all the arguments that have raged concerning its exact meaning. As a matter of fact,
nationalism is a *state of mind*. Nationalism is a
belief, held by a fairly large number of individuals,
that they constitute a 'Nationality'; it is a sense
of *belonging together* as a 'Nation.' The Nation, as
visualized in the minds of its believers, is a people or
community associated together and organized under
one government, and dwelling together in a distinct
territory. When the nationalist ideal is realized we
have what is known as a body politic or 'state.' But
we must not forget that this 'state' is the material
manifestation of an ideal, which may have pre-existed
for generations as a mere pious aspiration with no
tangible attributes like state sovereignty or physical
frontiers. Conversely, we must remember that a state
need not be a nation. Witness the defunct Hapsburg
Empire of Austria-Hungary — an assemblage of dis-

cordant nationalities that flew to pieces under the shock of war " (7).

The question we are approaching here is: Whence comes this sense of social unity; what composes it; how is it developed?

In the first place it does not emanate from a social mind (6, 9) nor a group mind in the sense of one distinct from that of each individual in the group but similar to it, which is alleged to have synthesized the individuals of a group into a social organism as my mind seems to have effected a synthesis which I call myself. In the second place this unity is not summed up in the possession by the group of a common language, common customs, common laws, art, literature, mental outlook, systems of political and religious thought, etc. These surely are signs that there is a social unity, and once they have been developed they facilitate the further evolution of that sense. But without at least a rudimentary consciousness of solidarity to begin with, it is doubtful whether a common language, etc., could ever develop. Nor, thirdly, is the principle of social unity to be found in the co-ordination of individuals in the activities of the work-a-day world (2). These co-ordinations, just as language, art, law, custom, etc., are objective products of a psychological unity that antedates them. Once we have found the psychological core of the phenomenon we are investigating, we can, I believe, account for the objective appearance. As we have already said of language, art, etc., so here we can assert a reciprocal influence between our co-ordination in everyday affairs on the one hand and our sense of

belonging together on the other; but the co-ordinations are not primary. We must make our appeal to
psychological analysis.

What then does analysis of the experience we have
under discussion reveal? Let each one take an illustration from his own experience as a member of a closely
knit club, society, or family. I have again and again
observed my fellow members in their reactions to a
great variety of situations and their reactions are
like or unlike my own in similar circumstances. Hence
they are like me or they differ from me. Today, even
though far separated from them, when this feeling
of belonging to them arises, I have in my mind's eye
an image of their behavior as it occurs in response to
a situation with which I am confronted, or which I am
creating; or I have an anticipatory image of their
behavior as it will occur later in response to the
situation that confronts me or to what I am at this
moment thinking, saying or doing. Their imaged behavior I may approve or disapprove. It may be like
or unlike my own in similar circumstances. More
important than this, however, is my anticipatory
image of what I deem their more or less inevitable
response to my reactions and *vice versa*. We do not
mean that this imagery need exist in great vividness
nor detail, as we have said in the preceding chapter;
it may be wholly marginal and in course of time as
the group interrelations become more and more highly
mechanized, the imagery may almost wholly fade
away. But all the while it seems to be an essential
feature of my sense of social unity or solidarity with
the group. A second element that analysis reveals is

a purpose or ideal, or a set of purposes and ideals
and felt needs that I cherish, and evidence of which
I observe in the behavior of other members respectively
of the group to which I belong. An individual may
consequently belong to several unities at one and the
same time: one that implies adherence to political
formulae; another, to a professional code of ethics;
another to a religious ideal, and the like. The third
and final essential element is affective or emotional.
At those moments when my sense of belonging to others
is most in evidence, there is a feeling of satisfaction,
or enthusiasm, courage and irresistibility that arises.

These elements are all illustrated in the experience
of the boy of '61 and the boy of 1917 as he trained
in camp and upon the village green. In his imagination he could see hundreds of thousands of other
youths like himself at military drill from ocean to
ocean (imagery of others' reactions) ; he realized that
all were doing so in order that they might the more
effectively obey the summons from Washington (purpose), and with it all arose the great swell of enthusiasm within him (emotional factor). He felt that he
was a part of a great closely interlocked and co-ordinated group. Without that imagery of others and
that realization of common purpose, there could have
been no enthusiasm in his make-up; no patriotism, no
loyalty. He would have been merely an isolated
drudge. This enthusiasm in each individual expresses
itself in easily recognized, easily imitated, and hence
easily imagined signs. Consequently the emotional
factor is an important contributor to the development
of a sense of social unity. Indeed without at least a

moderate emotional intensity, it is doubtful whether such a sense could persist at all.

From the foregoing, it is justifiable to draw an analogy. There is primitive man surrounded on all sides by evidence of natural forces, no one of which he understands in the sense in which we say it is comprehended by the more enlightened age in which we live. To that extent, in primitive man, the anthropomorphic disposition is unbridled. He stands in awe before the wind, the river, disease, life and death. He reads his own dispositions, greatly magnified, into these evidences of unknown forces. He observes that his neighbors are doing likewise — a sign that they too are moved as he is. By this token a psychological kinship or unity is established as a matter of course. Once a considerable group is included in this unity, it is but a short natural step to co-ordination in institutions for worship, for punishment, etc. This follows upon the realization of a common purpose or a common need. We do not mean to imply that this felt and observed reaction to the mysterious is the only psychological root of primitive social unity, but that among other roots this one looms large. It does so, no doubt, because of the prominence of the emotional element that is associated with it. This element makes the reaction especially observable and contagious. It contributes therefore to the individual's readiness in imagery of others' reactions, as described above, and therefore to the felt unity of the group. The mere perception of a similarity in bodily form and color, too, contributes to the same end.

Thus far the discussion suggests the "consciousness of kind" which Giddings calls the primary element that makes for social solidarity (4). Indeed, in the main, that is just what we are discussing. The consciousness of kind is a consciousness of likeness of form, appearance, purposes, needs, behavior, etc., and as such it is a primary factor in the sense of social unity. It antedates the organization of groups and therefore it precedes conflict among groups which some describe as the elementary social phenomenon. But ere long, as organizations become more and more complex, conflicts become more varied and intense and then the consciousness of difference as well as of kind becomes an element in our sense of social unity. This comes about as a consequence of numbers of experiences in which we have failed to satisfy our needs or attain our purposes; attainments which we have seen made successfully even by others whom we recognize as, at least in a psychological sense, very different from ourselves. From that moment we recognize the need for such persons and they, in our imagery, enter in with others, to the group of components of our sense of unity. In our mind's eye we see them, either as contemporaries or as belonging to a future generation, reacting to situations that we confront, in ways that we could not; responding to our behavior; coming to our aid and so contributing to the realization of our purposes and the satisfaction of our needs. Thus the *imagery of others' reactions* includes the *consciousness of kind*, antedates co-operation, organization and conflict, and later enters into reciprocal relations with all of these.

As the race has progressively gained control over the forces of nature, and specialization has followed upon specialization, social unities have multiplied within the group and we have the class consciousness of the commercial, the professional, and laboring sections, etc., and happily it may be, a larger unity including all of these and superimposed upon them. But in every instance it is a unity that is made possible only by reason of such mutual familiarity or understanding on the part of the members of the group or sub-group that each one can, and even does, represent to himself the reactions by which others of his class would respond, or are responding, both to the observer himself and to other situations. Obedient to the general law of automatization, the whole process, in course of time, becomes so highly mechanized that even the vaguest imagery suffices for the sense of unity which we have under discussion.

SOCIAL CONTINUITY. — In all the foregoing we have had in mind a unity among contemporaries. Obviously, if our analysis is correct thus far, our principle applies as well to social continuity or unity between or among successive ages. As we peruse the history, literature and other products of the civilization of a bygone generation, we become acquainted with the makers of that civilization; we know their natural dispositions, and other motives; their modes of thought, etc. Again and again we discover particulars in which they react as we do to similar situations. Our capacity for imaging them in one or other set of terms develops until we can put ourselves in their place and them in our place, so that our conscious-

ness of unity with them is made up of precisely the
same sort of components as those that enter into our
sense of unity with our contemporaries. The persistence of laws and courts and other institutions or
the modeling of institutions upon old copies is not in
itself social continuity: it is an expression or sign of
a psychological continuity. That we do not feel a
strong sense of unity with the Fijians of our time,
nor a sense of continuity with the ancient Egyptians,
would seem to be a corollary to the foregoing.

SOCIAL UNITY NOT INTELLECTUALISTIC. — All this
may appeal to many as over-intellectualistic. We do
not believe it is so. Surely we could hardly describe by
that term the unity among members of a profession.
There is an of-courseness about it that is not intellectualistic at all excepting that it rests in a vague
shadowy lot of images of others with whom we are
co-ordinated and so, as far as this is concerned, it is
in the same category as each one's consciousness of
one's self. It is no attempt to describe an aspect of
mind in terms of conscious stuff, exclusively. Indeed,
it is recognized here that automatic adjustments and
states, driven on by the great pushes of human nature
— an attitude of of-courseness — pre-eminently come
into consideration in this connection and that in
closely knit groups and societies the situation as far
as unity and co-operation are concerned is analogous
to that in the case of a family, or of husband and
wife, who have become one through years of association and co-operation. The intellectualistic aspect of
their unity and co-operation has been reduced almost,
if not quite, to the vanishing point.

AN INDIVIDUALISTIC CONCEPTION. — This is an individualistic psychological conception, but at the same
time it is social. In fact, no line can be drawn to
distinguish sharply the individual from the social.
It does not at all imply the direct transference of a
psychic influence from one mind to another which
Ellwood seems to fear the psychologist is approaching in a discussion of our subject (2), but only the
recognition of many signs as indicating that you and
others are in agreement. Neither does it imply the
mind of a social organism, nor anything of the sort,
which is by some assumed to co-ordinate and combine
the individuals. They co-ordinate because they are
receiving essentially the same set of stimuli, because
of an inter-stimulation among members of the group,
and because of a sense of belonging together. Each
and every member of the closely knit society to which
I belong would be completely isolated mentally; there
would be no unity among us were it not for the fact
that we are all responding to similar situations so that
in course of time each is able to represent the others
and each knows approximately what to expect of the
others.

What a student of psychology, in the light of the
foregoing, will have to say concerning the biological
or race factor and the institution, organization or
co-operation factor, to which Ellwood refers (2), as
determinative of a social unity or solidarity, is now
apparent. In as far as we are of the same race, we
can imagine one another with the greater facility; in
as far as we co-operate in the same organization or
institution our opportunities for observing one and

another in action and for comparing reactions are enhanced. By reason of these associations, therefore, our anticipatory and other imagery of interactions among our confreres become more rich and complete and the emotional or affective components of the sense of unity grow apace. In short, then, the factors named merely furnish an opportunity for the development of the elements that make the sense of social unity. These are a consequence of a felt unity that antedates them, and with which, from the moment of their inception, they are in reciprocal relation.

" Social Mind " an Unnecessary Concept. — As we have said above, this is a strictly individualistic position. If this point of view can be taken and maintained, it is unnecessary ever to use the phrase " social mind " or " group mind." The individual mind alone accomplishes everything that the " social mind " is assumed to bring to pass. The whole course of transition from the individual to the social is within the individual himself. The student of the philosophy of law may at first glance find nothing in this to support more than individual or private interest. But " public interest " is only a phrase. What he means by " public interest " is a series, so to speak, of widely overlapping private interests, or interests held largely in common, in the same outstanding objects, such as the right to life, health, property, freedom of speech, or in occasional subjects of political discussion, etc.

Because each one of us, judging by indubitable signs, realizes, or judges after immediate inference, that the people around him severally in the neighborhood or in the state at large cherish the same main interests that he cherishes, we have a public interest — of the only sort that we need. The way is then open for the pursuit of these interests in co-operation.

CHAPTER III

SOCIAL MOTIVES

PSYCHOLOGY as an account of behavior assumes that there is invariably a connection between mental processes and states, on the one hand, and certain implicit and explicit reactions on the other, by which the organism as a whole completes its adjustment to its environment. There is an elaborate group of such processes and states, each one of which, in a popular use of the word, is now and again called a motive. Thus perceptions, ideas, emotions, trains of thought, hopes, desires, ambitions, generosity, fears, and ill-defined feelings of tendency or disposition fall into the category of motives when they appear to occasion the final overt reaction on the part of the whole organism by means of which an adaptation or adjustment is completed. For example, the *perception* of a tennis racquet is a motive when it seems to occasion taking up the racquet and engaging in a game of tennis; a *train of thought* — particularly if it leads to a *conviction* such as that government bonds are the safest and best investment at hand — is a motive when it appears to occasion the behavior of purchasing them; the ill-defined *feeling of tendency*, likewise, is a motive when it appears to tie one up to conservative methods and purposes when the community is seething with revolt.

But the train of thought, ambition, or fear, etc., we conceive here as an intermediate link in a whole complex process of adjustment which is itself dependent upon a more remote motive; one that rarely or never, in ordinary circumstances, comes into the field of consciousness. At any rate this is undoubtedly true in so many instances that the conception deserves more emphasis than it has received hitherto. There may be motives of motives, therefore; motives of thought, emotion, etc.; or better, motives in various phases or aspects or levels, from unconscious mechanism to conscious process, or *vice versa*, and effective in all of them. Thus, for example, our impulsion toward feeding is effective upon the level of reflexes, and at the same time it gives direction to some acts of planning and thinking.

Those motives that lead up to a social consciousness and to social adaptation on the whole are what we call social motives. That is, whatever colors my thoughts, perceptions, ambitions, hopes and other forms of behavior, whatsoever they may be, with a consciousness dim or clear that I am a unit with a group whose members are responsive to my thoughts, behavior, ambitions, etc., or effective upon them, or both responsive to these modes by which I express myself and effective upon them in turn; whatever impels me, even blindly, to get upon a common footing with others, or to bring them to my footing; these are my social motives. The boy of '61 was acting under a social motive because he was responding to his immediate perception of others' behavior; or to his distinct or ill-defined idea or image of thousands of other boys, recognized as like himself, all over the land who were doing likewise; because he desired to induce others, then inactive, to do as he was doing, or to think, feel, etc., as he was thinking and feeling; or because he was acting in response to a tendency or a push from within resulting from long and interested indulgence in such activities, a tendency that leads him irresistibly to seek to occupy common ground with others in this particular respect. The reformer is acting under a social motive because he works for the adoption of his plans under stimulation, all the while, of the consciousness that future generations will react favorably to his work, even though the present may not do so, or by a sense of the distinctly or dimly expressed voice of human need.

The term " social motive " in psychological litera-ture has often not been made to appear more general nor less transitory than the particular forms of be-havior that it is invoked to explain, excepting in the case of such generalized motives as ambition, gener-osity, acquired tendencies, etc. The term is as ambig-uous as " cause." Each term has been conceived now as mechanical and again as " final." It is ambiguous, too, in respect to consciousness. It may, or may not be conscious. The motive is a distinct, conscious, deliberate purpose in which case the resulting phase of behavior is intended; or the element of conscious pur-pose is quite lacking, and in this case the consequent behavior is not intended. It is only when we get away from the attempt to find a motive that has its own characteristics distinct from those of other functions; when we come to think of any process as a motive provided only it is found in apparent causal connection with behavior; when, moreover, we take the genetic point of view and seek the developmental course of the motive — and only then — we escape the difficulties of certain writers in the field of ethics (9, 11), by whom the motive is described as the purpose of an act; again as the thought of a desirable end; the idea of an end which a self-conscious subject presents to itself and strives and tends to realize; the feeling excited by the idea of the end; and still further, as " that characteristic tendency or disposition of a man in virtue of which a given act possesses an attraction for him " (20).

Excepting the last instance, motive is hardly more nor less than the intention of an act; yet much of our normal and abnormal social behavior is not intended at all. The last characterization of motives above is a recognition of the unconscious factor which undoubtedly plays a large part, often apparently the whole part, in determining the course of human action, and which gives the motive a certain stability and breadth greater than that afforded by the conscious factor alone. Even ambition implies particular purposes and is subject to limitations when compared with human disposition, and unless it is anchored in a well-fixed disposition its social value is uncertain. In the light of this unconscious tendency or disposition, the motive is conceived as more general than the particular act or thought that it is invoked to explain.

From this point of view the purpose, desired end, idea, or thought or ambition, which are sometimes described as motives themselves, are only symptoms of motives (15). They serve only to complete and illuminate the account of an act. They indicate the individual's intention at the time at which a piece of behavior is projected and carried to completion, but this intention may have been stimulated by peculiar momentary or accidental circumstances, on the one hand, over which the subject had no control, and on the other hand, by a submerged disposition or complex that may never have worked itself out until now in any concrete, overt form of action.

Take, for instance, the case of a cashier, who misappropriates funds to pay a gambling debt. The purpose or plan to pay the debt is from one angle — the one most frequently accepted in legal procedure, for instance — the motive of the breach of trust. But there are many people who entertain the purpose to pay their debts whether they were incurred at gambling or otherwise. Such a purpose is honorable. It does not usually lead even to the temptation to commit a crime or misdemeanor as a means of accomplishing the purpose, but rather to a vigorous pursuit of what we describe as honest means. If, therefore, in a particular instance the purpose is followed by a criminal act the performance of which fulfills the purpose, it is obvious that it is at most only an aspect of the motive and that an analysis must be made to discover other motives; that is, the foundation upon which the purpose rests or the roots from which it grows. No sooner do we begin such an analysis than we find that the cashier, like most other gamblers, in all sincerity regards a gambling debt as one of honor. The ability to pay such a debt has precisely the same

positive emotional appeal for him as has the ability to
pay for a purchased house to one of the rest of us.
It is undoubtedly a habitual attitude, that is, a disposition that the individual has acquired, it may be,
through years of social contact; it has arisen from
mutual action and reaction amongst people who engage in commercial transactions and people who
gamble respectively. It is probable that if we had
always lived remote from any semblance of commercial
transactions the paying of debts against purchased
property would make no emotional appeal whatever —
excepting the negative one of aversion. Men who
practice gambling for money can doubtless describe
many a greenhorn who, outside the gambling art,
pays all his obligations with a relish, but who sticks
at a gambling debt.

When, therefore, the emotional appeal that is carried by ability to pay a debt has been described we
are not at the bottom of the cashier's motive, for this
appeal is common to both gambling and honest commercial debtors alike.

Precisely the same argument should be applied to
the proposition that it is the emotion of fear at the
prospect of losing caste with his associates or fear of
ruin or dishonor that led the gambling cashier to abuse
his trust. The honest purchaser fears losing caste
and other advantages when he is confronted with the
prospect of failure to make his payments when they
are due.

The trail of the cashier's motive leads to fundamental character traits: possibly an ego-centric disposition, more or less latent since childhood, against

which early training in school and home had erected insufficient bulwarks of acquired habits: possibly an inborn instability of impulses due to a lack of early training in persistence or in patient pursuit, against difficulties, of objects that have been made to appear desirable; perhaps the trail leads to a temporary unbalance arising from conditions of health or what not; again the quest may lead to dispositions that have been slowly built up by idle, and finally by more or less serious reflection upon ways and means of appropriating to his own uses the money that belongs to others, without his entertaining at any time the intention of misappropriation. At any rate a complete answer to the question of motives in this case calls for a thorough survey of a personality; it is not even suggested in the true statement that the cashier's purpose or intention was to find the wherewithal to pay his gaming debts.

The act of robbery involving murder is not explained as to its motive by the statement that the robber *intended* to obtain money to buy clothes and that he *intended* to escape arrest. Everybody intends to make such purchases and to avoid humiliation, disgrace and restriction of freedom, but few rob and murder to gain these ends. The distinctive and fundamental motives that actuate the robber-murderer may be found only by an analysis of his complex personality; which analysis will almost certainly reveal motives that do not, as such, come to the foreground of the criminal's consciousness at the time of the deed.

To take a more familiar illustration: when you fall into a discussion with A, whom you have met for the first time, and find yourself in violent opposition to him, your feelings are aroused; you raise your voice, gesticulate vigorously and leave your companion alone on the street where you found him. An observer might say that the opposed opinions in this case were the motive of your behavior. When you reflect upon the circumstances, however, it occurs to you that the same opposition of opinion that developed in this case exists also between you and B but that you and he can discuss the matter without a hostile demonstration. You account for the difference on the ground, not of opinion but upon the fact, as you express it, that there are some people with whom it is impossible to agree and that A is one of them. But why is it impossible?

You, yourself, in nine cases out of ten, are at a loss to account for your behavior in definite language that other people can understand. If you could go into the matter sufficiently you might find that Mr. A speaks with a nasal twang like that which character-izes Mr. C, who beat you meanly in a bargain a year ago; that the wart upon his face suggests a neighbor of yours who persistently argues to win, rightly or wrongly. In each of these cases the motive is an affec-tion; or it may be that an analysis would carry you back to your college days when the judges of a debate, as you for a long time bitterly interpreted it, robbed you of a favorable decision which you had fully won from an antagonist who bore the same name as your opponent today. In this case your motive is a revived complex representing the serious considerations and emotions that were associated with your earlier debat-ing experience. Or possibly your analysis will bring you to an unreasoned convention or prejudice relating to the subject of your discussion — one that you have never been able to defend successfully. If it has repeatedly brought you to confusion, you attribute to A the qualities that arouse your disagreeable emotion.

On the other hand, no such revivals as these occur when you are confronted by B and you get on with him satisfactorily.

Here you are appealing to that great unconscious, or almost unconscious background of your daily experience for an explanation of your behavior — in other words, its motive. You have invoked your predisposition or your prejudice as the final motive in this case.*

More or less unwittingly we repeatedly take advantage of such analyses as are suggested here when we forecast the probable social activity of an individual on the basis of an inquiry into his predispositions or prejudices — when we do not make our estimate merely upon the observation of particular instances of previous behavior. They are final motives.

The motives that the student of psychology discovers at the bottom of social phenomena are often described as of two groups, innate and acquired, by writers of psychological literature. So far as they relate to structure and function, at least, they are of the same nature; and to make a clear-cut distinction

* It is not intended here or elsewhere to emphasize the term "final" as many writers in the field of ethics do. It is not urged that here is the *ne plus ultra* among motives, but that the unconscious or marginal factor in the determination of human behavior must be brought forward more definitely than it has been hitherto in discussions of motives.

between the two, from the observer's viewpoint is often quite impossible.

THE QUESTION OF INSTINCTS AND THEIR ROLE IN SOCIAL LIFE. — Instincts are conceived as inborn mechanisms or dispositions that work together with other factors to determine the form and direction of our interactions in social life. It must be remembered that their existence is purely hypothetical. But, assuming their actuality for the present, they appear to be sources of impulses toward certain forms of behavior. Because it seems to be in virtue of them that certain forms of action have an attraction for us, we may call them motives and those instincts that perform this function in any degree in relation to our interactions among men will be classed among our social motives. More or less confusion has arisen in the use of the term "instinct." It sometimes refers to a form of behavior, simply, that has not been learned, and that is initiated without deliberation in each particular instance of its occurrence, as in the case of the dog that immediately starts in chase, even from a state approximating complete relaxation, upon sighting a rabbit; or as in the case of the man who immediately crouches and runs upon perceiving that bricks are beginning to tumble from a wall. In all such cases as these there is confusion with the reflex. Again the term is sometimes employed to refer to the natural *disposition* or persisting tendency that prompts the behavior we call instinctive and at least gives direction to other forms of action. Chicks following the mother hen, — and very often other moving objects for that matter; the hen sitting on eggs; the

beaver co-operating with others to build a dam; bees
working together to make and store honey; men in
primitive society working together at hunting and
fishing and engaging together in other activities that
are more or less supplementary thereto and controlled
or directed by the hunting and fishing situation, such
as building their villages upon their best hunting and
fishing grounds or closely adjacent to them, and
defending them in prolonged bitter warfare; all these
and the like are often described as " instincts " or as
" instinctive." Clearly in such cases there is confusion both with the reflex and with the acquired habit.
Once more: we sometimes use such forms of expression
as this: " When I was driving yesterday my horse
frightened and I *instinctively* drew up the reins."
Here is certainly a confusion with habit that has been
acquired, it may be, through years of training. The
only truly instinctive element in the performance is
doubtless the disposition to grasp something substantial, such as the arms of a seat, as a protection against
being thrown. But in the experience with the frightened horse there was not even the beginning of a movement in the direction of the seat arms or the dash
board. Instead the grasp at once was fixed upon
pliable reins: a habit that has grown up imperceptibly
in the course of a long experience at driving horses.

The term, instinct, we use to refer not to any form
of action but to an unlearned disposition that is part
of the natural equipment of animal nature. What is
properly called " instinctive behavior " is, strictly
speaking, a sign of instinct or of instincts.

The literature on the subject presents a formidable

list of so-called instincts. Each of the following is described as such here and there, and each one is expected to be interpreted as a sign of an instinct in the sense of an innate disposition which finds its outward expression in the form of activity named: sucking, biting, clasping, crying, grouping, standing, locomotion, vocalization, imitation, emulation, pugnacity, sympathy, hunting, fear, acquisitiveness, constructiveness, play, curiosity, sociability, secretiveness, cleanliness, modesty, love, jealousy. Even this list does not include all of those reactions that are sometimes described as instincts; and very often what are, in fact, highly mechanized habits are erroneously described by the same term. Indeed, as we shall see, such habits are perhaps invariably so tied up with the natural matrix of our personality that it is impossible to draw a line of division between the learned and the unlearned.

Students of behavior have described an instinct as a series of congenital or unlearned responses to the external conditions with which one is surrounded and to the metabolic changes, also, that are going on in one's organism. It differs from the reflex, as far as its outward manifestations go, in point of complexity, and in this respect too: that whereas the reflex is a momentary response to a momentary stimulus after which the whole process is at an end, the instinct, on the other hand, is a persisting tendency that, once aroused by an appropriate stimulus, results in a continuing state of activity, until the whole course has been run and final adjustment completed. No hard and fast line, for all of that, can be drawn between the reflex on one side and the instinct on the other. Some reflexes, the knee jerk, for instance, when often repeated, appear to result in a persisting tendency so that, once started by a single stimulus, it continues repeating itself for a period. It should follow from all this that instincts are no less modifiable than the reflex. The reflex eye-wink, as Swift has shown, may undergo modifications when external stimuli are placed under proper experimental control. Yerkes has shown that the reflex movement of the leg of a frog induced by an electric shock can be increased by applying an auditory stimulus at the same time with the electrical. Similar phenomena are well known in the case of the knee jerk. If the elementary reflex is modifiable to any degree, the more complex instinctive act should be expected to be even more modifiable, and less predictable. Similarly when one is emphasizing the background, the neurone pattern of the instinct and of the reflex respectively, the former may be conceived as the more complex and hence as the more liable to break down.

The foregoing sets out no clear-cut distinction between the reflex and the instinctive form of behavior. Furthermore, differences between forms of instinctive behavior themselves are much less clear than is popularly supposed (1, 4, 5). No particular set of reactions or part reactions constituting a pattern is confined to any one so-called instinctive act. Some reactions are common to the behavior that accompanies fear and that that goes along with anger. Fear sometimes appears as self-abasement, — looking at it from the explicit behavior side. For example,

the timidity, bashfulness or self-abasement of many a
youth and adult may properly be interpreted as a fear
reaction. His quavering knees, his stammering and
pallor upon the stage before an audience, or in the
parlor amongst strangers, his restraint of speech in
the deliberative assembly and the like are all of them
fear reactions and would be so recognized unquestion-
ably if the individual were making a display of them,
as he would, in the face of danger to life and limb.
In the behavior of fighting, that is invariably described
as instinctive, the emotion of elation that follows upon
the discharge of a successful blow may alternate with
that of self-abasement when one's antagonist for a
moment or more gets the upper hand or when there
flashes over one a realization of the undignified quality
of the business in hand. Introspective analysis will
bring other similar facts to light. It is clearly impossible to distinguish instincts by means of the accom-
panying emotions.

Moreover, as to explicit behavior, there is no hard
and fast line to be drawn between the so-called instincts of hunting and curiosity. The bodily attitudes
of searching and of expectation are characteristic of
each, and a general muscular tension prevails; a tension, that, whether in hunting or in the state of
curiosity, now and then breaks out into a definite form
of activity. Who has not seen, for example, a child
consumed by curiosity when packages from the market are being opened, standing tensed and with bated
breath, but finally climbing a chair, whence a clearer
view may be had? This is precisely characteristic
of the act of hunting as well. Not only so but sub-

jectively there are no sharp differences here. There is suppressed excitement, — it may be pleasurable or unpleasurable, or both alternately; and in each, likewise, there are more or less fleeting images of what may be the outcome of this hunting or of this state of curiosity. Acquisitiveness both in its outward expression and in its subjective aspect, has so many points of similarity with hunting and with curiosity that it cannot be put into a pigeonhole of its own. On another side acquisitiveness and pugnacity use the same arm in the same way. Constructiveness, also, certainly in its subjective aspect, is, very often at least, like acquisitiveness, and the two appear to merge in many a case in which a child brings together curiously shaped and colored pebbles for building a wall.

These considerations and the like have thus far proved insuperable difficulties in the way of a classification of so-called instincts by any more fundamental differentiae. The apparent purposes of behavior called instinctive, — but not of the thought-out variety, — seem to be the outstanding differentiae in such instances as the above; but purposes are so numerous as to discourage enumeration and they differ as day and night. One may fight *to kill, to hurt, to demonstrate strength, to gratify envy, to humiliate one's adversary or for many another purpose*. There is ground for the conclusion, therefore, that we should not attempt to base a system upon *instincts*, and even for the hypothesis that, in the plural, they do not exist.

This, however, does not run to the question of the existence of *instinct* in the sense of a generalized, unlearned tendency or disposition toward activity: such activity as will employ the natural structures and capacities of the organism. How this tendency shall work itself out; what natural structures and capacities shall be most employed, we may conceive as determined by the individual's desires and purposes. This determination may be immediate or remote; that is, the purpose of the youth of forty years ago to employ his capacity for hard work and logical analysis in competing (fighting) with his fellows for honors in the law school may have brought it to pass that today he is a formidable antagonist, throwing all his resources into the lists for no honor or prize, but as a matter of course. Historically, it was the purpose of forty years ago that opened up the ways through which *instinct* worked itself out. The outcome, we say, is a habit or a complex set of professional habits.

Without further elaboration at this point it will be sufficient to draw attention once more to the difficulty of drawing hard and fast lines — this time between the instinctive act and habit.

We have been using the terms *instinct, instincts* and *instinctive acts*. There are important distinctions here that will be apparent as we proceed. *Instinct* connotes a native undifferentiated structural or dispositional background, the source of undifferentiated drive toward activity: analogous to a dammed-up body of water that may be used to turn any one or all of hundreds of wheels. *Instinctive act* connotes a specific form of behavior that is assumed to have a tap root in the reservoir, and the term *instincts* is applied in the literature to particular inborn mechanisms or dispositions supporting specific forms of behavior. Clearly there may be *instinct* and *instinctive* behavior, but not *instincts*.

MODIFIABILITY OF INSTINCTIVE BEHAVIOR. — This brings us to the point that instinctive behavior admits of progressive modification within the lifetime of the individual, so that what we in many cases describe as instinctive is in reality a product of individual experience knitted into a broad but little differentiated instinctive basis. This amounts practically to modification of instinct. One of the best illustrations of this that is available in the literature of experimental psychology relates to the control of the so-called singing instinct in birds. The bobolink, oriole, and robin, when reared in the fields, develop songs that are characteristic of the species. In other circumstances, however, it appears that no characteristic song would develop. W. E. D. Scott (17, 18, 19, 20) segregated orioles before they had heard the songs of their species, and kept them in isolation for several years. They became good singers, and their earlier vocal utterances were similar to those of the free birds of their kind. During certain seasons they sang almost incessantly. " It was now a loud, clear series of notes of great brilliancy, poured forth in such rapid succession as to be like that of the house wren in the intervals, and lasting about as long as the warble of the wren. Except for the rattle, which was now and then a part of the repertoire, this song had nothing in it that reminded one of the song of the Baltimore oriole as heard in New York, Massachusetts, or at any other point where the birds occur. When orioles six days of age were shut up with adults that had been brought up in isolation they began at the proper age to sing the songs of their companions. When birds belonging to fifteen or sixteen other species were brought together and reared within hearing of one another's voices, more or less modification of songs occurred. Some birds resisted these social influences more than others. The robin and the wood-thrush each developed a song that was not original. A red-winged blackbird crowed constantly during two months in the year in imitation of a bantam rooster."

A second experiment of similar import was made by Conradi (2) upon a group of young English sparrows. Canaries with their song were an important element in the experimental situation. The sparrows were reared from incubation in the same room with the canaries and were isolated from others of their kind. The regular sparrow chirp developed at the proper time but the birds soon lost this form of expression and assumed the peep that is characteristic of the young canary. At the age of three and a half months one of the sparrows " constantly chimed in with the canaries in his own fashion, giving a low note followed by a few high ones, with now and then some slurring from a high to a low note similar to those that the canaries have in their overtures. He joined the canaries freely for a few days, when he became ill and was silent for a week." A fortnight later he resumed the foreign language. In general the song in the mouth of the sparrow resembled the confusion of notes that filled the room when the three canaries were singing together at their best. Other sparrows observed under similar conditions much more closely approximated the vocalization of the canaries. When these sparrows were returned to their own kindred they soon assumed the ways of the English sparrow, but they still retained traces of their earlier training which Conradi was able to observe after a few months when the birds were recaptured. Their voices were still more musical than those of untrained sparrows and when they were returned again to the canary environment they soon regained what they had lost.

Outside of the laboratory illustrations of the modifiability of what have been hitherto described as specific forms of instinctive behavior abound. The fear reaction has all but disappeared from domesticated cattle, horses, and sheep; so much so that these animals, — many of them, — far from running away at the sight of a human being will follow him quietly across the pasture.

The foregoing phenomena might quite well have been described later under the subject " acquired motives." They are serviceable here, however, because of the rather emphatic demonstration that they afford of the undefined or non-specific character of instinct.

What appear to be specializations of instinct are probably habits resting upon an instinctive basis: habits developed by repeated responses to the varied angles of the day's work. In the cases cited above we have the instinct for vocal expression in song; more likely only for vocal expression alone. It is assumed to depend upon a certain physiological mechanism which is heritable. What this mechanism will do — what notes will be sung — depends upon the influences that play upon it. But we will think of this further in connection with our discussion of the development of motives.

FUNCTIONS OF INSTINCTIVE EQUIPMENT. — In the introductory chapter it was pointed out that the student of social psychology is chiefly interested in the analysis of psychologic conditions that make for the development of interactions among human beings and for the growth of a sense of unity among those who live together in the same neighborhood, state, nation, etc. The customary mode of discussing the development of such interactions in the course of a chapter on instinct is to attempt to show how each one of a group of so-called instincts contributes its share. To begin with, there is the universal instinct of activity: an undifferentiated disposition toward activity, physical or mental or both. What forms the activity may assume, will be determined by the nature of the stimuli as in the case of the birds observed by Conradi and Scott cited above. It is impossible to conceive of a sense of unity among people grown up without a liberal degree of activity among them. It is only through the action of people and their interaction among themselves that their characteristics are brought to the attention of one another, and hence it is only through this means that we become acquainted with our fellows.

In the second place there is the disposition among individuals of a kind to group together: the instinct of gregariousness it is called, or the impulsive or motor aspect of the " consciousness of kind." There is ground for doubt whether there is a specific instinct of the sort excepting in so far as animals behave as if they prefer companionship to isolation. The attachment of the dog to his master and his master's family; the fact that isolated sheep in the field have been observed to become so attached to cattle and to horses — provided that association began in infancy — that they will not only follow them throughout the day but even stay with them when at last they have opportunity to associate with animals of their own sort; that similar behavior has been observable with respect to hogs, ducklings and the like; all this lends some color to the hypothesis that what appears to be a gregarious instinct is really a complex of habits: a series of acquisitions as truly as is the dog's behavior in lifting the latch of a door. But whether it is instinct or acquisition it is of social significance in so far as it implies, in the first place, a " consciousness of kind," or in the second place, a readiness on the part of an individual to react preferably to the stimuli presented by his own kind, or by others with which bonds of association have been created. Indirectly the gregarious tendency, whatever its nature, is of tremendous social value. In as far as its expression is a coming together of a group of individuals it presents opportunities for reciprocal stimulus and response; for observation of one another within the group and consequently for mutual acquaintanceship, for the development of an anticipatory imagery of others' responses which is the key to that sense of unity among the members of a group that makes the whole body seem kin.

The group reaction tendency, too, gives oppor-

tunity for the development of various pattern-like
forms of behavior commonly called the instincts of
acquisitiveness and constructiveness; and of what is
sometimes called the adaptive instinct of play, which,
as it develops with the maturing of the individual contributes to the sense of social unity among the members of the group.

For example, acquisitiveness: the primitive form
of this may be the hoarding of food among barbarians
and lower animals. It is expressed among children in
collecting all sorts of odds and ends: roots, leaves,
pebbles, birds' eggs, etc. In the adult savant it is
suggested in the mineralogical cabinet, the ornitho-
logical museum, the library of rare books; in the artist
the same tendency is displayed in the collection of
book-bindings, china, and what-not. In the miser's
hoard we have, at any rate from the esthetic and
moral point of view, a perversion. The whole institution of private property may be an outgrowth of
this same acquisitive tendency, together with that of
competition. Granting that this is the case, we are
prepared to see how it contributes indirectly to the
development of a sense of unity among, at any rate,
large groups of our population. By the very fact
that wealth has been accumulated by considerable
groups of our people they understand one another;
therefore they foresee one another's reactions to given
situations; insensibly there develops among them a
" consciousness of kind " and a class has so far been
formed. In such a way, too, development of a sense
of unity comes about in the academic group, the professional group, etc. The mere fact of the possession

of certain goods, whatsoever the goods may be, material, intellectual, or what-not, contributes to this sense.

Closely allied to this is another form of the individualistic tendency — competition: a primitive form of which may have been the struggle for food and for mates. In its crudest form it is expressed in unmitigated hostility between individuals and between groups. As the social consciousness develops, however, *i.e.*, as men develop the capacity to control their behavior in the light of the imaged reactions of others, or by the functioning of an all but unconscious background of their organizations, such as are the residue of countless experiences in which they have been controlled by imagination of the reactions of others; that is, by dint of the disposition that in time grows out of behavior so controlled: when all this transformation shall have occurred, the reaction is no longer unmitigated hostility, but manifold forms of competition in commercial, professional, and other activities. It is now a complicated disposition that controls. If the root of it is in instinct it is covered over and all but hidden by many acquisitions. These dispositions are supported by laws of the state and rules of procedure. Indeed, the criminal law, or the rule, with the penalty provided in case of its infraction, and the concrete presence of the officer of the law, are, properly considered, stimuli provided to occasion those reactions that will ultimately yield their fruit in a refinement of unmitigated hostility; in such a modification of crude pugnacity as will amount practically to its substitution by a disposition to compete as a matter of course according to the rules of the game.

Mutual acquaintanceship and the sense of social unity that grows out of it; the ability to foresee others' reactions and to adapt ourselves to them unconsciously or as a matter of course, favor competition instead of crude fighting. This same competition reacts in turn and contributes to acquaintanceship and hence to social unity. Perhaps it is the active competition to which they are accustomed that is principally responsible for the sense of unity or clan feeling that is alleged to exist among commercial men.

A corollary to all this is that the development of means of communication between portions of the state and between nations, and the removal of unnatural and artificial barriers by enlarging the scope of the expression of tendencies to competition, facilitate statewide and international acquaintanceship respectively, and therefore national and international unity.

In such connections as this some students of psychology would speak of what they call the instinct to imitate, and would elaborately describe the part it plays in the social life. The weight of authority, however, inclines to the view that we have here no instinct but that the term imitation refers to any one of a number of methods by which the original tendency toward activity is expressed. Students of animal behavior have failed to demonstrate that animals learn by imitation. The cases of the sparrows and the canaries described earlier in this chapter need not be interpreted as illustrations of an imitation instinct specifically. The particular notes and combinations of notes that are sung are responses to particular stimuli, which responses arrive in the course of time to the status of thoroughly rooted habits. Close observation of the sparrows might have revealed that they struck the canary's note immediately upon catching the stimulus of the canary's voice. At any rate the cat that has repeatedly seen its cooped-up neighbor open the door of the box and make an exit to a plate of food, has not obtained profit thereby if one is to judge by his behavior when he himself is placed within the box behind the closed door.

Without committing ourselves to the view that imitation is instinct, we may, nevertheless, briefly discuss the part that responses called imitative play in social psychology. In the first place there is the unconscious slipping into another's mental attitude or way of doing things: the root of conventionality and of custom — the subjects of a separate chapter. In the second place there is imitation in which the imitator is conscious of what he is doing but in which, nevertheless, he is serving no purpose beyond possibly the gratification of an immediate pleasure. In the third place, there is reasoned imitation in which the imitator copies another consciously and for the purpose of gaining an ulterior end, as when one business man imitates another's organization in order that he may diminish running expenses. Though this is designated in some texts as a type of imitation, it is doubtful whether it should be described in a way that connotes more than a broad, undifferentiated instinctive activity basis. Even this factor is undoubtedly very slight when compared with those of logical analysis and comparison. At any rate, in every form of imitation we have one more avenue through which an individual gains knowledge of other folk. He learns how it feels to do thus and so; consequently he is the better able to sympathize with others and to interpret their behavior; he arrives at a completer understanding of the motives both of himself and of others. In short, through the different forms of imitation, one becomes acquainted, in a deep sense, with other people, the number of whom is limited only by the breadth of one's sphere of activity, and therefore imitation has a tendency to contribute toward a sense of social unity, and by the same token to the capacity for effective co-operation.

Once a series of acts has got started the capacity for action in itself seems to supply additional motive. In fact it must do so, else the actor will succumb to the deadly routine of the performance. The young man practicing at football is driven to the training ground times almost without number, and always with a great deal of zest, because of his pleasure in the action itself; because he has discovered some capacities for physical prowess and he finds satisfaction in exercising them. In the course of time the push for satisfaction so obtained is the only motive that activates him. The unfolding of any other capacity such as for memorizing: for manipulating the abstractions of mathematics or of philosophy: for dealing with the practical situations incident to administration or what-not, may furnish an analogous drive in its own sphere — in fact, must do so if things are to be done effectively. This is a reminder, by the way, of the much-abused doctrine of interest in education, and it carries its implications into industrial problems. High wages and the prospect for promotion and participation in profits alone are of large usefulness only as far as they stimulate the motive that is suggested by the phrase " a feeling for the work itself."

To repeat: the discussion thus far points only to an undifferentiated native tendency toward activity, whether physical or mental, which may be termed instinct. *Instincts* are doubtful. No doubt many forms of action may be called instinctive for convenience, but this should imply only that a primary root of these actions is in an unlearned tendency toward reaction.

ANALOGY WITH THE COMPLEX. — Examination of motives, whether they are what have been called instincts or habits, suggests that they are not essentially different from the " complex " of the psycho-analytic school. In the sphere of abnormal psychological phenomena, the psycho-analysts seek to explain many forms of abnormal behavior on the ground of a suppressed complex, that in normal life is effective, if at all, unobtrusively. This term will be employed so frequently in this text, and the conception is deemed so important in connection with human behavior that an explanation is required.

We are accustomed to thinking of every impression upon the organism and of every reaction whether it be overt in the sense of muscular activity that is apparent to the on-looker, or as subjective in the sense of thinking or remembering as leaving a trace thereupon that is never entirely lost. Our personality is altered somewhat by each successive stimulation and reaction. This is, by no means, a new conception. It is only in recent years that it has received strong support of an objective nature. The analysis of the phenomena of automatic writing, of the imagery in dreams, and in the wild fancies of the fever-ridden patient and of the maniac and the objects of our phobias afford striking evidence for the hypothesis that while we forget much in the sense of becoming unable to recall voluntarily, we nevertheless utterly lose out of our personality much less than appears to be the case.

Dr. Morton Prince's patient (13), B, C, A, is a case in point. She suffered from an abnormal fear of white cats and she could not voluntarily bring to mind any memory images that could account for it, but she unconsciously or automatically wrote, under experimental conditions, a story of an experience of her childhood, thirty-five years earlier, in which she had been frightened by a white cat with which she had been playing. This, she said, in her automatic-writing state, she believed was the root of her present unnatural fear. In connection with her relation of the incident she described in great detail the furnishings of the room in which she was playing at the time, the designs in the floor and wall coverings, the window draperies, etc. She had never before related the circumstances, she said. In its essential respects, at any rate, the story was verified by members of the patient's family. The phenomena of dreams and of other hallucinatory experiences, of hypnosis, etc., afford other illustrations of what appears to be the actuality of the retention of the residua of many experiences which cannot be voluntarily recalled. Furthermore, many of us who are not professional mathematicians are today totally unable to recall at will many of the formulae that we learned and used freely in our youth. We no longer *know* the formulae. Yet with very slight expenditure of time and effort, as compared with what was originally required, we can regain complete control of all that has been thus temporarily lost. This statement and others of the kind that might be made about analogous situations are no doubt supported by the experience of every student and general reader.

Such situations as have been described or implied above obviously indicate that in some form or other the residua of certain experiences, — those with mathematical formulae, e.g. — have remained over in the background of the personality, in such form, to be sure, that they cannot be made use of on demand, but so that they give the individual a distinct advantage once he again attempts to work the field from which the earlier experiences were gained; that is, once we begin again to work in the department of mathematics we are at an advantage notwithstanding that we have completely forgotten, as we say, what we had well learned in that branch of science a score of years ago.

This something that remains over, this residuum of earlier experiences and adjustments, is a complex. It is essentially no different from a habit; or, more accurately, no different from the foundation of what we call the habit in every-day language; that is, an overt motor adjustment of a specific sort that next to unerringly occurs in a given situation; the man of the house, for example, inevitably reaches for his cigar after dinner as soon as he finds himself in his great armchair. In fact, a habit is a complex. But the former term has come to be used so exclusively to relate to overt reactions that the other should be a welcome addition to our vocabulary. It connotes the foundation of our acquired likes and dislikes, our religious, political, and other social prejudices, our professional dispositions, our morals, and the like. So far as its nature is concerned, as we conceive it, the complex is of the same nature as has been conceived to belong to the instinct excepting that as we use the term in this book, it is an acquired disposition rather than an inborn one.

Whether the residua that compose our complexes are physical in the sense of neurone arrangements or patterns that have acquired specialized functions; whether they are psychic or chemical, are queries that will be answered precisely as we reply to the same questions when they are related to our habits of overt reaction. Indeed, there is at present no ground of unquestioned fact upon which to fasten answers to these questions. It is sufficient that the phenomena of human behavior afford evidence to justify the hypothesis that at the foundations of our personality there are such arrangements as we conceive and to which we give the name "complexes." These are interwoven in infinite complexity with one another and with inborn structures.

Furthermore, the existence of a complex implies a corresponding "drive." Once it has been aroused to activity by an external stimulus or situation it expends its drive in bringing specific acts of behavior to pass or it imparts it to other complexes and to the whole network of arrangements within the organism so that each complex may be reinforced by others in respect to control over behavior. Thus the professional complexes of the lawyer make it inevitable that he will practice law or seek to do so. The sporting complexes of the man in the street impel him toward the bleachers even on a blustery afternoon to sit in the snow that he may see the game — or at least they father an *interest* in such behavior and a *longing* to escape to the athletic field. Similarly our town neighbor is impelled to ally himself with the prevailing political and religious life about him as a matter of course, or to set himself up against it. In short, we conceive of every commanding and persisting interest in our lives as resting upon an established complex in our nature which is normally interwoven with many others and with original nature.

It was pointed out above that the drive arising from a complex may be reinforced by that of others. But it may be opposed also and in such a case we are confronted by the " conflict " which figures prominently in psycho-analytic literature. Every normal process of decision is one of conflict which comes to an issue in satisfactory adjustment or at least in adjustment with contentment. But it is a conflict that comes into the clear light of consciousness of what one is about; not wholly into consciousness, indeed, for one who has just now reached a decision is often unable to relate even to himself clearly, all the devious paths he followed toward the settlement of the conflict. In a

measure the process is underground and unconscious.
It goes on unconsciously amongst the complexes of the
personality. Sometimes, indeed, the entire conflict
appears to be resolved beneath the surface as when
one falls asleep before an unsolved problem and awakes
to find the solution or the decision immediately at
hand.

But in many an instance insuperable barriers prevent the solution of a conflict. It therefore becomes a
habitual state and reacts upon behavior producing the
chronic grouch or the unrestful personality and the
like; and in extreme cases, a complete dissociation
amongst conflicting complexes occurs so that one or
a group of them independently control the behavior.
Normally this kind of thing occurs in states of rapt
attention and in fits of absent-mindedness, in which
case behavior may be even unconscious, that is, un-
controlled by the unitary personality. In the abnormal sphere persistent thoughts of a loathsome disease
from which one is suffering, or the haunting images
of objects of filth may be driven into the background
or margin of consciousness where they persist as complexes, — perhaps as neural patterns, — in conflict
with others that correspond to an interest in being
healthy and uncontaminated. The result is a dread of
contact and even an actual inhibition of touching certain objects. The memory of a humiliating failure,
driven from clear consciousness, may persist as a complex and occasion a distressing shrinking from public
appearance.

In like manner the positive advances of the abnormal
individual, his so-called insane, or anti-social acts, are

occasioned, according to the psycho-analytic hypothesis, by the influence of suppressed complexes in more or less dissociation from others that make up the total personality.

On a broad scale it is this dissociation or partial dissociation that has come to pass in the mob, in the war-fevered multitude and in the heated political campaign.

In every instance the particular act or thought or purpose or ambition is but a clue that must be followed up to find the final motive. When these complexes are once discovered, as sometimes they may be by means of psycho-analysis, and banished by suggestion or otherwise, the abnormality of behavior is corrected. As long as they exist we must think of them as predispositions or motives, which, given a particular sort of constitution, develop and are capable of being broken up again according to the laws of the development of habits, concepts, and of automatization in general.

Our thought is that the complex is a source of motive or of drive impelling the individual toward behavior, whether subjective, as feelings of preference or of unrest, or objective, as professional or occupational activity; and further that these complexes are capable of dissociation and of furnishing impulsions or drives more or less independently of the rest of the organism. So each of us has his political complex; his civic complex; his philanthropic, his religious, his moral, his educational, his occupational complex, and corresponding to each in turn, his antagonistic complex. These are again among what we may call final motives in our social life. They are not mutually exclusive.

Any more detailed classification of social motives would accomplish no more than to suggest those objects that have a peculiar attraction for us in virtue of one or another of our final motives. Thus we speak of generosity in those situations in which relief is extended to an indigent caller in whom we could not be interested but for our general philanthropic nature. It is by virtue of our educational complex, once more, that we are controlled by the motive of generosity in another sense; the sense of being open-mindedly interested in the opinions of others. Sympathy for others in distress is an expression of the philanthropic motive and is often aroused when it is impossible for us to do anything more practical than to approximate to the mental attitude of those to whom sympathy is extended. In another sense there is an expression of our educational complex when we adopt the same intellectual attitude as our contemporaries toward a given problem.

GENESIS OF MOTIVES. — The genesis of the motive in the sense of predisposition, prejudice, or " complex " as described above, may be compared with the development of a specialist in mathematics, for example. In the first years of his course the student elects mathematics because it is his purpose to become a civil engineer. The purpose of his activity at this stage is his motive. It represents a preliminary guiding of a generalized push from within. He becomes fond of his instructor and this fondness is another motive — in this case a feeling — that co-operates in the control of his behavior. These are conscious motives. They may have arisen accidentally. The story of a group of engineers surveying a line over the mountains for a proposed railway, and camping by the way, may have awakened the purpose or intention to become an engineer. The mere observation of such a motive, however, gives no assurance of its social value. It might be entirely possible at this stage to divert this prospective civil engineer from his purpose and to make a bricklayer of him. Let us suppose, however, that he persists in holding these motives vivid in consciousness, even while difficulties accumulate and the tedium of his work increases, by the aid of whatever other supplementary conscious motives may be presented, such as the purpose of competing for a prize at the end of the term. Ultimately he reaches the point at which he no longer requires such motives as these to hold him to his course. Gradually there has developed a mathematical habit, disposition, tendency, or " complex " in virtue of which the mathematical activity possesses a peculiar attraction for him and follows him throughout his life. He has lived through the period of accidental motives, and has developed a final motive. Any subject that can be approached by the method of mathematics elicits his ready response. The mere opportunity suffices. We now have a motive, the value of which we can estimate. It would be practically impossible, now, to make anything but a civil engineer of one who has had such a history. He can no longer be understood in the light of any particular act as a mathematician, stimulated by any specific problem.

It is hopeless now to describe his motive, simply as purpose or end in view. It was once no more than that, now it is much more. It is vividly conscious purpose and desire reduced to even more general terms than ambition which usually implies at any rate a frequent consideration of ends. It has become a settled disposition.

We may conceive a similar illustration in the growth of an individual into good citizenship in an American town. His psychological history first reveals a conscious purpose to be of public service in various respects. His motives are of the conscious sort. In course of time a disposition develops in the light of which those forms of activity, such as serving on school boards, election boards, expending time and effort toward the development of sentiment for public parks, etc., once objects of conscious purposes, have now acquired immediate attractiveness. The mere opportunity now suffices to set off acts of good citizenship. We cannot understand the good citizen by observing particular occasions of his activity. We must get his history. The history of the development of the antisocial motives of the criminal, as will be inferred, follows an analogous route. " It seems as if the isolated moments of desire sum themselves up in the course of time and then break out as the crime. In such cases the explaining motive of the deed is never to be found except in the criminal's past " (7).

REMORSE — SELF APPROBATION — CONSCIENCE. — From the point of view developed above, it appears that a motive or disposition or " submerged complex " is the root of remorse, self-approbation, and conscience. That these functions are controlling factors in behavior, inhibiting or encouraging it, should follow from their partaking of the warp and woof of final motives as already described. Whenever a clash of motives occurs, excited by a particular situation, and the one that has finally expressed itself in behavior contradicts that disposition that we recognize as our truest representative, or that that has been the object of our purposes, then there is remorse. When on the other hand, the motive that finally determines behavior after a struggle is recognized as in correspondence or agreement with this disposition, self-approbation occurs; but the well-knitted personality who plays his part without a struggle contemplates his behavior simply as a matter of course. The good citizen who has been reared from his childhood up in an atmosphere of disinterested community service, and who has steadfastly practised the art of citizenship has reason for being surprised when his friends commend him for his stand in favor of practical public improvement.

A corollary to all this will suggest itself in the case of the delinquent who has become what he is through a long course of development. Remorse, as a symptom of conflict when anti-social acts have been indulged, disappears in the same ratio as does the conflict among motives.

It is already clear from the foregoing what query will arise with reference to the social conscience. Does analysis reveal anything called conscience that has characteristics quite its own, distinct from what have been under discussion above? Or is it but another name for the feeling that follows the issue of a conflict? If the last question should be answered affirmatively, then it would appear that conscience has pursued exactly the natural course of development that has been attributed above to other motives. Indeed " promptings of conscience " and the " voice of conscience " would be the faint or strong incipient expressions of our final motives in cases in which there is an inner conflict.

CHAPTER IV

INTELLECTUAL LEVELS AND PSYCHIC STABILITY OF THE POPULATION

THE intellectual level of sections of the general population is another element that has a large bearing upon the problems of Social Psychology. In a similar category are the psychopathic nature and those instabilities of character that are recognized as signs of the hysterical disposition, mental instability, etc., and mental dullness such as may arise from infections that reduce the energy of the individual to a low ebb.

The term " intellectual level " suggests feeble-mindedness and moronity, which connote varying degrees of incapacity, by reason of a general mental defect, existing from early age or birth, to take ordinary care of one's affairs and to adjust one's self to the usual circumstances of life. The terms are believed to represent native conditions that cannot be overcome by processes of education, though in certain respects they may be relieved; for example those of the higher grades of feeble-mindedness may be taught to care for their persons and even to provide a living for themselves in simple manual occupations.

PROPORTION OF FEEBLE-MINDEDNESS IN THE GENERAL POPULATION. — Obviously it is impossible for such a group as this to become knitted into the general population and to become one with it. It is impossible to develop co-operation on any but the smallest scale between this group and the normal elements in the population. To whatever extent such a subnormal group exists in the general population it is a drag upon the effective co-ordination and progress of the entire group. Besides, it is potentially the source of very great embarrassment to the whole. It is pertinent, therefore, to attempt here an account of the extent and distribution of feeble-mindedness in the population.

One naturally turns to the United States Census Reports for whatever light they may throw upon the general question. But the manner in which the census is taken provokes a question as to the accuracy of any figure it may report upon this point. The heads of families of whom inquiry is made are not likely to report eagerly cases of feeble-mindedness in their respective houses, if, indeed, they know that they are there. The agents of the census bureau, furthermore, are certainly not, on the whole, skilled in making inquiry as to this particular point. Any ratio arrived at in this manner, therefore, is likely to be too small rather than too large. The same observation may be made with propriety as to the report of the Royal Commission of 1908 in England (13), which states that in the general population of England there is one feeble-minded to every 305. The Massachusetts report on the extent and increase of feeble-mindedness and epilepsy in that state is frankly an estimate, and it places the ratio at 1 in 171.

Another source of evidence is in studies of groups of school children. For example, Dr. Goddard reported (8) 2% of feeble-minded among 2,000 public school children in New York City. This figure is derived from an intensive examination of each of the 2,000 pupils by means of the Binet Tests, which, at the time investigation was made, were just coming into vogue.

Of much broader scope is the survey of 12,000 pupils in the Toronto public schools under the direction of the Canadian National Committee for Mental Hygiene during 1919. Of the number examined, 1.5% were found mentally defective with an intelligence quotient of 75 or less. Some very retarded children were not examined, owing to their absence from school. It is, therefore, the judgment of Professor W. G. Smith of the University of Toronto that the total per cent of mental defect, of the degree mentioned above, among the 12,000 children examined, would amount to about 2% (14). This would confirm Dr. Goddard's result in New York City, and would indicate further that among the 80,000 public school pupils in Toronto there are 1,600 mentally defective children, and 10,000 in the Province of Ontario. One cannot realize the barrier to social unity and co-operation that is created by such an army until one thinks of them as within a system such as the organized public schools of a city or state.

Other results obtained by the Canadian Committee show 3.34% and even 3.56% of defectiveness of the degree mentioned, in the school populations of Guelph, Ontario, and in British Columbia. These figures are based upon surveys of groups of 2,245 and 2,273 school children (12). They are the highest estimates

of the per cent of feeble-minded in the public schools.
The lowest, 0.42%, is that made in certain Australian
schools in 1912 (12).

These are widely divergent figures and their difference is doubtless due to a lack of standardization
of methods in large part, and in other part to the
personal equation amongst the examiners. Taking
all the variant circumstances into account as accurately as possible, Dr. Kuhlmann has estimated that
about 0.5% of the general population in the United
States is feeble-minded (10). Since this estimate was
made the World War has brought before the country
both the opportunity and the responsibility for making
an extended survey of the psycho-physical make-up of
the drafted men. This survey is the first careful and
very extended effort of the sort that had been attempted, and the result affords undoubtedly the most
comprehensive picture of the psycho-physical background of a people that is extant anywhere. " Nervous and mental defects, including feeble-mindedness,
mental deficiencies, paralyses, psychasthenia, constitutional psychopathic states, and neurasthenia were
among the defects, victims of which were most commonly rejected. These are the defects that are incom-
patible with the strain of military training and active
service. It doubtless would have been well had none
of these been accepted for general military service.
It is noteworthy that certain conditions, like psychasthenia, constitutional psychopathic states, neurasthenia, and hysteria, which are difficult to detect, were
passed over by local boards and were, therefore, an

exceptionally common cause for rejection at mobilization camps " (4).

We quote here from the " Memoirs of the National Academy of Sciences " which contains a detailed account of psychological examining in the United States Army during the World War (11):

" The psychological examiner is frequently asked this question: ' How intelligent is the Army? ' There is an inherent difficulty in making an answer, for there are no standards in terms of which the statement can be made. The most familiar measures of intelligence, (years of mental age as determined by the Stanford-Binet examination) are the results of investigations of a much smaller group (approximately 1,000 cases) than the group studied in the Army. For norms of *adult* * intelligence the results of the Army examinations are undoubtedly the most representative. It is customary to say that the mental age of the average adult is about 16 years. This figure is based, however, upon examinations of only 62 persons,† 32 of them high school pupils from 16 to 20 years of age, and 30 of them ' business men of moderate success and of very limited educational advantages.' This group is too small to give very reliable results and is furthermore probably not typical. High school pupils and business men of moderate success presumably do not represent the average American adult with respect to intelligence.

" It appears that the intelligence of the principal

* Italics ours.
† See Terman *et al*: The Stanford Revision and Extension of the Binet-Simon Scale for Measuring Intelligence, 1917, p. 49.

sample of the white draft, when transmuted from Alpha and Beta* examinations into terms of mental age, is about 13 years (13.08). Here we have a measure of the average intelligence of nearly 1,000,000 white recruits. We can hardly say, however, with assurance that these recruits are three years mental age below the average. Indeed, it might be argued on extrinsic grounds that the draft itself is more representative of the average intelligence of the country than is a group of high school students and business men. The draft, it is true, is highly selected at the upper end by reason of the fact that men of higher intelligence became officers without being drafted or constituted the greater part of the group of professional and business experts that were exempted from draft because they were essential to industrial activity in the war. It is impossible to guess the extent of this selection with respect to intelligence. It seems quite impossible that it could have reduced the intelligence level of the draft so much as three years. Considerably less than 15% of the draft lie above 16 years mental age. This discrepancy would mean that a very large number of men in proportion to the draft (considerably more than one man to every three of the draft, perhaps even so great a proportion as two to every three) would have been exempted because of service as an officer or because they were in some essential industry. No positive figures of the number of men exempted for these reasons are at present avail-

* See Appendix for a brief description of the Alpha and Beta tests used in the army. A complete and fully illustrated description of them may be found in the *Memoirs of the National Academy of Sciences* referred to at the end of the chapter.

able, but there seems to be no doubt that it was considerably smaller than these indicated proportions. Undoubtedly the intelligence of the draft is somewhat lower than that of the country at large, although it is quite unlikely that the difference should be so great. It must be recalled further that there was also selection at the lower end of the scale of intelligence. The low-grade feeble-minded were not in general included in the draft. This selection tends to offset the selection at the upper end, although presumably it does not completely counter-balance it, and thus to render the average intelligence of the draft more nearly representative of the population at large than would otherwise be the case.

" In general, then, we are forced to reply to the question ' How intelligent is the Army? ' by stating arbitrary figures that refer to the draft itself, and by arguing further that the draft is approximately a representative group which is presumably, however, a little lower in intelligence than is the country at large. . . . It may be necessary to revise our notion of the frequency of occurrence of these various levels of intelligence. . . .

" A moron has been defined as anyone with a mental age from 7 to 12 years. If this definition is interpreted as meaning anyone with a mental age less than 13 years, as has recently been done, then almost half of the white draft (47.3 per cent) would have been morons. Thus it appears that feeble-mindedness, as at present defined, is of much greater frequency of occurrence than had been originally supposed.

" Table 333 (Memoirs, National Academy of

Sciences, XV, 1921, p. 790), gives the best summary
of the intelligence of the draft that is available. It
will be noted that there are two sets of figures: one
a set derived from Groups I, II, and III,* of the principal sample as laid down on the combined scale, and
the other the actual percentages obtained in the Stanford-Binet examinations of the 653 native-born white
recruits of Group X. The former group is large and
representative but involves an error dependent on the
fact that these men were examined by Alpha and Beta
and not by a mental-age scale. The second group
suffers from the fact that it is small and cannot be
demonstrated to be representative. If the two distri-
butions are taken together the results can undoubtedly
be considered accurate within the limits of discrepancy
between them. It will be seen that a level of eight
years mental age for rejection would mean the elimi-

---

* Group I represents the draft of the United States at large,
pro-rated by states. (41,278.) Group II is intended to furnish a
basis for comparing the intelligence levels of states. In the
cases of a few states the pro-rata selection for the sample
groups did not furnish a sufficient number of individuals to
make an adequate basis. In those instances additional selections
were made so that no state was represented by fewer than a
thousand. (14,684.) Group III was selected by camps without
respect to states. (40,392.) These three groups together make up
a sample of 96,354 of the white draft.

Other groups forming additional samplings are as follows:

Group IV	Negroes pro-rated by states, 19,992
Group V	Northern negroes from Illinois, Indiana, New Jersey, New York and Pennsylvania, 5,400
Group VI	White officers, 15,528.
Group VII	Negro officers,
Group VIII	White established organization, various arms of the service, 24,205.
Group IX	Negro established organizations.
Group X	Special experimental group, 1,047.

nation of from 0.5 to 2 per cent of white recruits and approximately 17 per cent of negro recruits. Placing the level at nine years would eliminate 4 or 5 per cent of whites and presumably 32 per cent of negroes. A 10-year limit rejects from 10 to 13 per cent of white and 48 per cent of negro recruits. It would be totally impossible to exclude all morons *as that term is at present defined*,* for there are under 13 years 47 per cent of whites and 89 per cent of negroes."

Dr. Pearce Bailey, who during the War was Chief of the Section of Neurology and Psychiatry in the Surgeon General's Office at Washington, makes the following statement, in collaboration with Dr. Haber, with reference to the prevalence of mental defect (imbeciles and morons) in the draft army (1):

" Of the 72,323 cases of nervous and mental disorders identified by the neuro-psychiatric examiners of the Medical Corps of the army detailed in the United States, 22,741, or 31.4 per cent, were mental defectives. The mental defect was so pronounced that the bulk of these recruits were considered unfit for any kind of military service. They constituted nearly one-third of all the rejections for nervous or mental causes, and were far more numerous than any other single clinical group. If the mental defectives rejected at the local boards are added to those rejected at camps, the total number of individuals seriously handicapped by mental defect brought to light by the mobilization reaches 26,545.

" But while the figure of 26,545 undoubtedly represents the bulk of mental defectives originally called to

* Italics ours.

PERCENTAGE COMPARISON OF MENTAL AGE OF GROUPS FROM THE DRAFT

(From Mem. Nat. Acad. Sci. XV, 1921, p. 790)

Mental Age	White draft Groups I, II, and III		White draft Group X		Negro draft Group IV		Sheridan white individual examination		Sheridan negro individual examination		Grant, white discharge		Grant, negro discharge	
	Distribution	Sum	Distribution	Sum	Distribution	Sum	Distribution	Sum	Distribution	Sum	Distribution	Sum	Distribution	Sum
22–22.9	0.05	100.0												
21–21.9	.07	99.9				100.0								
20–20.9	.08	99.9		100.0	0.01	100.0		100.0						
19–19.9		99.8	0.9	100.0	.04	100.0	0.1	100.0						
18–18.9	1.5	99.8	3.7	99.1	.10	99.9	.3	99.7		99.8				
17–17.9	2.3	98.3	7.3	95.4	.27	99.7	.3	99.4	.2	99.6				
16–16.9	3.9	96.0	8.4	88.1	.79	99.4	.3	99.1	.8	98.8		99.8		
15–15.9	6.1	92.1	9.8	79.7	1.7	98.5	1.3	98.7	1.4	97.4	0.7	99.1		
14–14.9	9.3	86.0	12.0	69.9	2.8	97.2	3.8	97.4	2.7	94.7	0.7	98.4		
13–13.9	13.6	76.7	10.7	57.9	5.4	94.4	10.7	93.6	4.3	90.4	1.4	97.0		
12–12.9	15.8	63.1	12.6	47.2	10.0	89.0	21.9	82.9	9.9	80.5	0.7	96.3		
11–11.9	17.0	47.3	10.7	34.6	15.0	79.0	27.0	61.0	9.2	57.0	0.7	95.6		
10–10.9	12.7	30.3	10.4	23.9	15.0	64.0	21.2	34.0	22.7	37.0	0.7	94.9		100.0
9–9.9	7.6	17.6	9.5	13.5	16.0	48.0	8.3	12.8	20.8	37.0	3.5	91.4	0.6	99.4
8–8.9	4.7	10.0	5.4	4.0	15.8	32.0	3.5	4.5	24.9	12.8	9.2	82.2	4.4	95.0
7–7.9	3.15	5.3	.6		8.5	16.7	.6	1.0	9.3	1.2	15.6	66.6	11.4	83.6
6–6.9	1.75	2.1	.3		5.2	8.2	.1	.4	1.6	.6	29.1	37.5	22.8	60.8
5–5.9	.20	.4	.2		2.1	3.0		.3	.4	.2	11.3	14.1	25.3	35.5
4–4.9	.10	.2			.55	.8	.3	.3	.4		2.8	2.8	24.1	11.4
3–3.9	.04	.1			.26	.3	.3		.2				9.5	1.9
2–2.9	.05	.1			.04	.0							1.9	
1–1.9	.01	.0												
Number of cases	98,955		658		18,891		690		514		141		158	
Median mental age	13.15		13.25		10.1		9.6		8.9		7.4		5.6	

the colors, it does not represent all of them. It does not include the cases (afore mentioned) found in France and returned to this country from the A. E. F., or those found at the demobilization examinations. Also, some were discharged under a different diagnosis than mental defect; some were disposed of directly by the court; some were discharged as unfit under Paragraph 148–$\frac{1}{2}$ A. R. Also, numerous borderline cases were accepted by the examiners. Some of these higher-grade defectives became part of the army, settled to low strata of usefulness, and served through the war. . . .

"The most important question arising from this inquiry is: how many mental defectives are there in the United States? The answer to it, vouchsafed by the army figures, while perhaps not absolutely accurate, may be not far from correct. If the number of men examined be approximately 3,500,000 there would be a ratio of 6.5 defectives for every 1,000 men examined. The number of cases discovered at the local boards is so small that the preceding ratio may be used in estimating the number of mental defectives between the ages of 21 and 31 years, exclusive of those confined in state and private institutions. There were 10,101,506 registrants between the ages of 21 and 31 years, and the ratio of 6.5 per thousand would give, for this number, 65,650 male mental defectives of the given age period.

"If mental deficiency ran uniform among persons of all ages, there would be 353,210 male defectives in the United States; if uniform for the ages between

18 and 45, there would be 164,710 male defectives in this group.

" As a matter of fact, we know that mental defect by reason of the high mortality incident to it, especially in youth, has a greater frequency in groups under 18 years than in those over that age. So it seems evident that the estimates drawn from adults would understate the number as related to the entire population."

If Dr. Bailey's analysis is correct, somewhat under 1% of the general population may be assumed, on a very liberal basis, to be of such low intellectual level as to be classifiable with the mentally deficient — morons and lower.

Those of this group who are at any time and place confined in institutions and so are in very large measure removed from the possibility of obstructing the community as a whole, are the lowest grades of feeble-minded. Kuhlmann estimated that 18% of the feeble-minded were in confinement at the time he made his analysis, and that this included but 2% of the highest grade, the morons (10). But those of the highest grade, partly by reason of the fact that they are not easily recognized, are a particularly embarrassing element in any community. They may be pleasing personally. Those of the so-called verbal type, for instance, make a good impression with the result that they make their way into situations for which they are not fitted.

But after all our statistical reports upon the "intelligence level" of adults it is of fundamental importance to keep this qualification in mind: that whether we talk of a mental age of 13 years or of 16 years, more or less, as the general level of adult " intelligence," *we cannot be speaking in terms of absolute values.* The values are relative — and relative to the " intelligence levels " of children of given chronological ages. But children and adults differ so widely in point of background and hence in outlook, disposition and behavior, that it is extremely doubtful whether they are comparable, especially in the respect we are considering here. Indeed in our relations to adults and to children, respectively, as educators or as superintendents in any capacity we assume wide differences between juveniles and adults in respect to all their reactions to the same conditions, and the assumption, in practice, is justified.

Furthermore, we believe that in our testing for " intelligence levels," whether of children or adults, hitherto, we may not have been getting at " intelligence " at all (perhaps not more than glimpsing it) but have been testing *alertness* instead. That adults, even of broad experience and high social station, usually fare illy in the tests as compared with children and adolescents supports us in this belief. But employers and others who have for long periods been close observers of large numbers of men engaged in making their adjustments to complicated situations have undoubtedly found that *alertness*, apart from certain traits of character such as accuracy, persistency, honesty and good humor, is, in the long run, of very minor significance.

In this connection we believe it is in keeping with sound judgment to withhold conclusions at certain points in the reports upon the use of Army tests to determine the relative intelligence of large groups of recruits; to withhold it until we can answer, for example: " What is the probability that many thousands of white men from our remote Southern highland regions, and other thousands of negroes from the plantations of Georgia, Alabama, Mississippi, Louisiana, etc., have had the experiences that would make it likely that, in a picture completion test, they would insert a *filament* in the outline of an electric bulb and a *net* in that of a tennis court? " But these are only isolated instances. The details of any test should be narrowly examined before it is put into practical use, with a view to discovering what are the possibilities of reaction to its several sections, on the part of groups of people who are widely separated from one another in experience and geographically. And finally, when these possibilities shall have been stated, a scheme should be invented by which suitable allowances may be made uniformly when one subgroup is compared with another. A thorough procedure is complicated!

PSYCHIC DEFECTS OTHER THAN FEEBLE-MINDEDNESS. — Other groups included amongst those draftees who were found to be suffering from mental and nervous disorders are the constitutionally psychopathic, the victims of psychoses, the epileptics, those afflicted with organic nervous diseases, the inebriates and those who suffer from neuroses and from glandular disorders which had had the effect of retarding physical development. All these, together with the feeble-minded, according to the report, represent approximately 2.25% of the general population. This figure is probably too low. About the same ratio was found in the course of the examination of 28,000 recruits at the Great Lakes Naval Training Station.

The figures quoted, of course, mean that such portions of the population are definitely unfit for military and naval service according to the standards of the respective branches of the service. It is undoubtedly within the bounds of probability that there are many of somewhat mental and nervous instability in the region of the indefinite border of normality who, if added to the foregoing, would materially increase the total per cent. Many of the unfit for military service, by reason of nervous and mental defects, are capable of carrying a part successfully in civil life. These cases, other than the feeble-minded, may be superficially brilliant; they may appear normal by the criteria of intellectual progress in school, versatility, and range of information. As long as the affairs with which they come into touch are of the usual sort; as long as no special difficulties of long endurance occur, such persons may pursue their usual course, honored in their several communities and contributing usefully to the social and professional or commercial life of their time and place.

But let the unusual occur; something that induces a prolonged strain and diverts attention from the customary grooves — then the precarious character of the individual's adjustment becomes apparent. There is a sharp increase in these circumstances in the number of pronounced cases of mental disease.

The numbers of individuals who belong to the groups we have discussed in this chapter are not large in proportion to the general population. The great majority of those of low intellectual level are themselves alone altogether harmless, self-satisfied and incapable of leadership. The minority are a constant source of embarrassment. The difference between these groups is probably in what Goddard refers to as " that vague something that we call temperament."

The psychopathic group, however, is probably very much the more numerous of the two. Estimates are confessedly very unreliable. Many of these folk are brilliant, volatile, unsteady, attractive personally, capable of leadership, at any rate for brief periods, inciters to unrest, and therefore potentially and actually sources of grave concern to the social psychologist and to other students of social problems.

THE QUESTION OF HEREDITY. — The mental condition of the groups we have been considering is assumed, on many hands, to be hereditary and inescapable in the strains in which it may be discovered. The histories of the Jukes (5), the Kallikaks (7), the Nam Family (2), the Hill Folk (3) and many others of like quality have created presumed support for the hypothesis. It is very likely, however, that the conclusions are based upon incomplete statistics. For example, it is highly improbable that nearly all of the descendants of the feeble-minded girl of Revolutionary days who figures in the history of the Kallikak family are represented by the figure 1146 which is reported in the text. Furthermore such investigations as have been made respecting the families referred to, assuming complete enumeration, must necessarily gain what validity they possess chiefly from the accuracy of memory and statement of persons who have been interviewed, and secondarily from written records of extraordinarily questionable value. It is of little, if any positive worth, to be told as we are in reports of some of these families that individuals were " shiftless and neurotic " or " shiftless and alcoholic," or " a shiftless drinking fellow," or " a wild fellow," etc.

But it is of more fundamental importance in this connection that feeble-mindedness is most probably not a unit character at all; and if not, the formula for inheritance is at best doubtfully applicable to it. By the terms of the theory the determiners that carry the qualities of future offspring are segregated according to mathematical ratios. Therefore it is not to be inferred that because a person may be weak in one particular this particular form of weakness will be handed on to any or all of his descendants. We may expect a proportion of his progeny to be likewise affected, but which ones cannot be predicted. The laws of heredity in their present stage of development are useful to explain what has already happened, but are of little predictive value as to what will happen in respect to individuals as a result of a particular fertilization; this because we know so little as we do of the qualities of the germ plasm of the parents and more remote ancestors. Were we interested only in a mass of tens of thousands as is the wheat grower during each planting and reaping season, the situation would be very different. In our human relations we are emphasizing the family of two or three and the like in a single generation, and their ten or a dozen descendants in the next generation. Our regard for this small and at best slowly growing group we consider one of the finest fruits of our civilization and we are not prepared, forgetting them and the possibilities that lurk in even exceptional cases of defective heredity, as for instance the Edwards stock, to look abroad to the whole of tens and thousands in the very distant future.

THE QUESTION OF ACQUISITION OF MENTAL DEFECTS. — But leaving aside the question of inheritance of feebleness of mind and other forms of mental weakness, we are confronted by another situation: the belief that these conditions may be acquired in the course of life history has some currency. What appears in this light may be only mental dullness from physical causes, but even in that case it is undoubtedly often mistaken by the less skillful examiners for natural feebleness of mind or other mental defect — and in fact as far as the individual himself is concerned his adjustment in society may be equally affected whether he belongs with the high grade feeble-minded or with the dull for physical causes. Cases of this sort are an immediate but not a primary social problem. The possibility of the acquisition of feebleness of mind and other mental defects or mental dullness is properly one for the consideration of students of psychology, for whatever factor or factors are upturned may be looked upon as a situation or a stimulus that incites a reaction and repeated reactions which ultimately, under the general law of automatization or habituation, develop well fixed dispositions or " second nature."

The recent development of social and mental hygiene

has brought data to light that have been believed to add force to an argument that the hypothesis of acquired feeble-mindedness is a fact. Dr. William A. White (15), for example, looking at mental defect from the viewpoint of therapeutics says: ". . . the problem of feeble-mindedness and many other social problems intradigitate, as it were, and the resulting problems are not necessarily problems of feeble-mindedness at all. For example, not a few defectives are such because of the effects of congenital syphilis upon the central nervous system." The problem in this case is a much broader one than of mental defect. " Again — in the south many children are defective just because they have not the energy sufficient to enable them to give attention and to learn. The problem is again incidental to a larger one, namely, that of uncinariasis (hook worm infection) which produces these results as a consequence of its effect upon the general health. A similar situation arises as the result of adenoids with resulting serious interference with respiration. Causes which are distinctly more psychological are those defects in the sense organs — eye and ear — which make it impossible for the child adequately to perceive the environment and therefore adequately to react to it."

No better evidence of the prevalence of venereal infection in the population of the United States at large can be found than that that is available in the records of the drafted men in the World War. The maximum is 5.6%, based upon examination of the second million draftees, and but little lower than this is the result based upon over 2,500,000. The rate referred to includes all elements in the general population (4). The official report on the results of psychological examining in the army makes it appear doubtful whether this infection has a great effect upon the showing of intelligence. The infected white group is somewhat inferior to the unselected draft but not greatly so.

Intelligence Distribution of Whites (I) Negroes (II)	Intelligence Grade						
	E or D—	D	C—	C	C+	B	A
I. Venereals (1562 Cases)....4.2		22.6	22.6	26.4	14.6	6.7	2.9
Unselected draft (167,035 cases) 1.7		20.6	25.4	25.4	14.9	7.9	4.0
II. Whites, Groups I, II, III (93,973) 7.1		17.1	23.8	25.0	15.0	8.0	4.1
Negroes, Group IV (18,891) 49.0		29.7	12.9	5.7	2.0	0.6	0.1

In the above table at **II** we have inserted a comparison showing the distribution of letter grades of sample groups of white and negro recruits. It is apparent that the difference in intelligence so measured is much greater between the two races in the United States than between the infected and the non-infected whites as shown in Section **I** of the table.

A much greater difference in intelligence is apparent between a group of whites infected by hook worm and a group of the same race not so infected. The comparison is based upon the records of 632 who were infected with the disease and 5615 who were free from it.

HOOK WORM DISEASE

Weighted Score (Alpha)	0–49	50–99	100–149	150–199	200–249	250–299	300–349	350–414	mean	Prob. Error of mean	s. d.
Infected (501)	30.3	29.5	21.0	12.0	4.6	1.6	0.8		94.88	2.85	63.83
Non-infected (4792)	13.7	25.9	25.4	18.1	10.5	4.5	1.5	0.3	118.5	1.03	71.23

Weighted Score (Beta)	0–29	30–59	60–89	90–119	120–149	150–212	mean	Prob. Error of mean	s. d.
Infected (131)	32.0	42.8	18.3	5.3	0.8	0.8	45.38	2.46	28.19
Non-infected (825)	29.5	38.4	20.8	11.2	4.5	0.6	53.26	1.19	34.18

A similar table shows that 131 infected and 2877 non-infected negroes differ somewhat less in intelligence scores than do the whites. Reference to II in the preceding table indicates once more a considerably greater difference between the intelligence rating of white Groups I, II and III on the one hand and the negro Group IV on the other hand than appears between the infected and non-infected white groups.

The psychological examiners urge: "It is important, however, to guard against the assumption that data of this kind prove the existence of a causal relation between hookworm disease and mental inferiority. Low native ability may induce such conditions of living as to induce hookworm infection, or poor environmental conditions may be responsible for both the disease and the low test record."

It may be granted that hookworm disease is never a cause but that it is indirectly an effect of low native ability and at the same time it is probably a safe conclusion *a priori* that this disease and other long continued infections are causes of a mental dullness that is quite as serious in its effect upon the adjustment of the individual as is feeble-mindedness, technically considered, itself. More than that, by way of social inheritance, the dulling effect of this and other diseases may be passed on to succeeding generations; for the dull head of a family, from whatever cause he may be dull, creates an atmosphere in his home in which his children live and grow. This is equivalent to saying that he provides stimuli and creates situations to which his children are repeatedly reacting, implicitly or explicitly, until fixed dispositions are built up in them.

If this is a correct assumption Dr. White is right in his judgment that the larger problem is the correction of the conditions out of which devastating infections arise, for they occasion behavior that in the long run becomes crystallized into firmly knitted dispositions.

CHAPTER V

THE RACIAL FACTOR

AGAIN and again we have laid emphasis upon the fact that the unity of a people depends in very large measure upon the degree of their mutual understanding or acquaintanceship. Whatever favors or stands in the way of such a relationship indirectly aids or prevents the growth of social unity, and is, therefore, proper subject matter for the student of social psychology.

One of the great alleged barriers among people is found in racial distinctions. Everybody recognizes that such distinctions exist. We have no difficulty, ordinarily, in marking off the staid matter-of-fact Englishman from the stirring, ebullient son of Italy. The differences among peoples are in part as to color and form, and in other part as to dispositions, capacities, prejudices, and outlook. It is a question for the student of social pyschology how firmly these distinctions are rooted and whether they are hereditary or acquired in the course of a life history: an alternative that we do not attempt to settle in this chapter. Furthermore, we are interested in the possibility of transcending these barriers, and the means by which it may be accomplished, if at all. Neither do we attempt to derive a formula for this process; but obviously the issues of domestic and even of international co-operation and good will may, in considerable measure, depend upon the way we think about these problems.

There will be no question that differences as to color of races, at any rate, and of bodily proportions on the whole, are natural and heritable characteristics. As to this point, it should be remembered, however, that Franz Boas (1) has presented some very convincing data that go far toward establishing the proposition that even bodily proportions may be altered with change in surroundings in the course even of a single generation. This he was able to establish by means of extensive measurements of, especially, the cranial proportions of groups of Italian and Slavic immigrants into the United States. There is a tendency for the round head to become long and *vice versa*. This may appear to be of distinctly minor importance as far as our problem is concerned, but yet we must not forget that mutual relations are facilitated by the recognition even of physical likeness among people. More than that, there are many who maintain that on the whole physical development is indicative of mental development, and they point to the fact that school children of superior talent are, on the whole, of superior stature and proportions (See Chapter IX), and that on the other hand, delinquents and defectives are inferior in these respects. It is questionable whether the correlation of stature and other physical proportions is directly with mental quality or with developmental history and social status, and thus indirectly with mental quality. We are dealing here with questions that for the most part cannot be put to the laboratory in any justifiable hope for a satisfactory answer. Recourse must be had to statistical analysis of broad scope.

INTELLECTUAL QUALITIES OF THE NEGRO. — Only in respect to the negro as compared with the white race has there been any considerable attempt at experimental determination of mental differences amongst races. This has been the object in several American instances of the application of the Binet-Simon and other psychological tests. In no case, it should be said, is there assurance that the experimenters were dealing with pure representatives of the negro race. Indeed it may safely be assumed that they were not. In practically all cases in which the psychological tests have been resorted to as a means of comparing the races, the comparisons have been drawn between groups of school children belonging to them, respectively.

One of the first attempts of this nature was made by Miss A. Strong (24), who, in Columbia, S. C., made a comparison of three groups: one from schools for the colored, one of white mill-working children, and the third of more favorably conditioned whites from schools in the heart of the city and its outskirts. Comparisons were made only among the children of the first five school grades. The percentages of retarded and advanced pupils in the three groups respectively are as follows:

	City Children	Mill Children	Colored Children
More than one year retarded....	5.4%	18.3%	25.6%
Satisfactory	84.2	81.6	74.4
More than one year above........	10.4	0.	0.

Such data, however, are extremely unsatisfactory to the student of natural racial differences. There is no information available as to the faithfulness of the groups respectively in the matter of school attendance, and the quality of teaching in the schools respectively, nor are we informed whether the terms were of the same length in the three cases under observation. We are told that there are no marked differences in the way in which the white and colored children responded to the tests. Although no statistics are reported by the investigator, she does tell us what tests are most difficult for the colored group. They are precisely those that require home or school training or both for most successful performance, and are not, therefore, certainly indicative of native qualities.

Odum (14), Ferguson (4), Pyle (17), and others have contributed to the literature bearing upon the same subject. Odum points out that the Binet scale applied to a group of 300 colored school children in Philadelphia, chosen at random, would indicate that while those of the chronological ages five, six, and seven, test normal, those more advanced in years are far below normal, so that on the whole the negroes show 6.3% of feeble-mindedness as compared with but 3.9% among white children.

In Ferguson's experience with colored children their response to cancellation and maze or steadiness tests is not appreciably different from that of the whites, but they are inferior in their reaction to the mixed-relations and the Trabue form of the completion test: exercises that call upon a degree of facility in logic and language; and language, in its turn, is a social

product, in very large measure, at least. The young-
sters who figured in these tests were divided into four
groups according to the depth of coloration. Shade
was accepted as an indication of the proportion of
white blood and the author concluded that " in the
more intellectual tests, success increased with the proportion of white blood." We are not told whether
those with the largest percentage of white blood in
their veins were also most successful socially and
in the economic sense. Pyle distinguished two groups,
the socially inferior and superior, respectively, but
made no attempt at distinguishing greater and less
admixtures of colored and white blood. Those who
have been most successful in the social sense surpass
in memory, substitution, association, logical memory,
and imagination tests.

Pressey and Teter have concluded as follows from
an examination of 187 colored and 2800 white children of the same age from the same schools and geographical district:

" The colored children of a given age are at about
the average for white children (in the same city) two
years younger. . . . Analysis by test shows the colored children to average below white children of the
same age on all the tests."

It should be kept in mind that even between social
levels within the same race there are considerable mental differences — as such differences are measured by
psychological tests. Binet found that between Parisian school children of the same chronological age in
the public and private schools, respectively, there was
a difference of from one to one and a half years men-

tally. This difference may be attributed to the quality of the home life through which the groups respectively had grown up, and not to native characteristics. Those who stood higher in the tests — the private school group — grew up in the better grade of Parisian home. Allowance for this factor should probably be made in the comparisons we have at hand, especially in so far as the investigators were employing something other than performance tests. There is, on the other hand, the theory that blood will tell regardless of social advantages or disadvantages, and that, therefore, on the whole, those who belong to the lower levels of social and economic welfare are, by mental constitution, inferior. Galton, for example, who believes that the negro race has not had a fair chance to compete with the whites and at the same time that their capacity is about two grades below that of the Anglo-Saxon race, is of opinion that social and historical conditions are no more, on the whole, than disturbing factors in the career of genius. This, indeed, is the position assumed by most special students of heredity. Such judgments, in so far as they are derived from experimentation in the laboratory, as a matter of course, are based upon a narrow range of observation and should not be accepted as a final statement of fact. Further discussion of this point may be found in the chapter on progress, particularly in the section on intellectual leadership.

The Division of Psychology of the office of the Surgeon General has brought together data accumulated in the army camps in the course of the World War, which enables us to make a comparison between white and negro *adults* (13). The negro Group IV * comprising 18,891 individuals is made up of approximately a pro-rata selection by states and is therefore described as representative of the negroes of the country at large. It is comparable to Group I for whites and was selected in the same manner. The pro-rating was made on the basis of one recruit to every 250 negro males according to the census of 1910. The negroes of Group IV when compared with whites on the basis of the percentage who have made a given letter grade, appear to show a striking inferiority in intelligence of the colored troops.

The comparison is as follows:

	No. of Cases	D—	D	C—	C	C+	B	A
		\multicolumn{7}{c}{Percent Making Grade}						
Whites								
Groups I, II, III	93,973	7.0	17.1	23.8	25.0	12.0	8.0	4.1
Negroes								
Group IV......	18,891	49.0	29.7	12.9	5.7	2.0	0.6	0.1

These figures represent distinctly a massing of negroes in the lower grades and of whites in the middle grades. Had there been included in the samples a fair representation of high officials pro-rated by states it is probable that the showing would be still more to the disadvantage of the negro group.

It is important in this connection, too, to observe that 65.6% of the negro sample (Group IV) took the Beta test (for illiterates) as compared with but 24.7% of the whites in Groups I, II and III. The negro

* The basis for the groupings I, II, III, IV, etc., has already been explained (p. 72). (See the Appendix at the end of this volume for a sketchy description of the tests).

group who are represented in this calculation includes those who had taken the Alpha test (for literates), and who had been recalled for Beta, and those who had taken Beta alone. The figures are the more meaningful because all the negroes in the group are native born and speak the English language, whereas a large percentage of the whites who took the Beta test were immigrants who had difficulty with the language and were possibly at disadvantage for this reason alone.

The large difference between the negro Group IV and the white Groups I, II and III appears much less formidable when we take the colored Group V into account. This is made up of recruits from the following northern states: Illinois, Indiana, New Jersey, New York, and Pennsylvania. Owing to incomplete records there are no data for Ohio, and because of this lack suitable additions were made from New York, New Jersey and Illinois so as to make the total from all the states named equal to one in every fifty of the negro population according to the census of 1910. This provides a total of 4705 individuals in Group V and makes possible a comparison of the whites of Groups I, II and III, negroes of Group IV and negroes of Group V, showing the percent of each of the samples who took Alpha and were required to take Beta repectively for final rating:

	No. of Cases	Alpha	Beta	All Individuals
Whites				
Groups I, II, III.....93973	71.8	24.7	3.5
Negroes				
Group IV...........18891	30.1	65.6	4.3
Negroes				
Group V............4705	58.2	39.4	2.4

This table indicates a distinct superiority of northern over southern negroes. It is impossible, on the basis of data at hand, to state with any degree of satisfaction whether this is due to a difference in educational opportunity as between northern and southern negroes or to the probable fact that the northern group is composed of more intelligent stock — and the descendants of such stock — who had enough push to lead them to migrate from south to north. There is probably no ground for the argument that northern representatives of the race contain a relatively large admixture of white blood and that their superiority is due to this fact. Suffice it to say with respect to education that the report on psychological examination of recruits shows that 19% of southern and 7% of northern negro recruits report no schooling whatever; more than half of those from the southern states have not gone beyond the third grade and only 7% finish the eighth. In the northern states half do not go beyond the fifth grade, and about 25% finish the eighth. The median years of schooling of the white and colored draft, respectively, is shown in the following figures:

White draft, native born..6.0 (almost through grade 7)
White draft, foreign.......4.7(almost through grade 5)
Negro draft, northern......4.9(almost through grade 5)
Negro draft, southern....2.6(half way through grade 3)

On the whole the great disparity in showing of intelligence between northern and southern negroes may, in considerable measure, be accountable to differences in schooling, and by the same token this observation may apply to the gap between northern negroes and the white draft. After all, however, this observation applies best, if at all, to the findings on the Alpha test which certainly reflects, more than the Beta, the effects of school and home training. But yet the difference between northern and southern negroes is quite as great in the Beta (requiring little if any school and home training for successful completion) as in the Alpha test. This, on its face, suggests that in the northern group we are dealing with individuals whose migration is a selection on the basis of native intelligence, and that the test results are an index of such intelligence.

When now we compare negro recruits with 4007 foreign-born Italians (who comprise about one third of all alien recruits in the samplings on which the analysis is based) we arrive at the following figures showing the percent of negroes (Group IV) and of foreign-born Italians who received final rating on Alpha and Beta tests respectively:

	Number of Cases	Alpha	Beta
Italians	4007	14.4	72.0
Negroes	18891	30.1	65.6

The small percent of Italians finally rated on Alpha (14.4) and the large percent rated on Beta (72.0) implies an inferiority on their part, as compared with the negroes — given approximately equivalent educational opportunities — but, on the other hand, a distinct inferiority of the black race is indicated by the percent of negroes and Italians in the letter grades:

	No. of Cases	Percent Making Grade						
		D—	D	C—	C	C+	B	A
Italians	4007	23.4	40.0	9.1	24.4	2.3	0.6	0.2
Negroes Group IV	18,891	49.0	29.7	12.9	5.7	2.0	0.6	0.1

Certain alleged characteristics of the negro as compared with the white race have been brought forward from the basis of ordinary observation. Among these the so-called extreme emotionalism of the colored people has a prominent place. They are said also to exhibit an abnormally enlarged egoistic sense. It is questionable whether, in their emotional life as a race, they are less stable than, for example, the Mediterranean peoples, between whom and the various branches of the Teutons there is no such social barrier as that which exists between the colored and the white races in America. The evidence for their exalted ego, likewise, is drawn from casual observations of individuals, much as Charles Dickens obtained his widely heralded indices of the characteristics of the elements that made up the population of the youthful United States of America. Such eccentricities of character are — for all the evidence we have at hand — probably to be found in any group of people that is but beginning to sense its independence. It would be even more appropriate to draw upon the data, ready at our hand, that show conclusively the rapidly increasing economic competency of the negro in America, in the course of the brief space since the Civil War, as proof of the substantial quality of the negro and other races in America. Such facts as these have a value in connection with this chapter, comparable to that of statistics. They are signs, on the whole, of steady and persistent reaction tendencies, fixed purposes, self-denial and of normal intelligence level on the part, at least, of those who have become, or are becoming economically competent.

PROGRESS OF AMERICAN NEGRO IN FIFTY-SIX YEARS
(From the Negro Year-Book, 1922)

Some Lines of Progress	1866	1922	Gain in Fifty-six Years
Economic Progress —			
Homes Owned..................	12,000	650,000	638,000
Farms Operated................	20,000	1,000,000	980,000
Businesses Conducted...........	2,100	60,000	57,900
Wealth Accumulated............	$20,000,000	$1,500,000,000	$1,480,000,000
Educational Progress —			
Per Cent Literate...............	10	*80	70
Colleges and Normal Schools.....	15	500	485
Students in Public Schools.......	100,000	2,000,000	1,900,000
Teachers in all Schools..........	600	44,000	43,400
Property for Higher Education....	$60,000	$30,000,000	$29,940,000
Annual Expenditures for Education	$700,000	$28,000,000	$27,300,000
Raised by Negroes..............	$80,000	$2,000,000	$1,920,000
Religious Progress —			
Number of Churches............	700	45,000	44,300
Number of Communicants.......	600,000	4,800,000	4,200,000
Number of Sunday Schools......	1,000	46,000	45,000
Sunday School Pupils...........	50,000	2,250,000	2,200,000
Value of Church Property........	$1,500,000	$90,000,000	$88,500,000

* According to the report of the U. S. Army psychological examiners 65.6% of negroes in Group IV (18,891, distributed proportionally by states) were required to take examination Beta. In other words they were illiterate in the sense of the army: that is they could not read a newspaper and write a letter home. Evidently there is a difference here as to the criterion of literacy.

Among reports based upon more or less casual, but from all appearances, careful observation, is one in particular that must not escape the attention of the student of this subject. Ellsworth Faris (3) lived during a number of years in the region of the Upper Congo River where he visited villages in which whites had never been. The people in this region have no written language but their speech indicates that the natives think in abstract terms — contrary to the common opinion — and that they make many nice distinctions that we do not make in English speech; and nice distinctions of the sort are generally accepted as indicative of intellectual capacity.

Furthermore, the anthropologists have brought to light some interesting facts concerning the remote ancestors of our American negroes that are pertinent to our present subject (1). Their art as expressed in carving is said to be quite as worthy as that of primitive European peoples, whose handwork is now the prized possession of civilized nations, and their tribal government as nicely adapted to the circumstances of the times and place in which they lived.

All of this means, according to our interpretation, that in the background of the personalities of these people there is such a basis for the development of practical and symbolic expression as we recognize more clearly in more highly favored peoples. This assumes that primitive art is an expression of native capacities and dispositions which, therefore, persist from one generation to another, and that a race that has once demonstrated a given capacity does not lose it. however it may be eclipsed by the acquisitions of successive generations.

On the whole there is an appearance of inferiority of the negro as compared with the white race. It is most apparent in the results of psychological testing in the army. But this may be taken too seriously if we overlook the *immense* economic and educational strides the race has made in scarcely more than a half century, and the further fact that the mass of negro recruits are rural folk — southern representatives of the race particularly — who, owing to a certain lack of mental nimbleness fall behind their urban brothers in reaction to tests. An inferior endowment of the negro race may be acknowledged but that it has been exaggerated there is little doubt. The recorded difference between colored and white recruits is probably not greater than that between bodies of white recruits drawn from different geographical sections (11, Part III, Chap. 5). At any rate the claim can not be seriously advanced that there is a gap here so wide that *by itself* it constitutes an effective barrier against the development of a sense of social unity embracing the two races, and a spirit of co-operation. What barrier there is springs rather from differences in physical appearance and from the prejudice that attaches to the slave or, for that matter, to other menial servants. At any rate, this appears to be a hypothesis with sufficient warrant to justify openmindedness against the time when more conclusive data may be available. The hypothesis acquires additional support from the fact that in England and in continental Europe, where there is no history of African slavery as in America, there is no such closed door between the races as is found in this country.

PSYCHOLOGIC TRAITS OF OTHER RACIAL GROUPS — Le Bon (9) and Ross (20) have described the Chinese with slight reference to the psychological factor and Radosalevitch (19) has described the Slav. Stevenson (21) has discussed the Teutonic, Alpine and Mediterranean races of Europe, keeping before him the question whether anthropometric type equals sociologic type. He assumes that neighboring races should develop widely different types of institutions if they differ markedly by nature in point of anthropological and psychologic characteristics. But they do not draw strictly racial lines around their institutions. Whilst there are anthropologic differences among races yet the similarities predominate and it cannot be demonstrated that the same race will in all places meet the same problem of social adjustment in the same way. On the other hand each race is likely to solve its problems much as its neighboring races do, or in a way that is suitable in view of the total surroundings in the midst of which it is living. Left alone it will insensibly adapt itself appropriately. There is no assurance that a thousand Slavs planted in America will forever live the life of the old-country Slav and hand on their institutions, unchanged, to their successors. Yet this assurance should be forthcoming if they were essentially a peculiar people compared with other races.

A strong racial group is bound to make an impression upon constitutions and laws and other institutions. But when one group is imposing institutions upon another it must, for reasons of expediency if for no other, cut and fit the institutions; this, not because Semitic peoples, for instance, are lovers of authority and Aryans lovers of liberty; nor because one race is generous and the other selfish, nor one stubborn and another pliable. No such generalizations as these can be made with safety, and even if they could be the general trait will always bend before the particular

circumstance — as the young robin with its undifferentiated disposition for vocal expression takes on the
manner of singing of its constant and only companion,
the oriole. The cutting and fitting must be made because the racial group stands with a weight of convention or of tradition upon it. Each individual feels
as a matter of course, that he personally shares credit
for the achievements of the race and not only so but
for the accomplishments of the race's leaders. It is
this character of individuals that must be accommo-
dated and slowly bent when new institutions are imposed. It is the impact of this same character that
alters the institutions in the new country into which
the immigrant has come, and there can be no melting
of racial groups into a civilization very different from
what is customary — certainly no early melting —
until adjustment of this character or of those institutions, or of both together, occurs. Incidentally this is
one thing that makes government difficult in a population of mixed racial groups and relatively easy in one
of uniform racial character. It may help to account
for the complexity and variety of codes in the one
population and their simplicity and uniformity in
another.

Two recent studies of American Indians and cross-
breeds made altogether independently and by different
methods yield results that agree, as to this race and
the whites, with those already cited relating to the
negro. The Indians were literate pupils in schools
and colleges. Those of mixed blood, by one investigator were found to be superior to the full-blooded
in intellectual capacity by one full year of mental age.

The other compared white children with Indians of full blood and with those of one quarter, one half and three quarters of white blood, respectively. He found that the cross-bred approximate to the white level in proportion to their share of white blood. He concludes that the difference is probably due to race — and the conclusion is cautiously drawn. It is extraordinarily difficult in cases of this sort to make necessary allowances with due conservatism. There is always the possibility that the Indian of mixed blood owes a degree of his superiority to the *social* stimuli of one or the other parent dating from earliest infancy: stimuli that from the beginning have induced a level of reactions that otherwise would have been lacking, and have built up personality complexes that are next to original nature as respects substantiality. The social stimuli that are most effective in the long run are undoubtedly those that the infant receives from its mother, for the reason that the child, in its earlier years is in closer association with the mother than with the father. If the mother be white, therefore, and the father Indian it is probable that the personality complexes that have their rise in the infancy of the offspring will account for an individual more divergent from the level of the father's race than would occur if the situation as to parentage were reversed.

Whatever the value of the foregoing observation in this connection it should be equally weighty whatever races are concerned. Many observers of human affairs, and amongst them, Stoddard, have duly recognized the general principle involved (22). Speaking

of the improving status of women amongst oriental
peoples he says: " The social consequences of this
rising status of women, not only to women themselves,
but also to the community at large, are very important. In the East, the harem is, as Vambery well
says, the ' bulwark of obscurantism.' Ignorant and
fanatical herself, the harem woman implants her ignorance and fanaticism in her sons as well as in her
daughters. What could be a worse handicap for the
Eastern ' intellectual ' than his boyhood years spent
' behind the veil ' ? No wonder that enlightened Oriental fathers have been in the habit of sending their
boys to school at the earliest possible age in order to
get them as soon as possible out of the stultifying
atmosphere of harem life. Yet even this has proved
merely a palliative. Childhood impressions are ever
the most lasting, and so long as one half of the Orient
remained untouched by progressive influences, Oriental
progress had to be begun again *de novo* with every
succeeding generation.

" The increasing number of enlightened Oriental
women is remedying this defect. As Cooper in *The
Modernizing of the Orient* says: ' Give the mothers
education and you transform the whole situation.
Girls who are learning other things than the unintel-
ligible phrases of the Koran are certain to impart such
knowledge as daughters, sisters, and mothers, to their
respective households. Women who learn housewifery,
methods of modern cooking, sewing, and sanitation in
the domestic-economy schools, are bound to cast about
the home upon their return the atmosphere of a civilized community. The old-time picture of the Oriental

woman spending her hours upon divans, eating sweet-
meats, and indulging in petty and degrading gossip
with the servants or with women as ignorant as herself, will be changed. The new woman will be a companion rather than a slave or a toy of her husband.
Marriage will advance from the stage of a paltry
trade in bodies to something like a real union, involving respect toward the woman by both sons and
fathers, while in a new pride of relationship the woman
herself will be discovered.' "

How far the tests that have been employed to determine racial differences actually unearth capacities
or original endowments rather than acquisitions is yet
open to investigation; excepting, very probably, those
tests that are most' exclusively of capabilities for effecting concrete motor adjustments.

A study of the intelligence of oriental and American
student intelligence (27) has been directed especially
toward a comparison of (1) concentration of attention,
(2) speed of learning, (3) association-time, (4) immediate memory, (5) deferred memory, (6) range of
information. The following results were reported:

SCORES

Test	American	Chinese	Indian
1	75	75	62
2	66	62	45
3	46	38	58
4	58	..	54
5	80	..	88
6	23	15	24

The most significant thing in these results is the
low score of the East Indians on Number 1 — concen-

tration of attention which Professor James (Principles, II, p. 562) and many others have been in the habit of identifying with will — and which undoubtedly is, however we define the term, a very prominent aspect of the complex act of willing. The disadvantage of the lack of data of this sort when we attempt a comparison of races and peoples undoubtedly counterbalances much of the advantage that accrues from the possession of information relating to the remaining points in the table above. Observation of men in their relations to one another furnishes, again and again, support for the hypothesis that the superiority of one over another in such matters as the management of men and things; the solution of intricate problems of whatever sort and ultimately gaining the recognition of one's professional colleagues or what not, lies just in this capacity for sustained or concentrated attention. This amounts to saying that the superiority of one people or nation over another may be traceable to the same source — at least in their leaders. This is not passing over the obvious truth that in other respects psychic equipment must be normal.

Professor McDougall, commenting upon the scores quoted above, has the following to say in respect to the Indian people (12): "Now the more or less orderly and successful government of three hundred millions of India by a mere handful of British men, during more than a century, is one of the most remarkable facts in the history of the world. It is a marvelous achievement. And Englishmen have marvelled over it. And, when they have sought to explain how it has been possible, they have always come to the same conclusion. They have recognized that the natives of India, or very many of them, have much intellectual capacity; that they are clever, quick, versatile, retentive; that some of them have brilliant intellects. But such observers have frequently expressed the opinion that, as compared with their British rulers, the natives of India are relatively defective in character or will-power; and they have found the explanation of British ascendency in this fact. . . . If this conclusion is really well-founded, as it seems to be, may we not infer from it that, if the qualities of Indians and British had been reversed in this single respect — if the Indians had been as innately superior in will-power as they seem to be inferior — then, not improbably, a few Indians would at the present time be ruling over and administering the affairs of all Europe, and perhaps of all America as well? It is a strange reflection. It is not utterly fantastic and absurd. It may at least serve to suggest how profoundly peculiarities of moral constitution may affect the destinies of peoples."

Benjamin Kidd, who might be pardoned, by reason of nationality for partiality toward Britain, once described France as the " head of the intellectual nations of the west " notwithstanding that she was continually worsted in her struggle with England during the second half of the eighteenth century. England, during the period, continually enlarged her territory and cramped her adversary. The secret springs of success, as Kidd conceived them, lay in British character. He says: " The qualities which made these results possible were neither brilliant nor intellectual. . . . They are not qualities which impress the imagination. They are, above all, strength and energy of character, honesty, and integrity, simple devotion and the idea of duty. Those who attribute the enormous influence which the English-speaking peoples have acquired in the world to the Machiavellic manoeuvres of their leaders are often very far from the truth. This influence is largely the result of qualities which have nothing brilliant about them " (10).

These qualities are without doubt even more telling in the pursuit of industry and commerce in hum-drum peace-time than in the more romantic clash of military force and diplomacy. Le Bon, having commented upon the enormous inferiority of the French in industrial life as compared with the Germans — an inferiority that was elaborately demonstrated before the war in the report of the National Association for Economic Expansion in France — says (10) : " . . . The general causes of our industrial insufficiency are indeed of a psychological order, since this insufficiency results, as the inquiry has proved, from certain defects of character which are identical in all our industries.

" Among the most disastrous we may count the absence of solidarity, which renders the manufacturer incapable of disciplined and co-ordinated collective effort; the spirit of routine, which makes it impossible for him to introduce any change in established methods; and the dread of incurring risks, the timidity and the lack of initiative which make him fearful of large undertakings.

" Our lack of solidarity is a very old story. Colbert remarked upon it long ago. In one of his memoirs the famous Minister bitterly deplores ' that the French, the most civilized people in the world, should find it so hard to endure one another, that combination among them should be so difficult and their associations so unstable, and that the most favorable ventures should come to naught in their hands by I know not what fatality.' "

There is good reason to assume that in the future as in the past the race will be run successfully, not necessarily by the most alert, but by those who will not only map out their course, but who will persist in it.

Rigid racial unity has perhaps never survived in the period of advanced culture when two races are in contact. Variations there will probably always be and there is room for them in a civilization as complex as ours, but the widest of them are insensibly toned down when variant peoples breathe the same social atmosphere and are immersed in the same cultural system. The process through which this is accomplished is identical with the course of psychic events that terminates, on a smaller scale, in the conventionalities that make up much of the religious and political and other aspects of the social life of a neighborhood.

THE SCIENTIFIC ATTITUDE — The scientific attitude toward these problems of comparison of racial mental qualities is so admirably illustrated by Franz Boas that we quote below from him at length: (2)

" I will now select a few of the mental qualities which are most persistently claimed as racial characteristics of the lower groups of mankind. Among the emotional characters impulsiveness is considered the most fundamental. Most of the proofs for this alleged peculiarity are based on the fickleness and uncertainty of the disposition of primitive man and on the strength of his passions aroused by seemingly trifling causes. I will say right here, that the traveller or student measures the fickleness of the people by the importance which he attributes to the actions or purposes in which they do not persevere, and he weighs the impulse for outbursts of passion by this standard. Let me give an example. The traveller, desirous to reach his goal as soon as possible, engages men to start on a journey at a certain time. To him time is exceedingly valuable. But what is time to primitive man who does not feel the compulsion of completing a definite work at a definite time? While the traveller is fuming and raging over the delay, his men keep up their merry chatter and laughter and cannot be induced to exert themselves except to please their master. Would they not be right in stigmatizing the impulsiveness and lack of control of many a traveller when irritated by a trifling cause like loss of time? Instead of this the traveller complains of the fickleness of the natives who quickly lose interest in the objects which the traveller has at heart. The proper way to compare the fickleness of the savage and that of the white is to compare their behavior in undertakings which are equally important to each. Does not primitive man persevere wonderfully in the manufacture of his utensils and weapons? Does he shrink from privations and hardships which promise to fill his ambition of obtaining higher rank among his fellows? The Indian, fasting in the mountains, awaiting the appearance of his guardian spirit, the youth who must give proof of his bravery and endurance before being accepted in the ranks of the men of his tribe, may be adduced as examples. The alleged fickleness may always be explained by a difference of the valuation of motives and is not a specific characteristic of primitive man. Primitive man perseveres in certain pursuits which differ from those in which civilized man perseveres.

" The same may be said of the outbursts of passion occasioned by slight provocations. What would a primitive man say to the noble passion which preceded and accompanied the War of the Rebellion? Would not the rights of slaves seem to him a most irrelevant question? On the other hand, we have ample proof that his passions are just as much controlled as ours, only in different directions. The numerous customs and restrictions regulating the relations of the sexes or the use of the food supply may serve as examples. The difference in impulsiveness may be fully explained by the different weight of motives in both cases. In short, perseverance and control of passion are demanded of primitive man as well as of civilized man but on different occasions. If they are not demanded as often, the cause must be looked for not in the inherent inability to produce them, but in the social status which does not demand them to the same extent."

And again says Boas in the same connection:

" I will select one more trait which has often been adduced as the primary reason why certain races cannot rise to higher levels of culture, namely, their lack of originality. It is said that the conservatism of primitive man is so strong that the individual never deviates from the traditional customs and beliefs. While there is certainly truth in this statement in so far as customs are more binding than in civilized society, at least in its most highly developed types, originality is a trait which is by no means lacking in the life of primitive people. I will call to mind the great frequency of the appearance of prophets among newly-converted tribes as well as among pagan tribes. Among the latter we learn quite frequently of new dogmas which have been introduced by such individuals. It is true that these may often be traced to the influence of the ideas of neighboring tribes, but they are modified by the individuality of the person and grafted upon the current beliefs of the people. It is a well-known fact that myths and beliefs have been disseminated and undergo changes in the process of dissemination. Undoubtedly this has often been accomplished by the independent thought of individuals. I believe one of the best examples of such independent thought is furnished by the history of the ghost-dance ceremonies in North America. I am indebted to Mr. James Mooney, a close student of this subject, for the following opinion: ' Briefly and broadly it may be stated that the more primitive a people, the more original their thought. Indian prophets are usually original as to their main doctrine, but are quick to borrow anything that may serve to make it more impressive. Heathenism is usually tolerant and the Indian sees no inconsistency in adding to his heathenism anything that he can borrow from Christianity.' A few cases which have come under my own observation are entirely in accord with this opinion; that is to say, the doctrine of the Indian prophet is new, but based upon the ideas of his own people, their neighbors, and the teachings of missionaries. The notion of future life of the Kwakiutl of Vancouver Island has undergone a change in this manner, in so far as the idea of the return of the dead in children of their own family has arisen. The same independent attitude may be observed in the replies of the Nicaraguan Indians to the questions regarding their religion which were put to them by Bobadilla and which were reported by Oviedo.

" To my mind the mental attitude of individuals who thus develop the beliefs of a tribe is exactly that of the civilized philosopher. The student of the history of philosophy is well aware how strongly the mind of even the greatest genius is influenced by the current thought of the time. This has been well expressed by my friend Rudolph Lehmann in his work on Schopenhauer. ' The character of a system of philosophy is, just as that of any other literary work, determined first of all by the personality of its originator. Every true philosophy reflects the life of the philosopher as well as every true poem that of the poet. Secondly, it bears the general marks of the period to which it belongs, and the more powerful the ideas which it proclaims, the more strongly it will be permeated by the currents of thought which fluctuate in the life of the period. Thirdly, it is influenced by the particular bent of philosophical thought of the period.'

" If such is the case among the greatest minds of all times, why should we wonder that the thinker in primitive society is strongly influenced by the current thought of his time? Unconscious and conscious imitation are factors influencing civilized society, as has been shown by G. Tarde, who has proved that primitive man and civilized man, as well, imitates not such actions only as are useful, and for the imitation of which logical causes may be given, but also others for the adoption or preservation of which no logical reason can be assigned.

" Based on these considerations we believe that in the more complicated psychological phenomena no specific differences between lower and higher races can be found. By this, however, we do not mean to say that no differences exist or can be found, only that the method of investigation must be different. It does not seem probable that the minds of races which show variations in their anatomical structure should act in exactly the same manner. Differences of structure must be accompanied by differences of function, physiological as well as psychological; and, as we found clear evidence of difference in structure between the races, so we must anticipate that differences in mental characteristics will be found. Thus, a smaller size or lesser number of nervous elements would probably entail loss of mental energy, and paucity of connections in the central nervous system would produce sluggishness of the mind. As stated before, it seems probable that some differences of this character will be found between the white and the negro, for instance, but they have not been proved yet. As all structural differences are quantitative, we must expect to find mental differences to be of the same description, and as we found the variations in structure to overlap, so that many forms are common to individuals of all races, so we may expect that many individuals will not differ in regard to their faculty, while a statistical inquiry embracing the whole race would reveal certain differences. Furthermore, as certain anatomical traits are found to be hereditary in certain families and hence in tribes and perhaps even in peoples, in the same manner mental traits characterize certain families and may prevail among tribes. It seems, however, an impossible undertaking to separate in a satisfactory manner the social and the hereditary features. Galton's attempt to establish the laws of hereditary genius points out a way of treatment for these questions which will prove useful in so far as it opens a method of determining the influence of heredity upon mental qualities.

" On account of this difficulty I do not enter upon a discussion of the characters of nations. Much has been said about the hereditary characteristics of the Jews, of the gypsies, of the French and Irish, but I do not see that the social senses which have moulded the character of members of these people have ever been eliminated satisfactorily; and, moreover, I do not see how this can be accomplished without previous investigations into the question as to which groups of mental qualities are hereditary. A number of external factors may easily be named: climate, nutrition, occupation; but, as soon as we enter into a consideration of social factors, we are unable to separate cause and effect or external and internal factors. The first-named groups effect the physiological functions of the body and through them the mind. An excellent discussion of these influences upon the character of a people is given by A. Wernich in his description of the character of the Japanese. He finds some of their peculiarities caused by the lack of vigor of the muscular and alimentary systems which in their turn are due to improper nutrition, while he recognizes other physiological traits which influence the mind as hereditary. We may expect to find still more far-reaching effects of malnutrition which was continued through long generations among the Bushmen and the Lapps."

Without over-assurance we may say in the light of the evidence that there are no intellectual differences amongst races of the degree that should make it impossible for them to get together upon such a plane as to assure mutual understanding, sympathy and co-operation. If there are insuperable barriers they are of a different sort. With this statement Professor Thorndike appears to be in general agreement. After a review of studies in racial differences, in acuteness of sense perception and in intellectual capacity, he says: " Again, the civilization — the habits and customs — of a race need not be in a direct proportion to its intellect, even if entirely caused by it. A very slight difference in intellect might give one race supremacy over another, enable it to condemn the other to servitude and so free its own intellect from unconstructive labor. It would thenceforth progress in civilization much more rapidly than the other. What the mental ability of a race actually achieves is due to the conditions under which it operates, and a race may put on or put off such conditions or have them imposed or removed by other races, for all sorts of reasons.

" From all these facts each student may make his own estimate of the original mental differences of races, and learn at least the need of more actual measurements of race differences and of intelligence in interpreting them. My own estimate is that greater differences will be found in the case of the so-called higher traits, such as the capacity to associate and to analyze, thinking with parts, or elements, and originality, than in the case of the sensory and sensori-motor traits, but that there will be great overlapping. Calling the difference between the original capacity of the lowest congenital idiot and that of the average modern European 100, I should expect the average deviation of one pure race* from another in original capacity to be below 10 and above 1, and the difference between the central tendencies of the most and the least gifted races to be below 50 and above 10. I should consider 3 and 25 as reasonable guesses for the two differences.

" Even if the differences were far larger than these, the practical precept for education would remain unchanged. It is, of course, that selection by race of original natures to be educated is nowhere nearly as effective as selection of the superior individuals regardless of race. There is much overlapping and the differences in original nature within the same race

* Defining a pure race arbitrarily as one whose ancestry has less than 1 per cent of community with that of any other race for at least 20 generations back.

are, except in extreme cases, many times as great as the differences between races as wholes."

CONCLUSION — What insuperable barriers there are between races are not such as we have usually assumed. What radical differentia do exist *without doubt* are in respect to physical appearance. In so far as these form an inescapable mark of indentification they constitute a serious barrier because, on one hand, they are a constant reminder of race prejudices: prejudices that represent a defense reaction on our part toward a race that by crowding us may take our place in commerce, industry, agriculture, discovery or what not and thus edge out of our hands, a bit at a time, our means of living. They are attitudes that are assumed toward the strong or those who, we fear, may prove to be strong. But if these physical characteristics are not permanent and certain marks of identification we neglect them. They are not, therefore, constant reminders that keep prejudices alive and that maintain our reactions of defense. The way to amalgamation of races is open if differences in physical appearance are not striking. Witness the history of representatives of the Teutonic and Slavic and Mediterranean races in America.

But where indelible marks of racial identification do occur the situation is different. In this case it is less prejudice than revulsion, without deserving so strong a term. It is not directed necessarily against the strong who are able and aggressive enough to deprive us, nor against those whom we suspect of strength and aggressiveness. Whether we like to admit it or not it is often turned toward the weak.

There is more or less of hesitation on our part in the matter of approaching those who are like us yet markedly different in human form, as dwarfs and others who are deformed by nature. It is possible, too, that those of us who bear unsightly scars are at better ease when we have hidden them from view because we recognize the existence of such a motive in human kind. If there is any natural antipathy amongst races it is probably due to such causes as these.

Whether inter-racial barriers are due to different levels of intellectual capacity, to prejudice with its tap root in fear or to a feeling akin to revulsion because of striking differences in appearance, there is but one way around them; a way that will be apparent to representatives of the races respectively only when they seek it thoughtfully: let each representative do carefully what lies nearest his hand in the place where he may be. Then as we observe one another at work there will gradually emerge a recognition of each one's capacities, adaptability and usefulness. Inevitably, then, as in all social relations, they will draw together in a matter of course relationship, and then the barriers will have vanished.

" Under the influence of common environment, interest, language and religion these heterogeneous races may, by a process of fusion, become one homogeneous race.

" Fusion between different peoples is the work of centuries. Having insufficient time at their disposal, the founders of various empires — Turkey, Russia, and Austria notably — have simply replaced it by

CONCLUSION 121

force. Their work has always remained, for this reason, somewhat artificial, and the populations, however submissive in appearance, are not yet amalgamated " (22).

CHAPTER VI

SUGGESTION AND SUGGESTIBILITY

In this chapter we (1) discuss two definitions of suggestion and suggestibility, and (2) describe the conditions that affect both. This should enable us (3) to understand the limitations of suggestion and suggestibility as means of arriving at large social unities.

Titchener defines suggestion as " any stimulus, external or internal, accompanied or unaccompanied by consciousness, which touches off a determining tendency " (13). For example, in the simple reaction experiment the instruction to react on a given signal sets off a determining tendency which releases the reaction movement. What made the reactor ready to accept instruction? What brought him into the laboratory? What brought him to the university? What brought him to seek an education in any university? In each case a previous suggestion. The reaction to this train of previous suggestions, each in its turn, has developed a complex disposition because of which the reaction is made as a matter of course, once the stimulus is presented.

This definition makes suggestion no different from a command or a sensory stimulus. To understand the response to a command or a sensory stimulus we must assume that a tendency or a disposition has already been prepared which is of such a nature that it may be touched off by the appropriate word, gesture, or other stimulus. We would not command an ox to attend to the demonstration of a geometrical proposition because we assume that the animal has no disposition favorable to such a reaction. Nor is suggestion in this case different from any stimulus in the technical sense. A certain visual impression awakens the train of processes which ends in the emotion of fear. But the visual stimulus occasioned by the presence of a serpent, e.g., could have no relation to fear were there not already a determining tendency to be touched off by it. It is difficult to conceive of any reaction that is not a response to a suggestion according to this definition.

Again we have suggestion defined by Bunnerman, not as an external condition or stimulus, but as a mental state of expectancy or emotional disturbance: as an unusual working of the function of interpretation due to expectancy or emotional disturbance (1).

If we accept the view that expectancy is a state both of mental and physiological readiness or preparedness for response — more or less definite response according as attention is more or less sharply focused in a particular direction— then this definition confuses suggestion in Titchener's sense with the " determining tendency " that is " set off " by a stimulus, and with the act of interpreting the stimulus. The implication in Bunnerman's viewpoint is that the suggestion in Titchener's sense must be accepted by the person to whom it is addressed and that it must become a part of his personality, so to speak. Or as

certain practitioners in the field of mental therapy,
Coué and his disciples, for instance, put it: suggestion
must run into *auto*-suggestion in order that it may be
effective. The one — Titchener — emphasizes the
part of the stimulus or the one who presents it; the
other — Bunnerman — stresses that of the one who
reacts. Titchener's " tendency " is as substantial as
human nature. Bunnerman's " expectancy or emotional disturbance," as a state of consciousness which
is implied, is as temporary as the particular occasion
that elicits it. On the one hand, the usualness of
suggestion and response receives the emphasis, whereas on the other, it is described as " unusual." All
definitions of the term now in vogue closely approximate one or the other of the foregoing points of view.
There is, moreover, the definition of the term, intolerable because of its implications, as the transmission
of a conviction or an idea from one person to another.

An adequate treatment of suggestion and suggestibility must recognize the former as in the nature of a
stimulus and the latter as relating to a degree of
sensitiveness or of readiness to react on the part of
the more or less stable dispositions or tendencies of
human nature. The two are functionally related.
Suggestibility is the usual or normal, not the unusual
or abnormal state of the human organism. Suggestibility is sharpened temporarily by fleeting expectation
and by emotional disturbances, but it is not traceable
wholly to a temporary emotional condition.

As to the suggestion, only confusion results from
overlapping it with the command or with the " stimulus " in the technical sense in which this term is

employed in our chapters on sensation. It is not a direct appeal, such as a command, in the ordinary sense, issued by one person to another, in the full light of awareness of what is going on, nor as a sensory stimulus which, in its most technical sense is a *particular* vibration of a gas or a solid or a *particular* chemical reaction that produces a response in a group of nerve cells whose function has become so differentiated from that of other cells that they can react normally to nothing else. Thus one might suspend pictures until doomsday before the ears of one's neighbor without so much as beginning to excite his auditory nerve. So soon, however, as vibrations of air are reflected into his ears, that is, at the moment the atmosphere vibrating at a certain rate, is made to impinge upon his auditory apparatus a reaction occurs in it — a sensory response. The suggestion, on the other hand, is conceived as an indirect awakening of a determining tendency, not in full consciousness — on the part of the one who receives the suggestion — of what is going on. It is in consequence of this subterranean route by which the suggestion operates upon the subject that he, in reacting upon it, has more the sense of acting on his own initiative than of responding to external influence. He appears to be acting on his own initiative because there are no conflicting tendencies. Those that in other situations would conflict have become " dissociated " or thrown out of connection. He is, so far as his *suggested* behavior is concerned, in a state analogous to that of children and other immature persons whose sum of experience is small by reason of their having a paucity of contacts with many angles of life. They have, therefore, not yet developed a host of dispositions or tendencies toward reaction of many sorts which together insure a capacity for inhibition. We are using " dissociated " and " disassociation " in the sense of the psycho-analysts as relating to a disconnection amongst submerged complexes; complexes that have been repressed, it may be voluntarily, because the social atmosphere makes it urgent so to do, or because for other reasons there is no opportunity to give them an outlet in the course of behavior. Thus through mere lack of opportunity for outlet many a one submerges without destroying, those complexes that would otherwise express themselves in play and in the care of children. Most of us voluntarily submerge a complex that is the root of one or another ambition, but in neither case is it destroyed. It is described as, even in its submerged state, " intelligent " in the sense of being adaptable to circumstances, and as affecting the contentedness of the individual and as exercising more or less independent control of the ordinary forms of activity when restraints are removed or sufficiently reduced. We solve problems " in our sleep." The somnambulist climbs over the partially completed frame of a barn, or goes directly to the spot where he had placed his check for safe-keeping, and there he finds it after having spent days in fruitless, anxious search for it when the full light of awareness was on. These are intelligent forms of behavior that are performed through the agency of complexes submerged and dissociated. In normal waking life suggestion operates to reduce

restraint; remove inhibitions; in other words, to produce the state of at least partial dissociation. By this
we do not mean to imply that the dissociated state we
are considering is one of passivity. Obviously it is
quite the contrary. But there is a shifting of activity
from one department of the organism, so to speak, to
another.

SUGGESTIBILITY AS DISSOCIATION. — Suggestibility
is understood, therefore, as that condition of the
organism in which one or another determining tendency or disposition may express itself with relative
freedom. In extreme suggestibility this freedom of
expression is most marked. It is untrammeled by the
inhibitions that normally control. The active disposition or tendency has been, partially, at least,
dissociated from others, to use a phrase that is current among students of the abnormal mind. In other
words, it functions at least in a considerable degree
of independence of the whole system of dispositions
that make up the personality. This is the point of
view that is represented by Sidis (9). " Abnormal
suggestibility is a disaggregation of consciousness, a
slit, a scar, produced in the mind, a crack that may
extend wider and deeper, ending at last in the total
disjunction of the waking, guiding, controlling consciousness from the reflex consciousness; from the rest
of the stream of life." In normal suggestibility " the
lesion effected in the body of consciousness is superficial, transitory, fleeting. In abnormal suggestibility,
on the contrary, the slit is deep and lasting — it is
a severe gash. In both cases, however, we have a
removal, a dissociation of the waking from the sub-

waking, reflex consciousness, and suggestion is effected only through the latter. It is the sub-waking, the reflex, not the waking, the controlling consciousness that is suggestible. Suggestibility is the attribute, the very essence of the sub-waking, reflex consciousness. . . . Suggestibility varies as the degree of disaggregation, and inversely as the unification of consciousness." The conception is a reminder of the highly segmented animal. It gets on best when all of its parts are properly joined, each to each; but any one segment is capable of a more or less independent existence.

SUGGESTIBILITY DUE TO SUPERSTITIOUS NATURE. — If this is the correct view of the case we are prepared to understand that there are two large types of background for suggestibility. One is in our natural, the other in our acquired, dispositions.

There is our superstitious nature which is never quite held in leash by our scientific and professional habits. Signs and portents, shadows in the moonlight, etc., affect our attitude and our behavior more than we are often willing to acknowledge, and bring into the foreground of consciousness images and fears with their appropriate reactions which appear to the observer, in view of the occasioning shadow or what not, to be very far-fetched. They produce their effects by reason of the existence in the organism of a disposition fostered in us by years of wondering at phenomena which we are unable to understand. This disposition is never fully integrated with our acquisitions; it is always more or less dissociated from those dispositions that would control it, and it is, therefore, so to speak, upon a hair trigger and ready to be touched off upon slight provocation.

Rarely has suggestibility, resting upon this background of superstition-disposition, been so well illustrated on a large scale as in the witchcraft craze. Stoll (11), commenting on the atrocious witch trial at Zug, Switzerland, in 1737, shows how completely even some learned judges of the time suffered a dissociation between their superstition-complex and other complexes, which we usually think of as exercising control or restraint. They were under the spell of the universal witchcraft belief of the times. They did not, and could not in the psychological situation, recognize how perfectly the accounts that the accused gave of themselves tallied with the objective circumstances. One of them, Kathri Gilli, had a small bag of white powder. Her accuser declared it was a poison for the destruction of cattle. She explained that it was oat flour, showed that it had no ill effect upon a dog when a portion was fed to him, and she offered to prove it harmless by partaking of it herself. Nevertheless the witchcraft idea so obsessed the mind of the court that Kathri was found guilty and sentenced to the rack: a victim of the supersensitive superstitious nature of her neighbors.

A similar illustration is found in the great Kentucky religious revival of 1799–1800. (8) The same disposition-complex to stand in wonderment and awe before what is not understood and the natural disposition to seek alliance with a real or imagined stronger power in times of uncertainty or imagined distress compose the sensitive background which needs but to be touched to make it respond in the form of religious frenzy.

DISPOSITION TO AGREE WITH THE STRONG. — Again, it is the disposition to follow after the strong, or those who show evidence of strength, that makes us peculiarly open to suggestion from men and women of prestige, whether their prestige is due to social or economic, or professional position; to physical or mental qualities for leadership, or what not. The reports concerning testimony offered by children show how fatally the replies of the young are determined by the character of the questions that are put to them in court. Note, for example, a very striking case in Belgium in 1910: three little girls, aged nine and ten, had been playing by the roadside. In the evening they separated; two who were sisters went together to their home and the third set off in a different direction to her home. The next morning this girl was found by the roadside, murdered. The two sisters were awakened and asked of the whereabouts of their companion of the day before. They replied, " We do not know." Nevertheless the detectives in the case succeeded in putting into their mouths the statement that they had seen a stranger on the previous day, a man who stopped to speak with them. He wore a black mustache, a slouch hat, and black clothing. Such a man was then arrested and brought to trial. There was additional incriminating testimony by the two sisters: questions and answers aggregated hundreds of pages in typewritten form. The defense sought and obtained permission to try an experiment in testimony before the court. He brought a group

of school children into the courtroom and plied them
with questions concerning the man who, on that morning, had crossed their school yard and engaged their
teacher in conversation at the door of the school. The
children's answers built up a detailed account of the
appearance of the man, even to his necktie, and they
spoke of their teacher's agitation when the stranger
had gone. As a matter of fact no stranger had been
seen on the school premises on that day. The ques-
tioner had been able to play upon their sensitive complexes and to stimulate spontaneous expression. The
whole performance illustrates the play of suggestion
upon a suggestible make-up. (15)

Children have not the advantage of acquired dispositions, or the results of experience, that compose
complexes in conflict with their natural disposition to
ally themselves with the apparently strong, and consequently they give assent whereas they would otherwise withhold it. The effect would be the same if
these experiences had in fact been acquired but had
been dissociated from the more primitive tendency to
yield to the prestige of strength, position, or what
not.

But the testimony of adults, too, particularly if
it is offered with respect to an exciting situation, illustrates the response of the suggestible disposition.
The inclination to agree with the strong is not, however, so patent as in the false testimony of children.
A time of excitement is one of emotional instability.
One does not have one's self " in hand." Self-control
and even the unity of the personality are threatened.
It is a time of contending impulses to run away and

to stand firm; to fight and to surrender; of fleeting, unsteady attention to each one of many interpretations of the situation or adjustments to it. The whole behavior, both in the sense of conscious and of overt activity at such times comprises symptoms of an organism that is in turmoil through and through. On the side of conscious life at least partial dissociations are the rule. The whole organization of complexes can not be brought to bear for the purpose of interpretation. Hence the great variety of dispositions that are forth-coming from the members of a group respecting the same exciting event. It is essentially a case of suggestion and response.

Two classical illustrations are here presented of the reactions of the suggestible natures of adults of mature judgment as demonstrated by their testimony concerning exciting situations:

In Professor von Liszt's famous school of criminology in Vienna, several years ago, an attempt at murder was staged before a group of students of law in the final year of their studies. A pre-arranged altercation arose between two members of the school. Insults and threats followed. One seized a revolver and fired point-blank at the other. Other members who were present were then called upon to offer their testimony relating to what had happened. Some wrote out their depositions on the evening of the day of the occurrence; others, after one, three and five weeks, respectively. The event had taken them all by surprise. The extent of their errors more than doubled when they were describing what occurred at the culmination as compared with the beginning of the scene. That is, it increased from 9.3% to 20.3% (3).

A more striking demonstration occurred at a meeting of the Congress of Psychology at Göttingen. It was described originally by von Gennep (16):

" Not far from the hall in which the Congress was sitting there was a public fête with a masked ball. Suddenly the door of the hall was thrown open and a clown rushed in madly pursued by a negro, revolver in hand. They stopped in the middle of the room fighting; the clown fell, the negro leapt upon him, fired, and then both rushed out of the hall. The whole incident lasted hardly twenty seconds. The president asked those present to write a report immediately since there was sure to be a judicial enquiry. Forty reports were sent in. Only one had less than 20% of mistakes in regard to the principal facts; fourteen had 20% to 40% of mistakes; twelve, from 40% to 50%; thirteen more than 50%. Moreover in twenty-four accounts 10% of the details were pure inventions and this proportion was exceeded in ten accounts and diminished in six. Briefly, a quarter of the accounts were false.

" It goes without saying that the whole scene had been arranged and even photographed in advance. The ten false reports may then be relegated to the category of tales and legends; twenty-four accounts are half legendary, and six have a value approximating to exact evidence.

" Experiments on certainty, led to analogous results. Witnesses were asked to underline the passages in their accounts to which they would be prepared to swear before a tribunal. It was found there were as

many mistakes in the underlined passages as elsewhere. The important point to notice in this connection is that the underlined statements were of the
same type as legends; they were objects of belief."

Descriptions of any extraordinary event involve an
enormous measure of fantasy and error among us and
the tendency to error operates from the moment of
observation.

RACE AND SEX FACTORS IN SUGGESTIBILITY. — The
race and sex factors are other native determinants
of the degree of suggestibility, but they may very
easily be over-emphasized. It is true, as Ross says,
(8) that the American Indian, far from being a thoroughly impassive creature, is extremely susceptible
to suggestive influences. He cites the instance of the
ghost-dance religion that spread among the Indians
from 1889 to 1892, and took possession of probably
sixty thousand souls. The central features of this
phenomenon were a sacred dance and hypnotizing
operations upon the dancers who had begun to show
signs of ecstasy. " They kept up dancing until fully
one hundred persons were lying unconscious. They
then stopped and seated themselves in a circle, and as
each one recovered from his trance, he was brought
to the center of the ring to relate his experience."

This is a case in which a superstitious disposition,
or a crude religious nature, unhindered by the checks
that prevail among most cultured people, has been
able to express itself freely. It is probable that a
member of any other race, brought up from infancy
in an American-Indian environment, would behave in
like fashion. If so the case is not properly cited as

illustrative of a racial factor as a determinant of suggestibility.

The often-quoted data from Starbuck (10) to the effect that women are much more susceptible than men to religious influence; that in religious revivals " men display more friction against surroundings, more difficulty with points of belief, more doubt arising from educational influences, more readiness to question traditional beliefs and customs, more pronounced tendency to resist conviction, to pray, to call on God, to lose sleep and appetite " lend further support to the principle stated above — that suggestibility is to be explained on the ground of the degree of dissociation of a complex disposition, or system-complex from controlling dispositions. Practically such a dissociation is illustrated in the suggestibility of woman. Compared with man she has been in relative isolation from the affairs of practical life outside the home. Outside that sphere she has not acquired the disposition, therefore, to examine narrowly before judging or acting. She either does not possess those complexes, normal among active men in contact with the world, which express themselves in the control that characterizes the conservative, or if she has acquired them through such contacts she still lacks a strong unification of her personality. As Ross says, (8) " They are, in a sense, a social class shut out from many of the bracing and individualizing experiences that come to men. ' Nowhere in the world,' declares Thomas (9) ' do women as a class lead a perfectly free intellectual life in common with the men of the group like the modern revolutionary party in Russia.'

Hence woman is by no means synonymous with *human female*. Almost everywhere propriety and conventionality press more mercilessly on woman than on man, thereby lessening her freedom and range of choice and dwarfing her will. Individuality develops through practice in choosing. If women are mobbish, it is largely for the same reason that monks, soldiers, peasants, *moujiks*, and other rigidly regulated types are mobbish. Much of woman's exaggerated impressionability disappears once she enjoys equal access with men to such individualizing influences as higher education, travel, self-direction, professional pursuits, participation in intellectual and public life."

As women mingle more and more freely in the life outside of the home they will gradually build up and unify those complexes which will undoubtedly place them on the same level with men in point of suggestibility.

SUSPICION AND SUGGESTIBILITY. — Iago's deft handling of Othello when he and his master were left alone after Desdemona had intervened with her husband, Othello, in Cassio's behalf is an excellent instance of a suggestion tapping a native suspicious disposition that had been aroused by events immediately preceding:

Iago: My noble lord, —
Othello: What dost thou say, Iago?
Iago: Did Michael Cassio, when you woo'd my lady, know of your love?
Othello: He did, from first to last: why dost thou ask?
Iago: But for a satisfaction of my thought;
    No further harm.
Othello: Why of thy thought, Iago?

Iago: I did not think he had been acquainted with her.
Othello: O, yes, and went between us very oft.
Iago: Indeed!
Othello: Indeed! Ay, indeed; discern'st thou aught in
    that? Is he not honest?
Iago: Honest, my lord?
Othello: Honest, ay, honest.
Iago: My lord, for aught I know.
Othello: What dost thou think?
Iago: Think, my lord!
Othello: Think, my lord!
    By heaven, he echoes me
    As if there were some monster in his thought
    Too hideous to be shown. Thou dost mean some-
        thing;
    I hear thee say but now, thou likst not that
    When Cassio left my wife. What didst not like?
    And when I told thee how he was in my counsel
    In my whole course of wooing, thou criedst,
    " Indeed! "
    And didst contract and purse thy brows together,
    As if thou hadst shut up in thy brain
    Some horrible conceit: If thou dost love me,
    Show me thy thought.
Iago: My lord, you know I love you.
Othello: I think thou dost.
    And for I know thou'rt full of love and honesty
    And weigh'st thy words before thou givest them
        breath,
    Therefore these stops of thine fright me the more:
    For such things in a false disloyal knave
    Are tricks of custom; but in a man that's just
    They're close dilations working from the heart,
    That passion cannot rule.
Iago: For Michael Cassio
    I dare be sworn I think that he is honest.
Othello: I think so too.

Iago: Men should be what they seem;
  Or those that be not, would they might seem none!
Othello: Certain; men should be what they seem.
Iago: Why then I think Cassio's an honest man.
Othello: Nay, yet there's more in this;
  I prithee, speak to me as to thy thinkings,
  As thou dost ruminate, and give thy worst of
    thoughts,
  The words of words.

ACQUIRED DISPOSITION AND SUGGESTIBILITY. —
What has preceded will indicate that it is not only
the native disposition that determines the degree and
direction of suggestibility when it is partially or entirely dissociated from controlling complexes. It is
not possible to draw a sharp distinction between that
which is rooted in the native disposition and what
grows out of our acquired habits. It is impossible,
therefore, with entire satisfaction, to speak of the
relation of suggestibility either to innate or to acquired dispositions. It is usually a question which
background should be emphasized in a discussion.
Certainly each one and both together determine the
degree and direction of suggestibility when they are
partially or wholly dissociated from controlling
complexes.

The acquired disposition, or the product of education is a potent factor. If you seat yourself before
a bank of electric lamps and place your fingers upon
a coiled wire which is apparently in circuit with the
lamps, the coil will seem to the unsuspecting observer
to grow warm when the lamps are lighted, even though
a secret switch beneath the table may be so thrown

as to allow the current to pass only through the lamps and not through the coil. Here is suggestion that indirectly produces a thermal sensation. But the subject could not have been suggestible in this respect had he not acquired a certain disposition (an electricity-complex, we may say) in the course of his experience up to that time with electric currents and hot wires. We of our civilized place and time have so often seen the incandescent lamp. We have felt it grow warm when the current is turned on so as to light the lamp. We have made our morning's toast over coiled wires that have been made red-hot by an electric current passing through them. We have warmed our feet over coiled wires in the winter, and in many other ways the man and woman in the street have developed a substantial dispositional background by reason of which it is inevitable, unless they are very closely upon their guard, that they should report a warm wire. The lighted lamp is a stimulus adequate to occasion a visual sensation of brightness, not of temperature. It is only indirectly that it excites the behavior that comprises the vocal expression of the words: " Now the wire is warm." It is because of the round-about devious route of the stimulus and the excitation it arouses that we speak in such a case of suggestion and the response of a suggestible disposition; or as some prefer to say " suggesting " (the application, in this case, of the lighted lamp) and " suggestion " (in this case. the whole chain of inner and outer events that terminates in the spoken words, " the wire is warm.")

" The wire is warm " response is all the more likely

to occur if the operator introduces the experiment by giving the direction " Now tell me when the wire becomes warm." This, for the reason that the expectation element is injected into the situation, which is equivalent to heightening, temporarily, the sensitivity of the complexes whose activity is involved in the whole proceeding. In other words, the complexes involved are thus more completely than otherwise dissociated or disconnected from other elements in the organization that in different circumstances would bring to bear more or less of inhibiting influence.

If a native of the remotest corner of the South Seas could be suddenly transported to our laboratory and be there immediately confronted with such an experimental situation as has been described it is hardly conceivable that he would respond to the suggestion or the " suggesting " by the " Now the wire is warm " phrase as does the tutored product of our urban life.

The professional disposition or complex of the physician renders him suggestible in the face of situations that leave the carpenter untouched. He responds with enthusiasm to a movement for paving the streets because it " suggests " to him what never occurred to the proposers — the improvement of sanitary conditions. But why " sanitary conditions " ? Because the physician during the years of his practice and throughout his preparatory years has lived in an atmosphere that was charged with considerations of measures of sanitation. Thousands of situations during all these years have occasioned him to think and in other ways to do things relating to the protection and preservation of health by means of proper sani-

tation. In this respect he stands in a peculiar relation to his fellow-men. We say that his habits of
reaction — professional habits — are through and
through so thoroughly a part of his nature that he
cannot be rid of them if he would. His " sanitation
complex " is, just now, a controlling element in his
make-up, and one who has dealings with him must take
it into account.

The automobile salesman, even, has now and again
occasion for entertaining considerations like these in
the face of his prospective buyers. There is the
farmer who cannot be overcome by frontal attack.
A direct urging that he buy a car arouses an antagonistic reaction. Yet there are numerous complexes
in his make-up, any one of which, and all together,
may be brought to such a state of high sensitivity temporarily that by a skillful flank attack or suggestion
they may set off that behavior that will culminate in
the farmer's purchasing a car. Let us assume that
the agent knows at the outset that the farmer is of
an envious nature; that it stirs his pride to see his
family stand up with the best of them and enjoy life
as much as his neighbors do; and that he is disposed
to compete vigorously and by all means with his neighbors in the pursuit of his occupation. Because he is
aware, in advance, of these psychologic characteristics, the agent will not make it known at the beginning that he is a salesman but after some conversation
of a general nature he will, in an apparently casual
manner, bring the farmer's attention to the fact that
his neighbor up the road has lately purchased a car;
that he is now in the market with his produce and home

again in the morning in a quarter of the time that he
formerly required for the customary daily expedition;
that " the early bird catches the worm "; and finally
he leads the farmer to think of the pleasure that the
neighbor's family has in the new car. By all these
means the agent stirs up a group of sensitive complexes in the back-ground of the personality of the
prospective buyer. He makes it known that he is
authorized to take orders for automobiles, but not
until the farmer has begun to evince a real interest
in owning a car and when he says, it may be, that he
will some day make the purchase. The entire process
has been one of suggestions until certain complexes,
native and occupational or professional, have been
sufficiently aroused. Then it seems to the farmer that
his entire course of reaching a decision has been on
his own initiative.

MASS EFFECTS. — But suggestion and response are
of particular interest when they involve the large
group — especially when the individuals of the group
in reaction to suggestion are caught up into co-operative behavior and belief in common on a large scale.
Illustration is found in many situations that came to
pass in the course of the recent World War. Two
cases will suffice.

Before the year 1914 had passed Germany and the
German Army were filled with rumors, accepted as
facts, that Belgian and French priests and civilians
were committing all sorts of atrocities against German soldiers and civilians; that the priests were using
church towers, etc., for purposes of signalling for the
aid of the Belgian and French soldiery. These rumors

persisted during 1915 and the priesthood of Belgium and France became the objects of angry revilings. There were strong elements in Germany who were aroused to bitterness by the attacks against the clergy of their enemy countries and at last the situation became so tense that German civil and military authorities were ordered to co-operate fully with Pax (an association of German priests) in a thorough investigation of the whole matter. After an exhaustive examination of evidence a report was issued to the effect that the charges against the Belgian and French clergy were unfounded.

Such phenomena as these signallings and the like may properly be classified with illusions and they are so treated by many hands. But the essential feature of the response in illusory phenomena is precisely that that characterizes the reaction to suggestion. Furthermore, the stimulus or the situation that induces the illusion produces its effect only by a round-about route; as when the stump of a tree in the twilight by a lonely road appears to be a threatening robber when the timid traveler, fearful for his safety, sees it at a distance.

The whole web of tales relating to the alleged participation of Belgian and French priests and civilians in unlawful warfare and in atrocities against enemy wounded and prisoners is so instructive from the viewpoint of the subject matter of this chapter that we quote here liberally from van Langenhove, the Scientific Secretary of the Solvay Institute of Sociology at Brussels who, in " The Growth of a Legend " (14) has brought the stories together and along with them the reports of German civil and military authorities addressed to Pax, the investigating body.

" From R. P. Duhr in *Der Lügengeist*.

" PRIESTS WITH MACHINE-GUNS ON THE BELFRIES

" Priests armed with machine-guns, posted on the belfries of churches, appear by hundreds in the original tales from Belgium and France. The result is, each time, the execution of the traitor.

" Repeatedly already tales of this kind have passed from newspapers into books. (See, for example, Pauls, *Aus eiserner Zeit*, Elmshorn, 1914; Hans Leitzen, *Der grosse Krieg in Feldpost-Briefen*, Wolfenbüttel, 1914; *Feldpost-Briefen*, 1914, edited by Herm Sparr, Leipzig, 1915.)

" The novels are all engrossed with the theme. Thus Richard Sexau has published in his book, *Blut und Eisen*, a short story, *Der Zweifler*, wherein he depicts a fight for the possession of a village situated on the French frontier and defended by some enemy troops and some hidden *francs-tireurs*. The adversary finds his chief stronghold in the church of the place, on the belfry of which a machine-gun is in action. The German lieutenant Holk advances to the assault of the tower. ' Now he has attained the summit. A devil in a black robe is found there, his eyes fixed on the gun sights, his hand on the instrument of murder : it is the abbot.'

" This fragment is so suitable for the literary supplement of the *M.-Augsburger Abendzeitung*, the *Sammler*, (January 4th to 9th) for its ' series of the best novels written under the influence of the first weeks of war ' that it reproduces it and appropriates it. (Bayer, *Kurier*, No. 14, January 14, 1915).

" Many of these stories of church belfries **are** derived less from ill-will than from ignorance.

"Three facts are, generally, completely ignored: the first is the right of ownership of the parish over the belfry of the church; the second is the uniform of the Belgian town guard; the third is that many priests have been taken to Germany only as hostages who have not been guilty of the least fault or who are not even suspects.

"In Belgium, the church belfries are, according to the French decrees of 1809 and 1813, which are still effective, the property of the parish, whilst the rest of the church is the property of the vestry of the church (*Kirchengemeinde*). The parish has the right on certain days of national fêtes, etc., of ringing the bells which are in the tower. The burgomaster possesses the keys of the belfry for this purpose. The vestry of the church has only the right to use the belfry for the needs of the religious offices and for this reason the curé also possesses a belfry key. If one wishes to put the responsibility upon someone for the installation of machine-guns on the belfries it is then the burgomaster whom one should consider in the first place and not the curé. Moreover, neither of them should be held responsible. The machine-guns have not been put on the belfries either by the burgomaster or the curé but by military authority. When the latter considers it convenient, for military reasons, to place a machine-gun on a belfry it does not ask the permission of the burgomaster or of the curé. The burgomaster, no more than the curé, is then in a position to refuse the keys. In case of necessity, when they are not put rapidly enough at his disposition, the military authority simply forces the door leading to the belfry. The situation is entirely similar in France. In virtue of the well-known law of separation the churches have become completely the property of the State. The curé can then do nothing if the belfry is employed for military purposes. (Cf. *Kolnische Volks-zeitung*, No. 956, November 5, 1914).

" It is necessary to add to these considerations that the uniform of the Belgian town guard can very easily be mistaken for the religious dress by any man ignorant of it and, moreover, by any man not warned. The Belgian town guard wears notably a black blouse, more often a dark grey one which descends as far as the knees and which, in consequence, resembles in a striking manner the short cassock of our priests. A black hat, rigid, high, and round, serves him for head-gear. A black, yellow, and red cord is tied around and is only seen by an observer who is particularly attentive to it. The rifle is the only arm.' *

" At the beginning of Franco-German hostilities the town guard was particularly ordered to mount guard in the belfries of the places on the frontier and to inform the Belgian field army of the movements of the German advance.

" An example of defective observation and of faulty knowledge of events is furnished by a conversation which took place in a tramcar at Aix-la-Chappelle and in which a priest took part.

" A soldier of the Landsturm was concerned. He told how he had recently to escort a convoy of prisoners. As well as soldiers he had some civilians, also three priests who were accused of having taken part in the fighting against the Germans.

" ' How were they dressed? ' asked the priest. ' Had they long black cassocks? '

" ' No, not long ones but short ones coming nearly to the knee.'

" ' Was this robe really black? '

---

* " The description given here by R. P. Duhr of the uniform of the non-combatant town guard is not entirely correct. The distinctive signs of this uniform are essentially the blue blouse, the armlet, and the tricolour cockade. Many details belonging to this paragraph are therefore of a doubtful accuracy. We leave the responsibility for it to R. P. Duhr." (Van Langenhove.)

" ' No, brown,' was the response of the soldier.

" ' Then they were not priests; they must have been town guards. It is in this manner that these are dressed.'

" The soldier was silent, surprised; this truly he did not know.' (*Münchener Tageblatt*, September 20, 1914.

" Thus a whole series of these stories of machine-guns on belfries which involve the priests and which one has been able to follow up are shown to be pure products of the imagination.

" The curé of Arlon was said to have fired from the top of the belfry on the Germans and afterwards to have been shot. *Informations Pax* has received in reference to this subject the following report:

" ' Arlon, November 6, 1914.

" ' We have the honour to make known to you, whilst returning to you the enclosed letter, that the rumour in question is devoid of all foundation.

" ' Yours faithfully

" ' For the communal administration.

" ' REUTER '

" The rumor was current at Düsseldorf that the Curé of Orchamps near Neufchateau had been shot. With the sacristan and three inhabitants of the place he had fired from the top of the belfry with a machine-gun on the Germans at the moment of their passage.

" *Informations Pax* gathered from the Imperial Command at Namur the following information upon this subject:

" ' Military Government of the Province of Luxemburg, Arlon,

" ' November 21, 1914.

" ' Answer to the letter of the 21st of October, 1914, addressed to the Imperial Command at Namur:

" ' It appears from the observations made by the 4th mobile squadron of the Landsturm of Bonn, at present at Bertrix, that the news suggesting that the Curé of Orchamps, near Neufchateau, accompanied by a sacristan and three inhabitants of the place had fired from the top of the belfry with a machine-gun upon the German troops, is not correct. The curé and the sacristan were only shut up as hostages in the church; they were at once released.

" ' The Military Government
" ' ANDERHEID, Captain & Adjutant.'

" R. P. Duhr, *Der Lügengeist*.

" ' ATROCITIES IN THE CELLAR OF A MONASTERY
AT LOUVAIN

" ' *The Berliner Lokal-Anzeiger* reports in its issue of August 31, 1914, the following from Rotterdam, dated August 30th:

" ' A nurse who had arrived in Rotterdam from Louvain had spoken in the latter town with a German officer who gave her the following particulars of the punishment of Louvain. In the early days of the occupation of the town all was quiet, the inhabitants having put away their arms; the German visitors were not molested and were on sufficiently good terms with the population. Subsequently there were found in a cellar the bodies of fifty German soldiers who had apparently been killed by the brothers belonging to the monastery. The occupants of the monastery were arrested and the superior was shot. When he was led out he laughed triumphantly.'

" This horrible fable was quoted in numerous anti-Catholic journals. As it was likely to revive sectarian bitterness, the General commanding the 7th Army Corps sent the following note to these journals on September 6, 1914:

" Münster, September 6, 1914.

" ' Vague statements regarding the pretended mur-
ders of a large number of German soldiers by monks
at Louvain, like those which have recently appeared
in a series of journals, make it desirable for me to
remind you that such articles, which are calculated
to stir up religious or political discord, are forbidden.

" ' I insist that this interdict shall be observed in
the most rigorous way by journals, and I draw your
attention to the consequences of an infraction, as provided by my proclamation of August 27th, IIc. No.
2588.

" ' FRHR. VON BISSING,
General Commanding '.

" The *canard* continued its flight and the information bureau of the Catholic press at Frankfort endeav-
oured to learn something about it from the German
Command at Louvain. The reply was: ' We know
nothing here of this incident. The story is unworthy
of belief.' (*Bayer, Kurier,* No. 269, September 26,
1914).

" Shortly afterwards *Informations Pax* of Cologne
sent a similar inquiry to the Commandant at Louvain
and received the following answer:

" 'Headquarters of the Imperial Garrison,
" ' Louvain, October 7, 1914.
" ' Reply to your letter of September 29, 1914.

" ' It appears that the numerous statements which
the journals have reproduced in regard to events at
Louvain from August 25 to 27, 1914, are exaggerated
out of all proportion and are in part completely
imaginary. The article to which you make allusion
in your letter belongs to this category.

" ' (s) VON THIEL,'
" From *Kölnische Volkzeitung,* No. 247,
March 25, 1915.

" ' ANOTHER UCONFIRMED RUMOR.

" ' The following rumour was in circulation at Poppenhausen in the neighborhood of Cassel at the beginning of last December.

" ' At Vouziers, at the beginning of September, a French priest and a woman, who was doubtless his housekeeper, were condemned by the military authorities and hanged. This priest had been the curé of a village near Chalons-sur-Marne. He had welcomed into his house thirty-five wounded Germans and had then by means of a telephone in his cellar signalled to the French artillery to open fire upon the house filled with wounded. The propagator of this rumour even pretends that he saw the curé taken from Chalons to Vouziers with some French prisoners and *francs-tireurs*. He saw him hanged from a tree near the barracks in the former locality together with the woman mentioned.'

" ' On January 19, 1915, the Prussian Ministry of War sent the following communication to the *Pax* bureau:

" ' In reply to your letter of January 15, 1915 (*Akt.-Zeich.*, F. 51), the Ministry of War informs you that nothing is known of the rumour in question and that, without more precise details, it is impossible to discover anything.

" ' By order,
" ' (s) BAUER WAGNER.'

" *Informations Pax* wrote also to the commandant of the 9th mobile transport of the 3d army at Vouziers and received in reply the following letter:

" ' In answer to your enquiry of the 2nd inst. (F. 51) we have the honour to inform you that the rumour circulated at Poppenhausen, near Cassel, according to which there had been hanged here a

French curé and his housekeeper is a pure invention.
" ' The military tribunal sitting at Vouziers has not
up to the present sentenced any one to death.

" ' (Seal and signature,) ' "

In this manner throughout approximately one
hundred pages van Langenhove recites the tales and
sets down the answers as they were communicated to
Pax after investigation by German officials, civil and
military. In the following words he concludes this
section of his work:

" Such are the different categories of stories of
which a rigorous control has established the imaginary
character. Most of them, it is seen, have been surprised not far from their origin and have hardly
passed the first phases of elaboration. These indeed
are the only ones which afford scope for enquiry since
the data of place, time, and individuality have not yet
been lost and they therefore permit of checking."

The facts as they are related here are set forth
also by Dr. Albert Helwig, who was in the German
military service, in a pamphlet on the psychology of
mass suggestion. Both van Langenhove and Helwig
offer approximately the same account of the origin
of the tales as follows:

In the war of 1870–1871 the Germans were greatly
harassed by *franc tirieur* or " guerilla " warfare.
The formal discipline of the German soldiers had not
equipped them to engage successfully in this type of
individual fighting and it was correspondingly terri-
fying. Subsequently German military teachers and
writers gave a great deal of attention to methods of
engaging in this type of struggle. It is said that
each German soldier entering Belgium carried with

him a book of instructions, one chapter or section in which dealt with methods of meeting *franc tirieur* warfare. So it may be assumed that the German soldier, when he crossed the Belgian border, shaken by fear and uncertainty (activity of native complexes and of others acquired through training — and all made temporarily more sensitive than usual), easily conjured up the images that fitted in with the situation of the hour and the atmosphere created by his previous instruction. When, therefore, a party of them, approaching a position in the night, are fired upon by an unseen foe, and especially if approximately at the same time lights are seen in or about the church in a near-by village (suggestion of something afoot), the setting is complete for the mushroom growth of a story of clerical complicity with citizens in the much dreaded *franc tirieur* warfare. Fear throws off the inhibitions and one, more credulous than the rest, reported having seen suspicious lights in the village. It matters not at all whether he was merely the victim of his imagination or hallucination or not. His fellow soldiers throughout the army, and the civilian population as well, for that matter, have just such suggestible natures as his own; the same instinctive fears and the same acquired complexes growing out of reaction to circumstances similar to those he has met. When, therefore, he tells his tale of lights in the villages, it finds ready acceptance in thousands of minds and catches like wild fire throughout the nation behind the lines. Other tales have the same history and the whole people are caught up into a mad frenzy that in normal circumstances would be held in check.

The angels walking at Mons is a similar case. Fear has thrown off the inhibitions and the native superstitious disposition is aroused by the scenes of carnage around the soldier. He is excited by the fear of imminent death and his childhood's images of awaiting angels arise, in a dream or otherwise, and now a gray cloud moving across the horizon before the wind becomes, in his eyes, an angel or a group of angels. Others, prepared as he has been, take up the story as he renders it and thousands accept it.

CONCLUSION — If our analysis of these concepts of suggestion and suggestibility is correct, the possibility of successfully employing these means alone to build up large social unities is limited by three factors: (1) racial and other native differences, (2) prejudices due to social and economic position, (3) inequalities in education and want of uniform experience among sections of the population. All such factors as these tend to keep people apart and so stand in the way of a mutual understanding. They therefore maintain the people between whom such differences exist in a reciprocally defensive attitude. In this situation the suspicious nature is at high tension, and social stimuli, whatever their nature, are likely to be followed by an antagonistic reaction.

Wherever there is a group of people with so much in common that they constitute a crowd, a mob, an audience, the readers of a particular periodical or the disciples of a particular *ism*, there is opportunity for a fairly wide-sweeping interplay of suggestion and suggestibility. As the means and frequency of communication among men increase, and as localism becomes swallowed up in nationalism and more, we should expect an increase in the waves of phenomena of suggestion and suggestibility, were there no counterbalancing factor. Such a factor is provided, however, more and more generously as the years come and go, in our institutions for higher learning, in industry and commerce, in as far as they cultivate a disposition to seek first-hand data and weigh the evidence, pro and con, upon new problems.

It appears from the foregoing that a discussion of suggestion and the suggestible nature applies to the psychology of action and likewise to that of feeling and belief. As applied to action it is linked up with the development of the habits of individuals and the customs that prevail in groups. As applied to feelings and beliefs it is associated with conventions and morale in the individual and amongst peoples.

CHAPTER VII

THE CROWD AND ALLIED PHENOMENA

THE crowd is an unorganized or leaderless group. Its chief characteristic from the viewpoint of its psychological nature is that its members have their attention centered upon the same situation and are in an attitude of more or less expectancy with respect to it: for instance, a group of commuters in a railway station awaiting the appearance of a belated train at the close of a day's work. All have for the most part thrown off the immediately practical interests of the day: they have left their business affairs behind them in their offices. All are at the evening hour looking forward toward rest and recreation at home, and this attitude is intensified by the delay. Each member of this railway-station crowd sees every other member and hears his fellow-waiter's vocal expression of disappointment. Visual and auditory signs indicate surely that all are feeling and thinking as he is doing. Each one, therefore, recognizes a certain kinship between himself and the others and a sense of unity pervades the group. There is no idea held in common with respect to what shall be done about anything. This is the crowd state of mind. We are thinking here of the simplest form of crowd. We have referred to it as a *leaderless* group.

Whenever, in whatever circumstances, a leader comes forward the crowd becomes specialized. It may then be a mob, an audience, a deliberative assembly, or what not, according to the circumstances of the time and place, the purpose of the leader, etc. Distinctions of the sort serve mainly for convenience. The fundamental criterion — attention in common — is unaltered. Its direction is conditioned by different means: in the case of the crowd *so-called*, by a direct perceptional stimulus; in the audience, by ideals or situations presented by a speaker who holds the floor in a formal manner and directs the attention of each member of the group now to one and now to another aspect of a subject by a more or less systematic presentation of ideas; in the deliberative assembly, similarly, a presiding officer controls by recognizing one by one those who are permitted to present their ideas. Obviously the development of this crowd state of mind is facilitated by the ease of communication among members of the group in the railway-station-situation, e.g., and by another factor also: all the individuals are in such close physical contact — let us assume — that their freedom of movement is to some extent interfered with, and this, as Professor James has pointed out, goes a long way toward robbing each one of his individuality and bringing all to a common level of interest and desire.

It is a corollary to the foregoing that differences may be expected among aggregations of individuals with respect to the facility with which they may be made into crowds in the sense in which we are using the term. Persons who cannot understand one another;

whose background of experiences differ greatly or who have widely different prospects upon life do not readily mold into crowds. A group of newly arrived immigrants of different nations, races, languages and customs, whether jammed together or dispersed over a country can hardly be a crowd. An aggregation of such diversified folk will inevitably break up into crowds of smaller number unless they can quickly be brought to an understanding in which their fundamental differences are submerged.

It is often said that in a crowd the individual is of a different nature than in an isolated condition; that the " psychology " of the man or woman in a crowd is different from that of the same person in relative isolation. This in a sense is true, but when it is put in that fashion it carries untrue implications. The " psychology " of the man in the crowd differs from that of the man in his study in the very sense in which it differs from the same individual between a cold room and a hot room, or between a church environment and a base-ball environment. Amongst these situations there are wide differences in the pressure of desires, ambitions, and anticipations. The desire to pursue his business vigorously has been temporarily substituted in the railway station by a desire to reach home and family; the ambition to make a commanding impression upon the head of the firm, until tomorrow, takes a subordinate place. The physical surroundings in the railroad station provide stimuli that are quite different from those to which he reacts in the office. He behaves differently in the crowd than in his office or in his study, that is true.

But he does so because of a different set of stimuli, purposes, and the like, not because he is now of different nature than formerly nor because of a ' crowd self " that has somehow taken the lead.

But it is not necessary that a group of people should be jammed into physical contact in small space, nor even that they be within the range of sight and hearing of one another in order to be designated properly as a crowd. They may constitute the widely distributed population of a state and yet be a crowd, if their attention is bent in the same direction, if each one has a certain awareness that the attitude of others approximates to his own, and if all are actuated by similar motives. There is thus a stage in the development of a political party campaign, in the rise of a financial panic, and in the growth of a war spirit in which the population of a state and of a nation may be described as a crowd. The attainment of this condition in the state at large is facilitated by easy means of communication. Within the four walls of the railway station there is practically no bar to intercommunication among individuals. Each can see and hear his neighbors and mutual understanding is assured. Within the boundaries of the state or of the nation, the telegraph, telephone, and daily mail are the means by which communication is established and mutual understanding secured. Through these means, the conditions are supplied for the emergence of a nation-wide crowd. The possibility of the development of a crowd in this respect assumes such a level of training and intelligence on the part of the citizenship as will enable the people to make use of the means of communication, and further, it assumes that the population is not so divided in respect to race and other distinctions, including class prejudices, as to preclude the development of common interests. In spite of the existence of such antagonistic conditions the crowd may be developed and its life may span a brief space, but it must be maintained at the cost of extraordinary effort to stir the emotions of the people; to appeal to some of the most fundamental interests of men and women — whether for the sake of truth it is proper to invoke them or not — or at any rate to emphasize them at the expense of other interests. It is thus that "hearth and home," "our sacred firesides," "our households," "our flag" and such phrases or shibboleths attain their prominence in many a political campaign and during the stress of war time. There are many sharp and deep-rooted differences amongst the people of a state, but we all agree in our attachment to "our sacred firesides" above all else. If our attention can be distracted from our differences and centered upon some interest such as this that is held in common it is highly probable that within a limited period we will act in unison. But when the campaign is over or when peace has been declared and the multitude of our advisers have ceased bandying their phrases our divergent interests reassert themselves and we awake to find the large, apparently unified group of yesterday, broken into contending factions. Nearly every national and state campaign, preparatory to a general election, affords illustration, and on a larger and more tragic scale is the picture of world powers allied during the crisis of the war, broken apart and contending over minor problems since the peace was attempted at Versailles.

Some of the consequences of the emergence of the crowd are important. Individuality is lost or diminished: that is, the differences that set one off from another in ordinary circumstances, are toned down somewhat. This inevitably follows when a group of people are attending to the same situation and are moved by approximately the same purposes. Furthermore the group of conflicting complexes that make up the organization we designate by the term personality, is quiescent. The inhibitory effect of one complex upon another is allayed. Each person in the crowd is, therefore, in a higher state of suggestibility than in other circumstances. An appropriate stimulus may, as we have expressed it already, tap ordinarily submerged or inhibited complexes and excite them to the point of active control of behavior, after the manner with which we are familiar in the case of suggestion and response in the laboratory.

THE MOB. — When the crowd state has developed, the situation is prepared for the leader who may skillfully take advantage of the suggestible nature of the individuals who compose the crowd to harangue them, or by more subtle means to stir them up to such activity as will suit his own purpose. This may be a mad rush to destroy the railroad property or to wreck a newspaper plant down street. It may be a landslide to support a certain candidate at the polls; a craze for investment or a rush for the gold fields such as Down has described under the title " The Rush to the Klondike " (4): " On July 18 the Portland arrived in Seattle, on Puget Sound, having on board sixty-eight miners, who brought ashore bullion worth a million dollars. The next day it was stated that these miners had in addition enough gold concealed about their persons and in their baggage to double the first estimate. Whether all these statements were correct or not does not signify, for those were the reports that were spread throughout the states. From this last source alone, the mint at San Francisco received half a million dollars' worth of gold in one week, and it was certain that men who had gone away poor had come back with fortunes. It was stated that a poor blacksmith who had gone up from Seattle returned with $115,000, and that a man from Fresno, who had failed as a farmer, had secured $135,000.

" The gold fever set in with fury and attacked all classes. Men in good positions, with plenty of money to spend on an outfit, and men with little beyond the amount of their fare, country men and city men, clerks and professional men without the faintest notion of the meaning of ' roughing it,' flocked in impossible numbers to secure a passage. There were no means of taking them. Even in distant New York, the offices of railroad companies and local agencies were besieged by anxious inquirers eager to join the throng. On Puget Sound, mills, factories, and smelting works were deserted by their employees, and all the miners on the upper Skeena left their work in a body. On July 21 the North American Transportation Company (one of two companies which monopolized the trade of the Yukon) was reincorporated in Chicago with a quadrupled capital, to cope with the demands of traffic. At the different Pacific ports every available vessel was pressed into the service, and still the wild rush could not be met. Before the end of July the Portland left Seattle again for St. Michael's and the Mexico and Topeka for Dyea; the Islander and Tees sailed for Dyea from Victoria, and the G. W. Elder from Portland; while from San Francisco the Excelsior, of the Alaska Company, which had brought the first gold down, left again for St. Michael's on July 28, being the last of the company's fleet scheduled to connect with the Yukon river boats for the season. Three times the original price was offered for the passage, and one passenger accepted an offer of $1,500 for the ticket for which he had paid only $150.

" This, however, was only the beginning of the rush. Three more steamers were announced to sail in August for the mouth of the Yukon, and at least a dozen more for the Lynn Canal, among which were old tubs, which, after being tied up for years, were now overhauled and refitted for the voyage north. One of these was the Willamette, an old collier with only sleeping quarters for the officers and crew, which, however, was fitted up with bunks and left Seattle for Dyea and Skagway with 850 passengers, 1,200 tons of freight, and 300 horses, men, live stock, and freight being wedged between decks till the atmosphere was like that of a dungeon; and even with such a prospect in view, it was only by a lavish amount of tipping that a man could get his effects taken aboard. Besides all these, there were numerous scows loaded with pro-

visions and fuel, and barges conveying horses for pack-
ing purposes.

"A frightful state of congestion followed as each
successive steamer on its arrival at the head of the
Lynn Canal poured forth its crowds of passengers and
added to the enormous loads of freight already accumulated. Matters became so serious that on August 10 the United States Secretary of the Interior,
having received information that 3,000 persons with
2,000 tons of baggage and freight were there waiting
to cross the mountains to the Yukon, and that many
more were preparing to join them, issued a warning to
the public (following that of the Dominion Government of the previous week) in which he called attention
to the exposure, privation, suffering, and danger incident to the journey at that advanced period of the
season, and further referred to the gravity of the possible consequences to people detained in the mountain-
ous wilderness during five or six months of Arctic
winter, where no relief could reach them."

Even what, in popular language, is often erroneously
described as an audience is from our view-point properly a mob. Sidis, for example, describes such a case
in the following language: * "On the 11th of August,
1895, there took place in the open air a meeting at
Old Orchard, Maine. The business at hand was a
collection for missionary purposes. The preacher resorted to the following suggestions: 'The most
remarkable remembrance which I have of foreign lands
is that of multitudes, the waves of lost humanity who

* *Die Bedentung der Suggestion im Sozialen Leben.* Wies-
baden, 1905. (Quoted from Park and Burgess: *Introduction to
the Science of Sociology,* Chicago, 1921, 415 f.

ceaselessly are shattered on the shores of eternity. How despairing are they, how poor in love; their religion knows no joy, no pleasure, nor song. Once I heard a Chinese say why he was a Christian. It seemed to him that he lay in a deep abyss, out of which he could not escape. Have you ever wept for the sake of the lost world, as did Jesus Christ? If not, then woe to you! Your religion is then only a dream and a blind. We see Christ test his disciples. Will he take them with him? My beloved, today he will test you. (Indirect suggestion.) He could convert a thousand millionaires, but he gives you an opportunity to be saved. (More direct suggestion.) Are you strong enough in faith? ' (Here follows a discussion about questions of faith.) ' Without faith God can do no great things. I believe that Jesus will appear to them who believe firmly in him. My dear ones, if only you give for the sake of God, you have become participants in the faith. (Still more direct suggestion.) The youth with the five loaves and the two little fishes. . . .' (The story follows.) ' When everything was ended, he did not lose his loaves; there were twelve baskets left over. O my dear ones, how will that return! Sometime the King of Kings will call to you and give you an empire of glory, and simply because you have had a little faith in him. It is a day of much import to you. Sometime God will show us how much better he has guarded our treasure than we ourselves.' The suggestion had the desired effect. Money streamed from all sides; hundreds became thousands, tens of thousands. The crowd gave seventy thousand dollars."

In situations similar to either of the foregoing, once the quiescent crowd has taken on a fervor of unthinking activity in the wake of a leader, we have what is properly termed a mob. (The army and the like, *acting under discipline*, is in a different category.) The unconscious background of the personality of each member of the group is not only ready to express itself in action, but it has come into active control. Other controls are inhibited, and each individual is doing what in other circumstances he would not and could not do. There is a mutual exchange of stimulation among the members of the group. Because all are doing approximately the same thing the total volume of stimulation is large and powerful; the complexes that were aroused at the moment of the birth of the mob come more and more distinctly into the foreground and are increasingly sensitive with the consequence that the frenzied activity of the mob knows no limit until quiescence follows through sheer exhaustion, or until a counter stimulus arouses inhibitory controls or scatters the participants in the mob action.

Here, as in so many other connections that appear in the study of human behavior, it is impossible to draw hard and fast boundaries and to attempt it is to invite confusion. It is impossible to show just where the crowd ends and the mob begins. The distinction is in large part one of convenience, and in part one of traditional emphasis upon conscious states and processes on the one hand, and upon behavior in the narrow sense, on the other hand.

MOTIVES OF THE MOB. — The analysis of mob phenomena leads us to a great variety of motives, in some measure native and in others acquired in the course of life history. Let us take as an example the great religious revival in Kentucky in 1800. From the point of view developed in this chapter the Kentuckians involved in this case constituted first a crowd and then a mob. We will attempt to see what conditions gave rise to the phenomena. The pioneers of the day in eastern Kentucky had immigrated from the hills of Virgina and from farther east. They were on the whole of sturdy English and Scotch stock, such as is supposed not to lend itself easily to mob phenomena. Yet these people in this sparsely settled region, interested in common, and having a common purpose (crowd), came in throngs to the revivalist's services, fell to the ground under the spell of religious excitement that was aroused by the leader, shook the saplings in the wood and pawed up the earth in their religious frenzy. The group is now a mob.

In the towns and relatively densely populated rural districts in old Virginia, these people had been accustomed to meeting for the exchange of religious experiences and for social intercourse of other forms. Furthermore, at any rate among the Scotch and Scotch-Irish elements in the population, there is believed to be a natural trait that easily expresses itself in the guise of religious emotion. Such native and acquired dispositions are suppressed and inhibited by reason of lack of opportunity for their expression in a sparsely settled community such as eastern Kentucky in 1800 where the means of communication were few and precarious. But let the effective revivalist appear and make his vigorous appeal to even a small group, and the pent-up complexes are provided an outlet. The appeal comes to them bearing the color and atmosphere of the older days. The crust of indifference, bred of isolation, melts under the influence, and the Kentuckians throw themselves into the revival with zest and enthusiasm, reinforced by the unloosed complexes that lie at the roots of their natures: with reduplicated enthusiasm, in fact, for it is the way with men, on release from restraint, to give rein to a strong reaction. The repression of any complex implies tension and the psycho-analysts are repeatedly reporting and demonstrating cases in which the removal or breaking of an inhibition is followed by a vigorous, and sometimes blind expression of the repressed complexes.

It has been pointed out above that the members of a group may be widely separated and yet constitute a crowd in all essential respects, and for that matter a mob as well. Up to the moment of their coming together under the spell of the voice of the revivalist this condition obtained in the case of the Kentucky revival.

The circumstances leading up to a rush of home-seekers from the East to take up agricultural lands in the West will set forth once more, sufficiently, the characteristics of the crowd and the mob, in which the individual members are in relative isolation from one another.

We will first assume a promoter who is seeking to attract a large group of buyers to his western agricultural lands. He must advertise until his prospective settlers shall have centered their attention upon his lands practically to the exclusion of their ordinary, every-day interests. This advertising must be of such a nature that each person who is reached by it may be vividly aware of whatever favorable reactions others may be making to the appeal in behalf of western settlement. Thus a crowd consciousness will soon have been developed. To facilitate the process the promoter will judiciously select the group to which he will direct his advertising. He will not select the members of the legal, or the medical, or the clerical professions, e.g., because, while they may have the natural disposition favorable to *interest* in western agricultural life and successful adaptation to it, yet as a rule it is fair to assume that this natural background is not reinforced by such acquired or professional dispositions or complexes as will assure the skill and the interest in details needful to sustain the new westerner throughout the difficulties of the period of adjustment. Consequently the promoter will advertise amongst a group of farmers who may be assumed to have acquired an occupational complex, and moreover, amongst those who are not now satisfactorily exercising it, because of adverse economic conditions such as the high cost of land, because of sterile soil where they are now living, or for any other reason. Such folk are more likely to be his audience or his crowd than a group of farmers who are now satisfactorily expressing their professional or vocational motives and they are much more likely than others to sustain themselves in the course of the initial period of adjustment.

Let us assume that this group, now a crowd, caught up with eager interest, concentrated zeal for western homesteading, and fascinated by the mental picture of hundreds of persons like themselves preparing to set out upon the westward route, and let us asume that the movement has already begun with more enthusiasm than hard-headedness. Each one, in his own way, is making preparation for departure. He may know nothing of how others are going about the same task. All he knows — or thinks — is that he is one of a great number who are on their way. The group has assumed all the psychological characteristics of the mob — and it is a mob — notwithstanding that the individual members are isolated from one another, and notwithstanding that they are not madly rushing down the street bent upon destruction of life or property. Some of the deepest impulses in human nature have been freed from the restraints of conventional life and are in full control.

It is appropriate at this point to recall that when these home-seekers have once arrived upon their western lands the promoter has a new problem. He must hold his people during an unexciting period of adjustment during which their memories of what they left behind them in their old homes are very vivid. He must take account of the fact that they have in their make-up certain school-going, church-going, town-meeting and play complexes, and provide an outlet for each of them. They cannot, even if it were desirable, break completely away, and at once, from all that has been built into their natures in the course of their years in the old surroundings.

THE POLITICAL CAMPAIGN. — No doubt, as has been already suggested, the voters at the conclusion of many a political party campaign constitute a mob in as true a sense as in any other relation that may be described. [They have been caught up in a crowd state of mind by an arresting appeal: they have been bombarded with partisan paragraphs from platform and press: the band and the torchlight procession with banners have made their contribution and the voters in a jumble of excitement and zealous without knowledge, go to their polling places, no one thinking for himself: each one acting on an impulse or a tangle of impulses.] Once more it is important to remember that neither in the crowd nor in the mob are we dealing with what some have called a " crowd mind " or a " mob mind " distinct from the mind of each individual who is a part of the group.

In every case in which we have a crowd and a mob there is a concourse of stimulations peculiar to the situation as a whole. These have brought the attention of all to the same problem or related problems and later each one is borne upon, not only by the orginal, inciting stimuli, but by the additional excitations that impinge upon each one from every other in the group. All this arouses in every one the consciousness that all are concentrated upon the same end. Imagery of each other's actions and attitudes is vivid. Stimuli from without and impulses from within are infinitely reduplicated. It is the highly keyed up state of each one in the crowd: a state in which one " feels " and shares the attitude of many others, that

is erroneously interpreted by some as evidence of a
" crowd mind."

We have said that the voters in many a political
campaign constitute a mob. This is particularly true
of a brief but active campaign and of those persons
who, late in its progress, are caught up in its whirl.
In cases in which the moment of decision and action
is not imminent and pressure for action is felt to be
correspondingly weak, the trumpets, brass bands and
orators soon lose their power, and the eager, palpitat-
ing excitement of the people subsides — save, at any
rate, in exceptionally volatile natures that feed upon
the hyperbole: those of unstable constitution whose
will is the wind's will, and whose reliance is always
upon the new " ism."

FASHION. — The phenomena designated by the general term " fashion " are fundamentally of the same
nature as those that have been already discussed in
this chapter. Though we are gregarious, whether by
nature or by habit, and though we consequently are
disposed to sink our individuality by compromising
the differences between us and our neighbors, we nevertheless in divers ways assert our distinctness from
the common herd. It is in this way that fashion is
distinguished, as we think of it, from convention and
custom. Fundamentally it is not a matter-of-course-
like slipping into a compromise with our neighbors,
our contemporaries in general and our predecessors.
This is convention or custom, and the process of
reaching it is leveling. Fashion is a struggle or a
protest against the conventional. A group bound by
convention may be the " backbone of a nation " in

the sense that we can always depend upon them and know ever where to find them, but they are deadening. Where there are fashion-folk, on the other hand, there is vitality and stimulation. Such folk may not be the " backbone " of a people but in their changing fashions there is at any rate the possibility of improved adjustments.

We are probably all at once fashion-folk and conventional folk in one aspect and another. It is a matter of degree. Each of us, from the cradle to the grave, clamors for his neighbor's attention. The dead level is unendurable. There is a limit beyond which the spirit of compromise between our individualistic nature and our gregarious disposition may strive in vain. At some cost, be it great or small, each of us will be, in one respect or another, the center of a group of lookers-on, and more than that, a leader of a group. So the individual sets a fashion and bids for his followers. It may be a fashion in dress, house, manner of behavior or in theory.

What will determine its character? Obviously we shall have to seek our answer, in part, as in other instances, in the nature of the self. Professor James was wont to speak of the material self, the social self, and the spiritual self: three aspects of each personality. As a matter of course we cannot think of ourselves apart from our material possessions: our clothing, our watches and jewelry, our automobiles, our lands, our stocks and bonds. The sense of possession colors all our life. Take away our cherished material goods and we feel like different persons as compared with our former selves. We may voluntarily choose to make this so-called material self the outstanding feature of our character — or we may drift into such a choice quite as a matter of course. In either case the road has been laid along which we will travel. The acquisition of material goods will give color to our lives; leadership in activities relating to acquisition will be our ambition: we will follow the fashions set by those who are like ourselves and in as far as we ourselves may become the imitators of fashion we will create fashions in dress, house furnishing, automobiles, etc.

If we have chosen in any manner to emphasize what has been called the social self, our cherished fashions are once more predetermined and the way of our ambition for leadership is laid out. The manner of afternoon teas, of dinner parties, etc., manners of address, and all that, supply the material out of which, or in which, fashions will be made. Finally if we have chosen to emphasize the spiritual aspect of the self our fashions will be in the theories, cults, doctrines that we devise or espouse; in the variations in artistic expression that we affect, etc.

Once the new mode or what-not has been launched, the less ingenious or less independent persons into whose attention it falls become its followers. Thus for a period, at any rate, they satisfy their craving for differentiation from the common herd in whatever direction their preference may lie, and the country wide may be swept by the fashion, or fad.

Fashions tend to the extreme. When a large group of followers have caught up with the fashion leader, the individual's craving for distinction from the common herd is no longer satisfied. The line of least resistance by which satisfaction may be secured is in the direction in which the fashion is originally set. Hence the coats become longer or the sleeves larger, or the theory more radical, until a limit is reached, when the fashion breaks down of its own weight and a new direction, probably the reverse, is set.

The foregoing considerations account for the subversion of good taste in pursuit of fashion. It is assumed that good taste is a sense of proportion that is expressed in our loyalty to the fundamentals of aesthetics in form, color, tone, etc. In other words, good taste is a sense of harmony. Obviously, therefore, the pursuit of fashion — especially leadership therein — running as it does to an extreme — tends not only to break up established conventions in the arts and crafts, but even to the subversion of good taste. The resistance of the psycho-physical background, however, prevents the sudden onset of an extreme departure from the fundamentals of harmony. Its weight, furthermore, aids no little in reducing the extremities of fashion. It is more than a form of words to apply the term " ballast " to certain elements in the population in this and other similar connections.

THE AUDIENCE. — The audience is a specialized form of crowd. Its members have not come together fortuitously from every occupational and professional walk in the city as they came into the hypothetical railway station which served for illustration in the first pages of this chapter, nor yet as the thousands of prospective voters within the period of a political campaign come to their newspapers before breakfast and to the campaign tent where the orators hold forth. The audience is a selected group that has come together because its members are already interested in the subject matter that the speaker will present. There is already existing a defined intellectual craving to satisfy, and it is common to the members of the group. The demand for satisfaction overtops all else for the time.

To be sure, it is not solely the acquired intellectual motive that is stimulated in the audience. The speaker often appeals to quite different motives and finds them. For example, at the outset of his address he flatters his hearers by speaking of his own concurrence in certain " well-matured " views that he is told they entertain, and by the use of other phrases that are well known to the public speaker, he brings other motives into play such as will facilitate the development of a *rapport* between himself and his hearers and so enable him the better to direct the current of their thought.

DISCUSSION. — The leader of the audience may bring his hearers to a common opinion and to a common decision without further to-do. The members may go away with the feeling that nothing remains to be said and forthwith settle into inactivity. In the ideal situation, however, the leader presents many viewpoints and directs his hearer's thought without concluding it. He stimulates thought and discussion follows as a consequence. As this process goes on the kernel of the problem, whatever it may be, is approached from many angles and each participant has the opportunity to observe many reactions to each line of approach — in fact to experience those reactions himself. More or less formal analysis inevitably goes with discussion. In fact in may be said to be the essence of discussion. Points of weakness and of strength are made to stand out distinctly so that comparisons may be made. No weak cause can withstand it and every strong cause courts it. One person talking to or at a group can stir their emotions, reduce them to a common level of feeling and purpose, and develop a crowd or a mob. But when the members of the group begin to discuss seriously amongst themselves every crowd-mob-making factor is dissipated: the possibility of a mob developing has forthwith vanished into thin air; all this for the obvious reason, as already stated, that it is the essence of discussion to analyze, to bring not one, but many aspects of a problem successively into attention, to eliminate non-essentials, and to get down to fundamentals.

PUBLIC OPINION. — In the long run the upshot of the process of discussion is the emergence of a new phase in the psychological history of the group: a public opinion. It is more than the algebraic sum of individual opinions. As excitement is allayed, reflection ensues, and in such instances there is food for reflection for in the initial period of excitement individual opinions, formed at every angle of approach, of every degree of maturity and good sense, have been bandied about, and each wide-awake member of the community has observed many types of reaction thereto. Gradually there emerges, as a result of a slow, but more spontaneous than deliberate analysis, a certain apprehension of common and fundamental interests by all members of the group. This is a public opinion. It has no reference to all the varied contents of consciousness of the individuals who make up a community. It is rather, as we conceive it, a certain resultant that remains over from having entertained many opinions of more or less maturity. It is a sublimation from all that has been stirring individual natures during weeks of campaign commotion; one that has been helped on at many a cross-road and elsewhere by discussion, the genius of which is to sift; and because it is such a sublimation, attained by those elements in the community that are by nature capable of reflection and discussion and disposed thereto, rather than by the unstable cravers for excitement, or by those whose dullness blocks reflection and discussion, it can be safely assumed to touch more fundamental issues, and therefore to lie upon a higher plane than the average opinion or the algebraic sum of the opinions of all individuals in the community.

In the light of this it will be apparent why the clever manipulator who has his own selfish ends to pursue prefers a short campaign to a long one. He must force a decision and action as soon as the populace shall have arrived at the mob state of mind, and before a real public opinion shall have been developed. Conversely the statesman of broad vision has his advantage in a long campaign. Furthermore, if the above analysis is correct, it is safe to say that government by public opinion in the sense in which we are using the phrase, is a reliable government to follow. On the other hand, government by so-called public opinion, *i.e.* public opinion in the sense of general agreement as to objects of thought, and no more than that, may be a government by a mob.

Incidentally government by public opinion is bound to be more satisfying to the governed than any other form for the reason that the governed have had a hand and voice in creating the opinion and therefore in building the laws and other institutions which are crystallizations therefrom.

By this token government by arbitrary power and by experts is unsatisfying; it may even serve as an incitement to mob formation and action for the reason that no person nor institution can persistently neglect or refuse to recognize the fundamental demand of human nature to carve its own destiny: to find satisfaction of its craving for individuality, without sooner or later focussing the attention of all the people upon the objects of their fundamental demands to the exclusion of more immediate practical interests. At such a juncture there are always a few daring souls, devoted to an ideal, who will head a revolutionary movement.

We have attempted in this chapter to interpret the crowd, the mob, and allied phenomena, as forms of behavior that develop upon a basis of dispositions that respond in every case to more or less well-defined situations or stimuli in the social environment. The prevention and control of these phenomena are affected by creating situations or complexes of stimuli which, by inciting responses, are the occasions of those complexes or habit systems — public opinion in our sense of the word — that inhibit precipitate action.

CHAPTER VIII

CONVENTION, CUSTOM AND MORALE

THE terms convention, or conventionality, and custom, are properly applied respectively to two aspects of the same broad phenomenon. They are products of imitation of which one may be wholly unconscious, although it may have been conscious and voluntary at the outset. The finished product is always an automatism. " Conventionality " and " custom " are frequently used interchangeably. The term " attitude " may be substituted for conventionality. The whole subject is linked up with that of habits.

Strictly speaking, a convention or conventionality is a matter-of-course, silent, unthought feeling of acceptance, or approval or disapproval of a point of view or form of behavior or station in life; while a custom is an overt method, form or habit of behavior which gives outward expression to the feeling of approval or disapproval. Practically it is no more possible to separate the two than to effect a similar division in the case of any personal habit. For the most part we drift into our conventions and customs. Thus we acquire our class spirit; our political and religious complexions; our race prejudices; our feeling for capital and labor; our fixed professional preferences; the " spirit of the age "; morale, etc. These are, ordinarily, conventionalities. Most of us adhere

to one or another political party and to this or that
religious denomination or sect, not because we have
coldly analyzed the several political and religious
tenets respectively and thoughtfully arrived at a conclusion after the evidence has all been set in array, but
because we have been saturated with the atmosphere.
From the cradle onward we have seen and heard members of our own family and neighborhood in their
observation and discussion of the practices of their
political, social, and religious groups. We have heard
their points of view as to capital and labor and races
and have seen their behavior with respect thereto, and
our natures all the while were being formed in the
way in which they were being exercised The process
is closely analogous to that by which a group of
young men become professional lawyers. (Indeed in
the course of time any profession becomes conventional in so far as its members get into the way of
taking it as it is.)   Their natures have become inclined in that direction by repeated stimulation in the
home where the father, it may be, is a lawyer; later
accordingly in school and in college their attention
is caught by matters relating to that profession; later
still in the professional school the curriculum and all
other stimuli are selected, controlled, and brought to
bear as nearly as may be with the single purpose in
view to create in each young man in the group the
complex professional attitude or habit. The process
is carried on intensively in the practice of the profession until, before many years have lapsed, it is
difficult, if possible at all, to turn aside to a different
profession.

The outstanding difference between the method of arriving at the professional disposition or professional convention, and that of developing a convention of the lazy man's sort, is that in the former case voluntary choice and systematic effort predominate in the initial steps, whereas in the history of the other sort, drifting; casual, perhaps only implicit organic responses to repeated sets of stimuli, that is, responses of an " inner " sort like the sub-vocal speech that accompanies thinking or to the " atmosphere " of a time or place is the rule. The finished professional man can give reasons for his attitudes and behavior in particular instances, though as a matter of fact, they probably rarely occur to him, and he is a matter-of-course creature much the same as others are. The conventionalized product of sheer drifting cannot support himself upon cold reasons. He, too, goes along as a matter of course.

But it should not be understood that either the non-professional or the professional man invariably accepts completely the lot of the group in which he has grown up. In fact it is often as a matter of course that he struggles against the social atmosphere around him: he is in it but not of it: he is as a matter of course under an inner compulsion to ally himself with others whose lot is cast elsewhere than with him. For example, not only does the four-hundred look upon manual labor as degrading and as the symbol of ill success or of positive failure, but the manual laborer himself often assumes the matter-of-course attitude that pecuniary well-being is the culmination of a successful career and that one's civic worth is meas-

ured by one's bank account. This resistant convention is being bent in these latter days — but slowly.
It rests upon a strong natural foundation: the tendency to gravitate toward the strong — or toward
what displays accepted evidences of strength that
reach the eye of the observer — and they are inclined
to accept the testimony at its face value. Miss Jane
Addams (1) cites an illustration in point. " During
one of the Chicago (aldermanic) campaigns a clever
cartoonist drew a poster representing the successful
aldermanic candidate with pretentious dishes and surrounded by other revelers. In contradistinction was
his opponent, a bricklayer, who sat upon a half-fin-
ished wall, eating a meager dinner from a working-
man's dinner-pail, and the passer-by was asked which
type of representation he preferred, the presumption
being that, at least in a working-man's district, the
bricklayer would come out ahead. To the chagrin of
the reformer, however, it was gradually discovered
that, in the popular mind, a man who laid bricks and
wore overalls was not nearly so desirable for an
alderman as the man who drank champagne and wore
a diamond in his shirt-front. The district wished its
representative to stand up with the best of them, and
certainly some of the constituents would have been
ashamed to have been represented by a bricklayer."
This is clearly a case in which a community of manual
laborers were conventionally striving against their
own plane rather than slipping along within it — and
in this particular instance to their own hurt, probably; in which they have leaned in the direction of
what has gripped their attention and presented ac-

ceptable signs of strength and power. On the other hand the bricklayer is drab; he wears no diamonds, no great watch chain, and he does not drive a limousine. He does not attract attention and he presents to his colleagues no evidence of strength more than they themselves possess. With the development of class leadership and the clearer understanding of class needs that inevitably follows upon liberal and general education, the convention we have been discussing is in process of crumbling in the group of manual tradesmen, and the class spirit — another convention — is taking its place.

Conventions arise then, first, from lazily drifting into an acceptance of prevailing conditions and viewpoints and sentiments as they are found in our immediate place and time, as when we drift into our political and religious life. Secondly, they arise from an opposition to prevailing conditions as when the population upon the lower economic levels, as a matter of course, looks upon the possession of material wealth or the attainment of a place in the public eye — especially the former — as the criterion of civic worth, of success, of usefulness; or as when they look upon conspicuous leisure or the conspicuous display of leisure and wealth as evidence of civic worth, etc. In the third place their history is that of the professional or occupational spirit; it is a result of a voluntary control of circumstances; of voluntarily copying an ideal to the end that it may be attained or approximated at least, leading finally to the matter-of-course professional or other occupational spirit.

Obviously the intelligent leaders of a community

prefer to see their neighbors growing into and expressing conventional attitudes that are out of accord with
the real situations in the midst of which they live —
so long as the variance is in the direction of what they
are rightly or wrongly pleased to call " progress," and
so long, furthermore, as the rebellion is not merely the
feverish unrest that is an expression of unadapted, because unstable, human nature that is discussed in a
subsequent chapter. In the natural course of events
a people of low degree mingled with a community of
persons of better estate (provided the obstructions are
not well-nigh insuperable, and provided further that
they are gifted with a modicum of the spirit of discontent), will gravitate upward through the almost
insensible processes of the growth of conventions. This
upward gravitation is an expression of the *élan vital*
of healthy natures which is assumed here as the
" going " power of individuals in all their relations.

Professor Pillsbury's observation upon the growth
of the spirit of nationality among our immigrants, to
be discussed later, is to the point. The very fact that
they feel a certain oppressive atmosphere from being
looked at askance by their new neighbors is a stimulus
to which the more sensitive and adaptable among them,
at any rate, respond by adopting native manners, voluntarily in large part, and gliding into the new spirit
by exercising the new manners. The process described
by Pillsbury goes on largely, no doubt, without their
recognizing it and some day they wake up surprised
to find how far along the way toward naturalization
in the real sense they have already gone. The analogy
is close to the formation of any automatism.

SPIRIT OF THE AGE. — The spirit of the age is conventional. " We see nothing ' dogmatic ' in the inspiring, but certainly most startling, theory of physical science, that we should collect facts for the sake of facts, even though they seem as useless as sticks and straws. This is a great and suggestive idea, and its utility is, in the abstract, quite as disputable as that of calling on oracles or consulting shrines which has been in times past said to prove itself. Thus, because we are not in a civilization which believes strongly in oracles or sacred places, we see the full frenzy of those who killed themselves to find the sepulchre of Christ. But being in a civilization which does believe in this dogma of fact for fact's sake, we do not see the full frenzy of those who kill themselves to find the North Pole. I am not speaking of a tenable ultimate utility which is true both of the Crusades and the polar explorations. I mean merely that we do see the superficial and aesthetic singularity, the startling quality, about the idea of men crossing a continent with armies to conquer the place where a man died. But we do not see the aesthetic singularity and startling quality of men dying in agonies to find a place where no man can live — a place interesting only because it is supposed to be the meeting place of some lines that do not exist " (13). The great body of scientists individually accept this spirit and act upon it, scarcely thinking why. It is their second nature. It is " in the air " and they are imitated by the novices who will develop and perpetuate the spirit after them. Various departments of science have startled us so often by their discoveries that they have acquired a glamour of their own, by reason of which the masses of the people expect to be startled again and are predisposed to give their silent, matter-of-course, or conventional approval to the projects of men of science. Besides, because each branch of science has a glamour of its own, grown out of its startling accomplishments, it appears to the outsider to be a vital, powerful thing, and for this reason there is a predisposition on the part of observers to consent, conventionally, to the proposals that men and women of science may make from time to time, unusual though they may be.

The spirit of the age described as economic is a confession that in the background of our consciousness the economic motive plays a large rôle. It is next to inevitable, especially in the case of that great multitude who must continually struggle for daily bread, and of that other group who are put to it to maintain a family tradition by holding together and increasing a swollen fortune and managing large affairs, that the economic activity should after a while resolve itself into second, in this case conventional, nature.

Once a convention has been developed on a broad scale in a group of people, a bond has been created among them that contributes to the sense of unity that was the subject of an earlier chapter. A group of lawyers, of physicians, of commercial men, of farmers, plumbers, or day laborers, in part by reason of their professional or occupational conventions which they hold in common, understand one another, and take one another and the group into consideration in relation to their daily work. In consequence of all this they are able to co-operate toward ends that they value in common.

NATIONALISM. — The formation of conventions amongst the members of a family or neighborhood or profession is, on a smaller scale, the same phenomenon as the assimilation of the diverse elements in the mixed population of a state or nation. It has a relation, therefore, to the Americanization of immigrants, or to the Germanization of a population. As soon as one people have begun, on a voluntary basis, to act and think as their neighbors do assimilation has begun. No deep-reaching alteration of their personalities has yet come to pass. They may be shaken apart on slight provocation. After sufficiently prolonged co-operation on a voluntary basis, deep-seated changes take shape. Both implicit and explicit habits are formed that involve the organism through and through in infinite permutation: a psycho-physical change has been perfected, and assimilation is a fact. The assimilated and the assimilators figuratively look through the same eyes and stand in the same shoes. From this new psycho-physical disposition, according to a hypothesis widely accepted among psychologists, arise impulses that lead to matter-of-course overt behavior.

It is a question how far the process of assimilation can go. Undoubtedly it will vary with individuals and with groups. It will vary, too, with the manner of distribution of the foreign groups amongst the would-be assimilating population. If colonies are planted down here and there so that the persistence of inter-stimulations common to the homeland is assured, assimilation may not even have a beginning. But if there is no such grouping: if each and every individual immigrant is so isolated from his countrymen that he can be played upon uninterruptedly by stimuli that are peculiar to the new society into which he has come: if necessity compels him to learn the new language: if getting on with his new neighbors compels him to take on new forms of behavior, and if he is brought into contact in season and out of season with the traditions and ideals of American institutions, he will sooner or later inevitably become a matter-of-course naturalized member of the new community.

Professor Pillsbury has made an attempt at selecting the most potent situations that lead to the ultimate transforming of the foreigner into the naturalized citizen (11).

" In estimating the relative importance of the different influences, one may probably put first the desire for the better social standing and higher degree of physical comfort enjoyed by the native. That the superiority of wealth and ordinarily of education is an important factor in inducing the amalgamation, becomes evident if one thinks what the probable course would be were the immigrant to go among an inferior people. It has been the history of the settlement of countries inhabited by inferior races that they were merely driven out or exterminated. Where the native and immigrant are more nearly on a level or the natives are strong enough to hold their own, as in China and in certain of the more backward Latin American countries, either the races live entirely apart or the two fuse into a new race to which each contributes its share.

" Many of the altruistic social workers, and Zimmern among the theorists, have criticized the American people for assumption of superiority and for their contempt of the foreigner. It must be admitted that it has no defense on theoretical or moral grounds. One must admit that the American is full of conceit as to his superiority and that the conceit is largely based on ignorance. In every city there are undoubtedly many men who are passed by with contempt, or more likely never noticed at all, who, by their training and ability, are entitled to a high place in literature or art or political theory. This attitude is taken not by the superior Americans but by the ordinary man, very much inferior in every respect to the men he is looking down upon. Much as we may deprecate the unfairness of the American in this respect and lament the opportunities that he misses on account of it, we must still grant that by it the process of naturalization is hastened. The unreasoning race prejudice which shows itself in repugnance toward the strange speech, customs, and standards of the immigrant is one of the strongest forces in compelling him to be absorbed. How the opposite course of accepting all as equals, with manners and clothing and standards that were merely different but just as good, would work, we cannot say because it has never been tried. Probably one would find that if the newcomer were not repressed he would dominate and soon oppress. At the best he would not be assimilated. Whatever its ethical value, even its logical truth, race prejudice is one of the most important forces in the amalgamation of the stranger.

" It is, of course, granted that the more independent minds among the newcomers see the injustice of the native attitude; the more self-reliant resent it. The prejudice accounts in part for the strong socialistic and anti-governmental political beliefs among them. The great majority, however, feel that steady pressure of implied inferiority that meets them on every side and in every field. They respond to it both in essentials and non-essentials. Their costume may be affected first. The native dress is discarded as soon as possible. The women are ashamed to be seen without a hat; the native costume, however attractive in itself, soon becomes a mark of inferiority and a matter of reproach. All of the external manners and customs yield in the same way. The methods of salutation, and habits in connection with the toilet and table are gradually given up or modified to meet the prevailing American usage.

" Many of these are superficial and unimportant in themselves and serve only to indicate the way in which the assumed superiority of the new compels the change in old customs. In the more essential respects the same forces are at work. Between manners and hygiene there is a close relation. The reason for abandoning overcrowding in sleeping quarters, unhygienic food and personal habits is usually the social disrepute in which they stand rather than any rational consideration. To be able to receive friends in a room not used as a bedroom, to say that the wife does not keep boarders, is a mark of social distinction, or a plea for social recognition, quite as frequently as it is an acceptance of rational hygiene or a consideration

of the well-being of the wife. Even the possession of a
bathroom is frequently, among the lower circles, more
a mark of social superiority than a means of cleanliness. When the change, whatever its nature, has been
introduced as means for the attainment of social distinction, habits develop that have a hygienic value.
Cleanliness in its different forms becomes essential to
comfort and cannot be easily dispensed with.

" Frequently the change has been worked with slight
recognition on the part of the individual. He may
still look back with fondness to the good old ways.
It is only when he tries to return to the old that he
appreciates his change and the advantage of the new.
I remember a relatively young Greek at Patras, who
had been recalled for service during the Turkish war
and had gone back to the shepherd's life of his parents
while waiting for induction. Before his return he had
looked back upon the shepherd's life as idyllic, even
as ideal. When he experienced it, the hardships, particularly the dirt, were insufferable. After a few
weeks he gave up the life and came to Patras and
worked as a porter about a hotel. Even there he could
not endure his accommodations but rented a room at
his own expense to obtain the cleanliness that had become essential to him. Once the standard of comfort
has been raised by the social forces, the new habits
and the emotions that develop with them prevent slipping back to the lower level."

It would probably be going too far to assert that
Professor Pillsbury has named here the most potent
factor universally. But whatever that factor is in a
given case it is the one that best succeeds, in the

long run, in paving the way toward a certain emotional reaction of at-home-ness on the part of the immigrant in his new environment.

MORALE. — The term " morale of a people " is descriptive of a state that is not greatly unlike that to which we apply the term " convention." The difference seems to be that the former implies something more of a recognition of aims and purposes than does the latter, and that the people look upon those aims and purposes with warmth of emotion. They are the only objects that seem worth while. If this is correct, morale may be interpreted as a partially fixed convention; or as a phase in the development of a convention which it fully becomes when novelty has been displaced by accustomedness. We are repeatedly saying in war time that the morale of the people must be bolstered up or maintained at all costs and that the morale of the army must not be allowed to suffer, whatever circumstances may befall. We use the same term in peace time in political campaigns, etc. The leader of an army or of a people in time of peace can execute his plans only on the assumption that the morale of the army or of the public is at a sufficiently high pitch. If it is not so the leaders must first set about to develop it. How it grows up may be appreciated by reverting to some of the experiences gained in the World War.

It was necessary in the last degree to weld all the people; to create a nation-wide spirit of co-operation toward a well-defined end, and a common determination to brook no interference with such co-operation. All of this was covered by the term " morale." It was

pre-eminently the function of intellectual leadership to
develop it. Once secured it afforded opportunity, both
to intellectual and executive leadership, for other
accomplishment.

In the course of the war there were special difficulties before the leaders of the people of the United
States who were attempting to assure such a morale
of the whole population as would insure victory. Their
difficulties and the way they were met are full of meaning for the morale of peace time as well as for war
time.

The people of the United States are sometimes described as lacking in national traditions. There is a
measure of truth in this but there is at least one
important exception. We have from the first cherished an aloofness from Europe. This is traditional.
That we should have no entangling alliances with European powers was, up to 1917, an ideal that was
cherished by natives and immigrants alike. This had
to be overcome and it could never have been accomplished had advantage not been taken of the sinking of
American passenger vessels, other acts of violence on
the part of the Central European powers, and of the
timely cry, "Make the world safe for democracy."
The latter carried with it always the suggestion that
our vaguely conceived ideal of democracy was being
endangered and that we must take up arms to insure
its development abroad if we would protect it at home.
Overt violence to our lives and property and real or
imagined violence — it matters not which, for our
purposes — to our ideals: these alone could grip the
attention of practically all of the people. Nearly all

the exceptions were to be found in that considerable group of immigrants whose sympathies naturally lay with their homeland in Central Europe. And this is the first and most essential condition of morale in war or in peace: the attention of practically all the people must be gripped by one thing, or by a group of several things, to be accomplished — whether the act of accomplishment is to be protective or aggressive — and the people must be made to feel that the accomplishment is the one thing worth while: that by the side of it everything else fades into insignificance. The love of fighting and of the chase are so strong in human nature that in other circumstances it would not be difficult to bring about this result. In this case, however, the disposition to fight and the love of adventure plus the strong resentment of the hour had to be reinforced in order to overcome the national regard for our traditional isolation and the divided sympathies of the people that were so manifest in the early period of the European struggle.

Resort was had to many expedients — among others to millions of posters to stimulate enlistment with the Marines and the Navy, and to support drives for the Red Cross, for loans, for the promotion of the moral and physical health of the soldiers, for the conservation of food, etc. — all for the one great end of winning the war " to make the world safe for democracy." Dr. G. Stanley Hall (5) lists fifty of these posters, all of which have had circulation in the United States. At least forty were drawn by American artists for use in our country. The Clark University Library, says Dr. Hall, has on exhibition about 6,000 of them collected from the *entente* powers — including proclamations. The German government used the same means to bolster morale amongst the Teutonic population. All of these, from whatever country they have come, were used to stir up the emotions: to " uncap impulses that may be made to spur men on to great decisions," for it is the nature of emotion to dispel doubts by suppressing the alternatives to decision and action that lie in the background. On every corner these posters met the eye with their compelling appeal. Says Dr. Hall: " Not until the history of this great conflict shall have been written up shall we realize to what an amazing extent art has simply been the very *incarnation* of war morale. Many of these artists have already been decorated, and the end of the war by no means marks the end of their influence or of their work." In England " some of the best artists were engaged, and a series of about 150 posters were soon conspicuously displayed all over Great Britain with a message it was hard to ignore. All agreed that they were a prominent, if not the chief factor in raising a volunteer army of over three million men. When and before recruiting was superseded by the draft the same method was applied to war loans, and by its aid over three billion dollars were raised in two weeks." By all these means, and by the aid also of countless three-minute snappy speeches and other varieties, morale was developed and maintained at home. The essence of the whole proceeding consisted in giving the people one great, clear-cut aim to think about, and not only so, but in reiterating the aim in countless ways and by many devices, and in stirring up the emotions of the people until all alternatives to the one great decision and action were suppressed. On a broad scale the process was similar to the first type of decision described by Professor James (7), excepting that in this case the materials for decision are being set in order deliberately by the leaders of the people with a view to obtaining the reaction they themselves desire.

The problem of developing and maintaining morale among the soldiery at the front and in the camps, is not widely different from that at home. It may be assumed that there were no pronounced differences in sympathy to be leveled. It was their job to fight and their decision to that end had already been made. But to keep up the fighting spirit — meaning to maintain the desire or love for fighting and the enthusiasm for all hard work and drudgery preparatory thereto — this was the special problem relating to morale among the fighting forces.

Several expedients were resorted to. As has been indicated in an earlier chapter there was never such a gigantic system afoot for eliminating from a group of men those who were mentally unfit at the very beginning of an enterprise, as we saw in this war — particularly in connection with the participation of the United States in it. The Surgeon General's Office, as has already been indicated, maintained a force of psychiatrists and psychologists to weed out in every camp those who were unfit in mental and nervous organization for living the life of a soldier. Such unfits or misfits never contribute to a steady morale. Arrangements for sanitation and hospitalization in the camps

and at the front were so extensive that at home the
people were in danger of serious deprivation of medical attendance in case of widespread need; this pro-
vision was an official recognition of the fact, so well
known in smaller circles, for a long time, that the
spirit of accomplishment, or the will to do, is dependent upon mental and physical well-being and even upon
brawn. Not only so, but the sordidness and the tedium of an immediate environment are strongly inimical
to high morale. If sordid surroundings and tedious-
ness are inevitable, every device must be employed to
enable the soldier to forget them. Pawlow's studies
of emotional life, and those of his pupils, have shown
us how fundamental are normal appetite and proper
metabolism for healthy and vigorous mental states,
To quote again from Dr. Hall: " War, of course,
needs intense physical energy, and the labor of drill
and camp work, which has toned up so many men of
poor physique, has left a bequest to morale that ought
long to outlive the war. To be weak is to be miserable
and to be strong and well predisposes to true virtue.
The muscles are nearly half the body weight. They
are the organs of the will, which has done everything
man has accomplished, and if they are kept at concert
pitch the chasm between knowing and doing which is
often so fatal, is in a measure closed. There is no
better way of strengthening that class of activities
which we ascribe to the will than by cultivating muscle,"
and he might have added, " general health."

By means of the spirit and expression of humor
men and women lift themselves out of the humdrum
of every-day life and escape from the ugliness of a

situation that they would have ordered otherwise if they could. By its means they create for themselves a symbolic sphere of existence that is more tolerable than the actual. It is a defence mechanism. There is no one, certainly, but finds his burden lightened thereby. Fewer there are who are able to give it expression. Those who possess this capacity are worth more than their numbers to the regiment that is so fortunate as to possess them. The Irishman sitting smilingly in his trench when enemy shells are bursting round him and others in his vicinity are shattered by fear, is worth more than can be estimated because he has just finished explaining that he is not afraid for the reason that " my fortin teller has towld me that Oi'll have sivin more years o' bad luck." Besides, humor is almost instinctively accepted as a suggester of reserve power and resourcefulness. The person who can indulge in humor is not quite down or " all in " and if he bobs up with his cordial wit and humor when circumstances are of the most desperate sort, when he and his companions are not yet accustomed to them, he is justifiably the hub of all around him. Wherever he goes and whatever he does, others will go and others will do likewise. Thus far he is the stuff of which successful leaders are made. He lifts his fellows with him instead of dragging anchor after them.

Reading played its part in the maintenance of morale in the camps. The strong demand was for fiction including tales of adventure. The leading motive seemed to be for diversion and for living in imagination through the exciting scenes of battle for which they were preparing, or at any rate for living a life that is recognized, for the time being at any rate, as more nearly approximating an ideal than the actual present existence. Reading in the camps, therefore, in large measure, was for providing the materials for a defence reaction. (8)

But this is not all, for there was always a demand upon camp libraries to furnish books that may be described as technical: relating to the French language and literature; the science and art of warfare, etc., and thus more or less directly associated with the new profession upon which our soldiery had entered. This suggests an acquired or professional motive, perhaps the conscious, choosing phase of the development of the matter-of-course, unconscious motive which we have discussed heretofore.

MORALE IN PEACE.—At the outset of this rehearsal of the methods of developing and maintaining morale in camp and at the front, and in the civilian population in war time, the statement was made that we should be able to draw important inferences therefrom for the development and maintenance of morale in peace. And at this point it is appropriate to say that the process of Americanization, of developing better codes of commercial and professional ethics, and a strictly non-partisan and non-commercial attitude toward the selection of school-boards — all this and the like is a going toward the development of morale which, as Dr. Hall says, cannot be defined. It can only be felt.

We have seen that in war time the first great essential is to grip the attention of the soldiery and of the public at large by the aims and purposes of the struggle. These must be made to appeal personally to each individual to insure the morale that will make victory possible.

Morale in time of peace, and the conditions that foster it are essentially in no wise different from those in time of war excepting in the aims and purposes that are the objects of attention. In peace it is more difficult than in war to inject aims and purposes of such vividness that they can hold attention against competitors and assure the emotional reaction that is essential to pursuit of those aims. From the angle of the psychologist the Boy Scouts, the Camp Fire Girls and many of the activities of the settlements amongst the immigrant population of our great cities and the like, are so many organizations that are attempting, through their varied programs, to make good citizenship appear so much worth while to everyone in touch therewith that no deviation from it can be tolerated. Their success in developing morale will depend in great measure upon the vividness of their appeal to widely-held motives and upon the vigor with which their members repeatedly react to the ideals and duties that are implied in membership.

Religion, both in war and in peace, bolsters morale because in the religous attitude all eyes are turned toward a being whose greatness and power are conceived as embracing everything. Brush aside all dogma as to the nature of God and His relations to men, and all ceremonial, both of which are superficial and conventionalized, and there still remains the core of religion which implies a conviction that there is something superior to men and to all the forces of nature; *something* that *somehow* is in control of everything. Millions personify that *something* and endow it with the most beneficent nature that can be conceived. Then when health and fortune fail, when armies are crushed and governments totter and every other visible support is in danger, we lean back upon religion, and this process has undoubtedly been the source of many victories both in war and in peace. In such a case our religion is our morale. It depends for its effectiveness upon precisely the same conditions as affect morale in any other relation; aims and ideals must be made vivid and our behavior must square with them.

CHAPTER IX

SOCIAL PROGRESS

WERE our instinctive and conventional or customary attitudes or states the sum and substance of our social psychology, we should have a static system; we should ignore the most important feature of community life: the altering face of social phenomena.

The upward push is the great central fact in life. It defies analysis. We may call it " the will to do " but the phrase is not descriptive. It is not instinct nor habit nor does it comprise only the intellectual capacities of men. These are avenues through which the push finds outlet, and in every discussion of these elements it is assumed that the *élan vital*, as the French describe the upward urge of human nature, is the fundamental thing. Some students are likely to be unhappy whilst reading of social progress from the psychologist's angle unless this assumption is made at the outset.

Customs or conventions are crusts that tend to limit the extent and direction of the upward push and of adjustments among individuals, and at the same time they are the results of repeated reactions to these forces. They are, in fact, as has already been pointed out, habitual mental attitudes and habitual modes of behavior; they are, therefore, essentially, not different from a habit of speaking or a habit of writing, and just as a habit of speaking the English language stands in the way of the acquisition of French speech, so the conventional or customary attitude of a class stands in the way of adopting or of appreciating the attitude of another class. It, by the same token, stands in the way of those changes that we describe by the term progress.

Progress, as we use the word here, implies movement or change in the direction of a goal chosen and approved in advance; if chosen by the wisdom of a group with an eye to the unity and co-operation of members of the group it is social progress. We do not wish to emphasize the deliberateness of the choice in this connection. It may or may not be deliberate in the technical sense of the term. The " change " involved in progress is essentially and in the very last analysis, an inner alteration of the personality of which other changes in the external relationship of persons may be signs.

The methods of organization and co-operation in business, political and other forms of social life are sometimes described as comprising progress in so far as, by common consent, they are understood as effecting improved adaptations to the conditions of life. But we are interested in these matters and in the invention and adoption of mechanical and other devices — invention in the narrow sense of the term — first, because we interpret them as *signs* of progress or the reverse; it is impossible to conceive of a mechanical device whose inventor was not, at the time of invention, in a social attitude of mind. He must in some terms or other have imagined a need for the device and have pictured others using it when completed; secondly, because we conceive of them as so many stimuli that occasion new reactions and bring people into contact with a large number of hitherto unknown phases of their environment; or at any rate as making possible the larger and more varied stimulation by surrounding circumstances. Thus the invention of the steam engine, the telegraph, the democratic form of government, etc., brings people into new relations among themselves and with the surrounding world, and facilitates directly or indirectly the growth of new customs and conventions; new unconscious backgrounds of personality which, as we have already seen, determine largely the course of human social behavior.

Furthermore, we are interested in the persistence of these inventions because it is a sign that there is in the personality of the individuals affected a disposition that is capable of reacting to the new order. Thus the persistence of the democratic form of government of nations and other institutions is a sign that the people among whom it thrives have a disposition that is favorable to co-operation for the advantage of the whole, and that they have the capacity, as we say, each one to put himself in the other's place; all of which, no doubt, grows very largely from the fundamental factor that we have attended to hitherto: viz., our capacity to imagine our neighbor. If an invention such as a method of government, *e.g.*, not only persists but is gradually adopted more and more widely, after a period of earnest try, try again, the student of psychology interprets it as an indication of the development of dispositions that existed earlier only in embryo. Conversely, the failure in this direction and consequent retrogression to more primitive forms means to him that the people either had not the suitable background to begin with or that they were crowded forward more rapidly than dispositions to react to the new situation could be developed through education or otherwise.

One essential thing then, in social progress, is the suitable psychic or psycho-physical disposition: the unconscious psychic background as distinct from the conscious psychological aspects of life. It matters little whether this disposition be a heritable trait. It is equally effective if it is acquired in the lifetime of the individual. But the favorable disposition must be there ready to spring into activity when the suitable stimulus or stimuli are presented.

It should be apparent from the foregoing that we think of the goal of social progress as implying those changes in the personality of individuals that are comprehended in complete mutual understanding among the members of the social group and the ultimate extension of that group to include all peoples. It implies further the approach of a complete matter-of-course co-operation among men such as will naturally arise with complete mutual understanding. We are dealing with internal modifications but not solely in the sense of the eugenist.

We do not deceive ourselves by accepting a conception of " general progress." Undoubtedly progressive and retrogressive movements go on coincidentally. If the theory of progress that underlies this chapter is correct we should expect that generation after generation retrogressive movements should become relatively fewer and fewer.

Obviously we do not presuppose the existence of a social mind that comprehends all individual minds, perceives various possible courses of social evolution any one of which may be pursued by society at large, and makes a selection among them. Such a presupposition is in the minds of many students. It has hardly arisen from the employment of scientific method. We have not found it necessary to employ it hitherto in these chapters and we shall not be compelled to resort to it in connection with our discussion of social progress.

Not too great steps at any one time, may be required with impunity of those dispositions the development of which we describe as progress. A Jovian intervention from without, even though it may be aimed at what those of our civilization would describe as ideal, is doomed to failure. All deliberate intervention must be preceded by an intelligent appraisal first, of what dispositions may be counted upon for reserve power and as steering gear, and secondly of what stresses and strains they may be expected to endure, and of the spans they can safely cover in each successive adjustment.

The very hub of social progress then is a growing psychic background of such a quality that the people who possess it are growing daily more and more capable of mutual understanding and co-operation, and more and more inclined thereto. Practically, we may be permitted to say that social progress is the increasing occurrence amongst the personnel of a community

of sympathetic co-operation toward a common goal.
This is equivalent to the statement that social progress
is always a slow, gradual process. There are accele-
rations and retardations as in all processes of growth
and decay, but these are never sensationally abrupt
like a flash from the clear sky. The great political
campaign, the stirring religious revival, the war craze
sweeping the land, are not progress but ripples upon
the surface of the great silent current of progress or
reaction in every normal personality, occasioned by a
leader's or agitator's interference with its accustomed
course.

Failure to recognize these fundamental truths
breaks many a reform movement which in more auspi-
cious circumstances might have been the means, in the
course of time, of developing new dispositions, expressed in enlarged outlook and sympathy among millions of people. Such failure it is that leads to social
reaction and disaster. A case in point is that of Emperor Joseph II of Austria — attempted reformer
(22):

" He was permeated by the characteristic ideas of
the eighteenth century as to the duties of an absolute
monarch, and began at once to give effect to them in
a fearless and almost revolutionary spirit. His first
step was to combine the various nationalities subject
to him into a single state with thirteen administrative
districts. He refused to be crowned King of Hungary,
and would not summon the Hungarian diet, insisting
that the country should be governed as a province,
and causing German to be used as the official language.
Among other reforms he proclaimed the abolition of

serfdom, substituted various punishments for the capital penalty, established common tribunals, and issued new codes based on the principle that all citizens are equal before the law. He transferred the censorship of books from the clergy to laymen of liberal sympathies, and granted complete freedom to journalism. He instituted public libraries and observatories, founded a medical college in Vienna, a university in Lemberg, and schools for the middle classes in various parts of the monarchy, and encouraged art by offering prizes in connection with the academy of the plastic arts. Industry and trade he fostered by destroying many monopolies, by aiding in the establishment of new manufactures, by raising Fiume to the position of a free harbor, and by opening the Danube to his subjects from its source to the Black Sea. . . . In 1781 he issued an edict of toleration, granting freedom of worship to all Protestants and to members of the Greek Church; and between 1782 and 1790 about 700 monasteries were closed, the members of religious orders being reduced from 63,000 to 27,000. All these changes were well meant, but the emperor, in the ardor of his philanthropy, shot too far ahead of the prevailing sentiment of his people. Moreover, his good intentions were often rendered fruitless by unskilled or unsympathetic subordinates. In nearly every part of the monarchy discontent soon manifested itself, and some of the inhabitants of the Tyrol broke into open rebellion. The Hungarians bitterly resented the suppression of their ancient privileges, and in 1787 the emperor's new institutions led in several districts to a furious conflict between the peasantry and the nobles. The

estates of the Austrian Netherlands persistently
opposed the execution of his schemes, the clergy
being especially active in stirring up popular in-
dignation. . . . In Hungary there was so dangerous
an agitation that in January, 1790, Joseph had to
undo almost everything he had attempted to accomplish in that country during the previous nine years;
he succeeded only in maintaining the decrees by which
he had abolished serfdom and established toleration.
Thus his last days were rendered miserable by the
conviction that his career had been a failure."

Of the same order is the group of phenomena referred to by Aschaffenberg (2) in his discussion of
the relation of juvenile delinquency in Berlin to the
economic level of the people concerned. It had been
urged, and is yet on many hands, that if the pinch
of poverty could be removed; if people in general
could but receive a good wage, delinquency and crime
would disappear. This hypothesis was the more widely
accepted in Berlin because during the decade following
1882, when juveniles of working age were not generally employed owing to industrial depression, the wave
of delinquency waxed at an alarming rate. But during the following decade of industrial prosperity in
which practically all of working age were profitably
employed, delinquency continued to increase at a rapid
rate. The difference between the two periods is that
in the former thievery ran high whereas in the latter
this type of offense became less frequent relatively,
and personal violence increased almost as if without
let or hindrance. Offences of assault and battery, for
instance, increased 123% over the preceding period,

breach of the peace 128.6%, insult 105%, resisting
an officer 50%, malicious mischief 55%, fraud 40%,
offenses against chastity 19% and theft only 8%.
Undoubtedly this disappointing phenomenon appeared
for the reason that the youths concerned were not
equipped with either native or acquired dispositions
such as would enable them to take advantage of the
best opportunities that economic prosperity placed in
their hands. The economic improvement in this case
was only an illusory show of progress. The essential
groundwork had not been completely prepared, and
society, as far as it was represented by the youths in
the case, was in no better situation, if indeed it was
not worse off, than before.

Social progress cannot be forced from without. It
must wait upon developments within. The liberal industrial or commercial organization establishes a welfare bureau which is interested in all that the name
implies: recreation, health, education, home management, etc., among the workers. But the employees,
especially if they are native Americans or of British
origin, resent what seems to them to be paternalistic
and set their faces toward forms of recreation, etc.,
of their own devising. The promoters of the welfare
enterprise are in danger of running counter to fundamental tendencies in human nature.

The like observation may be made properly of an
industrial plant, the management of which institutes a
profit-sharing plan, participation in which on the part
of employees is conditioned upon their living in certain
localities; in certain types of house; in spending such
a portion of their income for insurance, purchase of

home, clothing and so on. As a general rule people are not made continuously happy thereby, because their personal initiative is sacrificed. Their sense of self-management is shocked; they are offended by paternalism.

There must be exceptions to these statements when one bears in mind large blocks of individuals who are near the edge of normality like the constitutional inferiors, whose philosophy is of the *laissez-faire* type, and of other large groups immigrated from paternalistic regions. Even as to the red-blooded ambitious element in the population the paternalistic devices referred to above cannot be utterly condemned in the name of progress. Such devices may properly now and then be interpreted as stimuli adequate to call out desirable behavior such as ultimately will result in a complex of acquired dispositions favorable to good housing, to recreation, insurance, mutual understanding and co-operation, etc. The process of approximation toward such a result is progress. It is the part of unusual wisdom to discern how far paternalism may go without endangering the process.

LEADERS. — Progress assumes the activity of leaders; and the nature of leaders and the sources whence they come are of prime importance for our consideration.

EXECUTIVE LEADERS. — A distinction may properly be made between two types of leader: the executive and the intellectual. It is not pretended that this division is altogether exhaustive. One might mention many subtypes: the ward leader, the labor agitator, the religious leader, etc. But all of these and whatever others may be suggested are probably comprehended in the two types we have named.

The first in this classification is illustrated in many military men and responsible heads of large commercial or industrial establishments. Such men have a capacity to grip the attention of their followers by a certain physical appearance of vitality, a vivid statement of purposes and means, and withal an inviting rather than an antagonistic personality. The entire make-up of such an individual is suggestive of strength. For that reason the native impulse of his followers is to go with him without questioning why. Aided by his vivid portrayal of ends and purposes and methods, each follower catches a vision, not only of what he himself is doing but of what is at the hand of every other in the group as well. Perhaps he catches a view of a thousand others who are doing almost precisely as he himself is. At any rate he sees, even though meagerly, how they all fit into a general scheme. Mutual understanding and sympathy arise in the group and we have a degree of morale which may be so " high " that nothing can stand in the way of the expenditure of the last ounce of energy by each individual follower for the attainment of the common purpose. It is meant to be implied in the foregoing that the successful executive leader exercises a capacity for inciting enthusiasm in his followers. But this could not be accomplished were he not able also vividly to portray aims and ways and means (16).

Furthermore, such a leader as we have in mind skillfully estimates the morale of his followers and is able, therefore, to determine within reasonably accurate limits, how far he may expect them to go with him in a given enterprise. He is able, also, to seize upon the " psychological moment," as we say, for launching his program; in other words, he recognizes the times at which the psychic disposition of his followers will most favorably respond to active leadership. He thus takes a hand in fixing and developing those dispositions because he gives them an outlet and exercises them.

TRUE WIT AND MADNESS. — It is at least an interesting phrase from the pen of Dryden that suggests the alliance of true " wit and madness." Much has been written, not strictly apropos of this dictum, but yet in support of it, especially as applied to the executive type of leader. Ireland, for example, in his description of the characters of Mohammed and Joan d'Arc (21) recites at length the evidence that these leaders were victims of hallucinations in waking life and that they accepted their hallucinatory experiences as representing actualities. He presents evidence, too, that the first named, at least, was an epileptic. According to tradition, when " Mohammed was walking in the defiles and valleys about Mecca, every stone and tree greeted him with the words, ' Hail to thee, O messenger of God!' He looked round to the right and to the left, and discovered nothing but trees and stones. The prophet heard these cries as long as it pleased God that he should be in this condition; then the angel Gabriel appeared, and announced to him the message of God in the mountain Hira, in the month of the Ramadan."

Again, on Mount Hira, he heard a voice from

Heaven. " He stood still, for he felt faint on account
of the voice, and he turned his face upwards, and be-
hold, Gabriel sat with crossed legs upon a throne between heaven and earth, and cried out, ' O Mohammed,
thou art in truth the messenger of God, and I am
Gabriel ! ' The prophet then turned back. God had
gladdened his heart and filled it with courage. Then
followed revelation upon revelation."

These quotations run to the question of hallucinosis.
As to alleged epilepsy in the case of Mohammed, Eman-
uel Deutsch writes (quoted by Ireland) :

" Mohammed was epileptic ; vast ingenuity and
medical knowledge have been lavished upon this point,
as explanatory of Mohammed's mission and success.
We, for our own part, do not think that epilepsy ever
made a man appear a prophet to himself or even to
the people of the East ; or, for the matter of that,
inspired him with the like heart-moving words and
glorious pictures. Quite the contrary. It was taken
as a sign of demons within — demons, ' devs,' devils,
to whom all manner of diseases were ascribed throughout the antique world : in Phoenicia, in Greece, in
Rome, in Persia, and among the lower classes of Judea
after the Babylonian exile."

Yet whatever was Mohammed's pathological condition, says Ireland : " We do not seek to explain the
nature or success of Mohammed's mission by his epilepsy. These lie in the character of the man and the
circumstances of the times ; but we think that the start-
ing point of his hallucinations came through the nervous
disorder which affected him, and of which the epi-
leptiform fits were the visible proof. It was this

which held before his eyes, and made sound in his ears, the hallucinations which led him to believe that he had a message from God. Without this, no amount of religious fervour or abstract monotheism would have made him take such a view. The message once granted, each step becomes easy. We are inclined to believe that the fits were rather rare, as a frequent succession of them would be fatal to an active and difficult career; yet Mohammed had to encounter much opposition, both before the flight to Medina and after it. He showed great activity in war; he led twelve military expeditions, underwent much exposure, and was many times in extreme danger. Setting aside his claims to Divine communications there is no proof that he was in the least deranged. He evidently possessed an intellect of the highest order for managing and controlling affairs, and was skillful both in conducting war and treating with his adversaries."

As to the alleged hallucinatory experiences of Joan d'Arc, Ireland writes:

" In a letter of Perceval de Boulainvilliers to Philip Visconti, Duke of Milan, dated 21st June, 1820, there is an account of Joan, which was probably taken from original observation — for Boulainvilliers held a high office at the court of the Dauphin. He writes that the first revelation made was when Joan was twelve years of age. She agreed to try a race with some of her companions. She ran with such swiftness that one of the girls cried, ' Joan, I see you flying over the ground.' She stopped to take breath at the end of the meadow.

" She thought she heard a boy's voice saying, ' Joan, go home, for your mother needs you to help her.'

Thinking it must be her brother, or some other boy, she hastened home. Her mother asked her why she had left her sheep, to which the girl answered, ' Did you not send for me? ' Her mother said, ' No.' Then, believing herself mistaken about the boy, and wishing to return to her companions, suddenly before her eyes a bright cloud or haze appeared, and from the cloud a voice came, saying, ' Joan, you must lead another life, and do wonderful actions, for it is you whom the King of Heaven has chosen for the succour of France, and the help and protection of King Charles expelled from his dominions. You will put on male attire, and, taking arms, will be the leader of war. All things will be ruled by your counsel.' It seems likely enough that these two accounts reproduced different circumstances of the same story, for Joan may have thought that the first voice, calling her to her mother, was not worth mentioning or it may have been suppressed in the truncated notes of her trial.

" These visions returned again. The angel Michael brought with him St. Catherine and St. Margaret, who often visited her. She knew their voices which were gentle and sweet, said that she had embraced and kissed them, and felt that they had a good odour. They exhorted her to lead a pure life, and to go to mass, and she made a vow of virginity to them. At her trial a great many questions were put to her about the appearance of these angels and saints, whether the angel wore a crown? and whether he had hair beneath it? and whether the hair was long or short? or whether the saints had rings in their ears, or wore dresses of the same cloth? When it came to such particulars

Joan refused to answer, sometimes saying she was forbidden to answer, perhaps because the visions had a
vague form, or that she feared some snare under their
captious questioning.   A few months before Joan's
trial a woman in Paris had been burned because she
said that the Maid was doing the will of God, and that
she herself had seen God, and that He wore clothes,
which was treated as blasphemy.   Joan, however,
firmly maintained the reality of the apparitions.   She
said that Michael had the form of a proper man. ' I
saw them,' she said to her judge, ' with my own eyes,
as plainly as I see you; and when they retired from
me I wept, and much I wished that they would take
me up with them.'   She kissed the ground over which
they had passed.   Joan told no one of these visions,
not even her confessor; but apparently her parents
had their surmises or fears, for about two years after
her first vision, when she was about fifteen, her mother
told her that her father had dreamed that their daugh-
ter would go away with armed men to France.   He
told her brothers that he would rather she were
drowned than that this should happen to her.   She
said that her father and mother watched her, and kept
her in great subjection and that they almost lost their
senses when she went to Vaucouleurs.   She said she
had never disobeyed them save in the case of the young
man who wanted to marry her.   He summoned her to
the court at Toul, saying she had promised to marry
him, which she denied on oath.   The voices told her
that she would gain her process.   Apparently
this young man had seen Joan at Neufchateau, where
she had gone for fifteen days to live with a woman who

kept an inn. Her enemies made a good deal of this
residence at the inn, saying that she used to take
horses to water, and thus learned to ride. It is not
very clear how she learned to be so expert at riding,
as it seems she was, when she appeared before the Dauphin at Chinon.

" As time wore on the tumult of war came nearer
and nearer, and the prolonged siege of Orleans kept
the whole of France in a state of excitement. The
voices told her twice or thrice a week to go to Robert
of Baudricourt, the commandant at Vaucouleurs, and
that he would help her."

And again in the course of her trial at the hands
of her English captors:

" Joan boldly defended the truth of her revelations,
even when threatened with torture. She said that she
had heard the voices every day in her prison, and that
light accompanied the voices. Visions, if they appeared at all, were much less frequent. The angel
Gabriel conversed with her on one occasion; the voices
told her that it was he. But the voices of St. Catherine and St. Margaret were often in her ears. They
told her to answer boldly. Sometimes they came without her asking; sometimes their voices were drowned
by the noise made by her guards. They told her
what to say, and when she prayed to God for them
they came immediately. Sometimes the saints would
ask God what she should say, and return with the
answer. They promised that she should be freed from
prison, but in what manner she did not know. ' Take
everything cheerfully,' they said. ' Do not distress

yourself about your martyrdom, you will come at last into the Kingdom of Heaven.' "

It is unthinkable, however, that it was *because* of these abnormalities that these characters were the great executive leaders that they proved to be according to the record of history; it was, on the other hand, in spite of them. Rather it was because of their rare intellectual acumen (it is reported, for example, that no trained artillery captain could excel Joan d'Arc in the placement of guns) coupled with unbounded religious enthusiasm: an emotional reaction that often accompanies the psychopathic disposition. But it need not, of course, be a *religious* enthusiasm to be effective; whatever its object or complexion, enthusiasm linked with intellectual acumen — even of average measure — will make the executive leader.

A while back we said of the executive leader that he seizes the " psychological moment ": that he recognizes the times at which his followers will best respond to his active leadership. This is true of our successful political leaders. We sometimes say of them that they " have their ears to the ground ": by which we mean that they are catching indications as to the trend of the people's thought and sounding their morale preparatory to the execution of a plan. We say that a secret of their success lies just in their ability to listen accurately " with their ears to the ground." They know the common people and such knowledge quickly becomes mutual. They can interpret what to others are inconspicuous signs of the people's meaning as one member of a family interprets the meaning of his brothers and sisters.

INTELLECTUAL LEADERS. — The intellectual leader points the way for his collaborator of the executive type. We do not mean to imply that the two are wholly distinct. There is more or less overlapping of types. The inventor of devices and of theories; the expounder of viewpoints; the investigator in science, history, art or what-not, is an intellectual leader and often, though not always, he is able to put his discoveries and theories to work. But whether so or not he is a leader. By the fact that he is pushing out the frontiers of knowledge and building an accumulation of data in his laboratory or library far from the limelight, though the people at large have the vaguest understanding of the data and only a cloudy grasp of the fact that the frontiers of knowledge are being disturbed in any manner, the spirit of the age is maintained in a plastic state; the formation of unyielding conventional crusts is thwarted or delayed, and the people are therefore in an adaptable and sympathetic state of mind with respect to leaders of this sort. From the viewpoint of a psychological conception of social progress the development of the condition described above in itself represents a measure of social progress.

There are others who as intellectual leaders stand out from amongst the investigators behind the scenes. These are men and women with a capacity for a quick grasp and analysis of masses of details. They catch the meaning — or at least *a* meaning — of it all and have a certain facility for bringing it to public notice, and developing a consuming interest therein, in such manner as to hasten the reshaping of customs, viewpoints and dispositions in consonance therewith. Or they give expression in music, in carving or upon canvas, to the inarticulate, half-conscious backgrounds of human nature. Forthwith they are recognized as leaders. Under their hand what was inarticulate becomes articulate on the tongues and in the behavior of thousands of people who thus are brought a pace nearer to a realization of a common interest and to a mutual understanding and spirit of co-operation.

STATISTICAL STUDIES OF MEN OF SCIENCE. — A part of the general question as to the nature of the executive and the intellectual type of leader, respectively, are the more specific questions relating to their racial characteristics and their national and sectional origins, and the circumstances of their development.

Let us consider first the national and sectional origin of American leaders in various departments of science and later their racial affiliations. A careful study of data relating to these questions may be found in Professor J. McKeen Cattell's studies of the families of American men of science (7). The table below shows the nationality of the parents of 917 leading scientific men:

NATIONALITY OF THE PARENTS OF AMERICAN MEN OF SCIENCE

	Both Parents	Father Only	Mother Only	Total Families
American	628	23	42	660.5
English	48	36	28	80
Scotch	9	13	15	23
Irish	4	10	12	15
Canadian	14	3	7	19
German	54	23	12	71.5
Norwegian	6	0	0	6
Swedish	6	0	0	6
Danish	1	2	1	2.5
Russian	6	0	0	6
Dutch	3	3	5	7
French	6	6	2	10
Swiss	6	4	0	8
Italian	0	1	0	0.5
Japanese	2	0	0	2
Total	793	124	124	917

Six hundred and twenty-eight, or more than two-thirds, have both parents of native American (United States) birth, 23 others have an American father only and 42 only an American mother. Foreign men have married American women more frequently than the reverse. In 165 cases both parents are foreign born and of the same nationality. Including Americans there are 124 marriages in which the nationality of the parents was mixed, but they were largely British. The American-born parents are mainly of British and New England descent; of foreign-born parents, 137 fathers and an equal number of mothers are English, Scotch, Irish or Canadian. Germany contributes 77 fathers and 66 mothers. Other nations contribute in all 51 fathers and 44 mothers — fairly equally distributed among Norwegians, Swedes, Russians, Dutch, French and Swiss, with several from Denmark, Italy and Japan. The parents of American men of science are thus predominantly British-American (American, English, Scotch, Irish and Canadian), with an admixture of nearly 8 per cent. of Germans and about 5 per cent from other nationalities (including French, approximately 1 per cent).

Twelve and six-tenths per cent of our leading scientific men are foreign-born, 12.6 per cent are native born of foreign-born parents, and 7.1 per cent have one foreign-born parent. In the general population of the United States 14 per cent of the people are foreign-born, 13.5 have both parents foreign-born and 6.7 have one parent foreign-born. The foreign-born and those of foreign-born parentage thus contribute less, but only slightly less, than the native population to scientific productivity. There is a great difference in the different nationalities. Those born in Great Britain contribute 1.2 per cent to the population and 3.4 per cent to our scientific men; Germany contributes 2.7 per cent to the population and 1.9 per cent to the scientific men; Russia 1.7 to the population and 0.6 to the scientific men; Italy 1.5 to the population and 0.1 to the scientific men. These differences are not, however, necessarily due to any racial superiority of the British and Germans. This will be apparent as we proceed.

In the following table Professor Cattell sets forth the per cent of scientific men in each of four grades according to the nationality of their parents (the grades represent relative degree of attainment in science) :

THE PERCENTAGE OF THE SCIENTIFIC MEN IN EACH OF FOUR
GRADES ACCORDING TO THE NATIONALITY OF THEIR PARENTS.

	No.	Percentage of Each Grade			
		I	II	III	IV
American	652.5	7.7	18.3	57.9	16.0
British	137	6.6	17.9	56.9	18.7
German	73.5	10.2	20.4	57.1	12.2
Others	48	8.3	20.8	56.3	14.6
Total	911	71	169	525	146
Per cent		7.8	18.6	57.6	16.0

The showing of a certain superiority of foreign
groups may be accounted for on the ground that a
number of European men of science, highly trained,
had been imported by universities into the United
States. This in itself therefore is of no significance
in relation to our problem. For the matter of that,
whether immigrants as a whole in this country — and
their children — contribute more or fewer than their
proportionate share to the total number of intellectual
leaders in America is of no definite significance in
this context. It may reflect, not the qualities of a
nation or a race, but of the social strata from which
our immigrants come — in some cases the best, in
others the worst strata. It should be said for all adult
immigrants who do not speak our language and who
do not understand our customs that they are at a disadvantage in the matter of establishing leadership.

Of more significance are the sectional origin of men
of science in the United States and the occupations
of their parents (10). The table below from Cattell's
Study of American Men of Science shows the birth
rate of men of science per million inhabitants in that

year, based upon the census of 1860 in nineteen states:

Mass.	108.8	per	million	inh.
Conn.	86.9	”	”	”
Me.	46.1	”	”	”
N. H.	46	”	”	”
Vt.	57.1	”	”	”
N. Y.	47.2	”	”	”
Pa.	22.7	”	”	”
Va.	8.8	”	”	”
N. C.	5	”	”	”
Ga.	2.8	”	”	”
Ala.	2.1	”	”	”
Minn.	1.3	”	”	”
La.	1.4	”	”	”
O.	32.1	”	”	”
Mich.	36.	”	”	”
Wis.	45.1	”	”	”
Ill.	24.5	”	”	”
Mo.	11.8	”	”	”
Ky.	6.9	”	”	”

Massachusetts has produced many fold as numerous scientific men as the average of the southern states in this list. In other words, the probability of a youth born in Massachusetts becoming a leader among men of science in his generation was 50 times as great as that of a youth born at the same time in Georgia or in Alabama. It would be rash to conclude therefrom, however, that New England stock is 50 times as fertile in this respect as southern stock. If this were true the average attainment of Massachusetts-born men of science should be as many times higher than that of the product of Georgia and Alabama. But this, as Professor Cattell says, is by no means the case. Indeed, from an impartial viewpoint, the one stock is as substantial and fertile as the other.

The social life of the two groups at the time in ques-

tion and after, was vastly different and their traditions
differed widely. The southern family lived in a
considerable degree of isolation upon a large plantation, and the young men of the foremost families were
brought up in an atmosphere that accustomed them
to the management of things and men rather than to
the management of abstract ideas and the details of
science. It was an admirable matrix for the growth
of the publicist, the statesman and the military leader,
as the northern states learned to their discomfiture.

Massachusetts, and New England as a whole, on
the other hand, was a region of towns, factories and
small farms. There was a relatively dense population. There were strong churches, schools, lecture cir-
cuits and periodicals accessible to the masses. Personal contacts and interstimulations of a variety of
sorts were constant. In a word, the conditions for
the development of the particular kind of intellectual
leadership we are now considering were of the best.
It appears to be the social environment, not solely
the biological nor the psychological factor in the narrow sense, that developed the picture.

The distribution of this same group of American
men of science, according to the professions of their
parents, shows that 21.3 per cent have sprung from
the agricultural class, 35.7 per cent from the manufacturing class and 43 per cent from the professional
group.

In detail, Professor Cattell divided the men of science into four groups in the order of their superiority
and showed that the sons of clergymen, physicians,
lawyers and teachers have a considerable advantage

over all others in the struggle for a place in the upper ranks of scientific men. On the whole, the professional classes named contribute, in proportion to their numbers, 14 times as many scientists to the nation as do other classes. But it would be extreme to say that this disparity is a result of a fourteen-fold superiority of stock among the professional as compared to the non-professional folk. The only plausible accounting for such a difference as this is on the hypothesis that the social environment in the homes of professional classes affords mental stimuli that are so powerful as to turn even intellectual mediocrity toward intellectual leadership. The isolated life of the farm and of the plantation; the mechanic's bench and the desk of the manufacturer and the merchant are not conducive to intellectual leadership in science because their social environment does not supply such stimulation — at least not in sufficient measure.

In the light of all the foregoing it would appear that one of the very first obligations of a state should be to supply the conditions or stimuli that will contribute toward developing dispositions for intellectual leadership, and stimulate effort for accomplishment.

SUPERIOR CHILDREN. — The recent investigations among exceptionally bright children in the schools contribute more or less directly to the psychology of leadership, especially of the intellectual type, assuming that the unusually bright pupils of today will recruit the supply of intellectual leaders, and the few outstanding ones among them whom we call geniuses, of a quarter century or more hence.

Support for this assumption is principally in the

nature of impressions. There are many examples of intellectual leaders (28) who, according to their biographers, were very precocious youths. John Stuart Mill, Thomas Macaulay and others are cases in point. In no instance has an attempt been made at a quantitative estimate of the intellectual level in youth of these leaders excepting in the case of Francis Galton. Terman has estimated his intelligence quotient at 200 (25). The estimate is based upon the biographer's account of Galton's intellectual attainments at the chronological ages of 3 to 8 years and upon the known intelligence quotient of normal and precocious children of our own day whose chronological age and attainments are comparable to those of Sir Francis Galton at the time of which the biographer was writing. There are undoubtedly many who are properly classified as intellectual leaders who were not precocious children — perhaps it is more accurate to say that they were, at any rate, not recognized as precocious.

A fairly widespread popular belief that such children are mentally unstable and physically unfitted to endure the strains incident to preparation, and later for the responsibilities of leadership, is hardly borne out by the facts developed in recent studies of such classes. On the whole, children of superior intelligence in the public schools are of superior physical development, and there is no evidence of greater or of more frequent liability to failure of mental equilibrium in the group of exceptionally bright children than in an average group.

Professor Terman is authority for significant data

relating to fifty-nine superior school children of whom
eighteen were girls (26). Their average intelligence
quotient was 149.7 and the median was 145. Reck-
oned on the basis of chronological age the average
acceleration of this group was slightly more than two
years.

Apropos of the popular suspicion that very bright
children are afflicted with such instability of character
traits as to interfere with their prospects for attain-
ing leadership, the rating of Terman's group with
reference to such traits as obedience, conscientiousness,
dependability, unselfishness, evenness of temper and
will power is in point. The ratings of teachers on
these points were 1.51, 1.61, 1.56, 1.73, 1.90, and 1.50,
respectively, — compared with average children, and
Terman interprets this as meaning that the group is
as superior morally as intellectually.

As to their physical condition, Professor Terman
has the following to say:

" Only four were said to have defective vision, and
only one defective hearing. Twenty-one had undergone operation for removal of adenoids, and two others
were known to have more or less adenoid trouble. The
record for tonsils was similar. The fact that approximately half of our superior children have had either
adenoids or diseased tonsils suggests that these defects
may not be as injurious to mental development as
common opinion would have us believe.

" One had chorea a few years ago but has recovered.
Two others had noticeable muscular twitchings. There
were two stutterers in the group, both of whom at
the time of the investigation were taking corrective

lessons. There were no cases of abnormal fears. A part of the nervousness and restlessness occasionally mentioned was probably due to their not having enough school work to keep them busy. One boy, asked how he liked school, said he liked it in the morning but not in the afternoon, because by noon he always knew his lessons and then there was nothing to do! So much has been said about the nervous unbalance of precocious children that it is surprising to find over two-thirds described as free from symptoms of this kind. The symptoms of most of the others indicated nothing serious. The proportion of stuttering and chorea was not far from that which is usually found for unselected children.

" All but three of the children were said to sleep ' perfectly.' The average time of sleep for the children of each age was found to be slightly greater than the Terman and Hocking average for 2692 unselected school children. There was no case of marked sleep deficiency.

" Of the nine cases who were said to have occasional headaches, eight had them very seldom, not more than two or three times a year. One had long been subject to serious recurrent headaches.

" Five were described as ' not strong.' One of these had always been sickly and at the age of eight years had attended school only one year. In that year, however, he did the work of the first three grades. Another of these has also had insecure health from birth. He did not enter school until the age of fourteen. Between the ages of six and twelve he had only one hour per day of private instruction, and in that time completed the work of the first eight grades. The other three of the five were apparently just not strong enough to endure serious physical strain or excitement. Only three were seriously handicapped by ill health, a record which would probably not be excelled by an equal number of school children picked at random."

Tentatively Professor Terman offers the following conclusions concerning the nature of superior children:

" 1.   That intellectually superior children are apparently not below the average in general health;

" 2.   That in the vast majority of cases their ability is general rather than special or one-sided;

" 3.   That the superiority is especially marked in moral and personal traits;

" 4.   That ' queerness,' play deficiency, and marked lack of social adaptability are the exception rather than the rule.

" 5.   That while superior children are likely to be accelerated on the basis of chronological age, they are usually two or three grades retarded on the basis of mental age;

" 6.   That their school work is such as to warrant promotion in most cases to a grade closely corresponding to the mental age;

" 7.   That the superiority tends to show early in life, is little influenced by formal instruction, and is permanent;

" 8.   That superior children usually come from superior families."

As far, at any rate, as height and weight of normal and superior children are concerned, Baldwin and

Stecher (4) have confirmed the high correlation between superior physical development and mental
normality and acceleration. Their report is based
upon 143 studies of individuals who had been followed
up from 1917 to 1921 by methods of such refinement
that the commonest sources of error were no doubt
elminated.

Lacking more extensive evidence on either side of
the question, it is a good hypothesis that our intellectual leaders arise from a group of exceptionally bright
pupils and that this group will continue to be the
source of supply.

Evidently, to assure us of progress we must, at the
earliest possible moment find who amongst the young
folk in any group are the most capable; and, having
found them, we must do our utmost to surround them
with such conditions as will help on their development.
To discover them is the proper function of a personnel service in our educational institutions. But having found them in high school or in college we believe
it is a mistake forthwith to feed their interests in a
particular occupation to the exclusion of other occupations or professions. To do so is to ossify them or
to conventionalize them in a narrow sphere when they
should be cultivating the most inclusive possible range
of interests. This view, we believe, is justified by considerations of utility even, if by no other. The best
satisfied, and the most efficient workman in any sphere
is one who has the habit of observing broad relationships among even widely separated areas of human
interest, and the leader *must always* keep them in
view. He dare not be over-specialized.

CHAPTER X

SOCIAL ADJUSTMENTS AND MALAD-
JUSTMENTS IN RELATION TO
MENTAL QUALITY

THE data presented in the chapter on Intellectual Levels and Psychic Stability of the Population are of first rate importance for the behavior or adjustment of groups in the organization of society as a whole. The various levels of intelligence and other psychic qualities that occur amongst a people must be conceived as correlated with certain broad aspects of social adjustment and with progress.

These correlations are inevitable phenomena — inevitable, that is, assuming the fixed nature of the intellectual levels and degrees of psychic stability of the elements of the population. People of the same quality tend to drift into the same eddies and back bays, or to rise to the same heights approximately, as the case may be. We do not mean to imply it as a statement of fact that the people of the slums, for example, would make a slum of the avenue and *vice versa*, if their positions were exchanged, but that there is a tendency in this direction cannot be gainsaid; the backwardness of sections of the population, however — mountaineers for illustration — cannot, without debate, be attributed to a low intellectual level. This may be attributable to the personal qualities that we are in the habit of grouping under the illy-defined term "individualism," which, generally speaking, stands in the way of unity and co-operation on a broad scale. Hence it is in the way of successful achievement in the usual sense of "successful." "Individualism," however, as applied to the mountaineer is probably a product of age-long social and physical conditions in the midst of which the people of the rugged highlands have to live. Where the roads are few and so precarious in every sort of weather that even walking and riding on horseback from place to place are fraught with extraordinary difficulties, it is the nature of things that those human characteristics should develop that, taken together, make up our picture of the individualist. But "individualism" is entirely consistent with a high order of native, untutored general intelligence. It is expressed in self-reliance, in the loyal cohesion of small groups in matters of local and even of broader concern in exceptional circumstances, in whole-hearted respect for the rights and claims of others, and in vigorous defence thereof on occasion, even though such defence may now and again run to persons who in common knowledge may be known as transgressors of recognized and even generally respected law. These qualities are all outstanding in our southern mountaineers and they have earned their reputaton as individualists. That such folk are, moreover, capable of intense enthusiasm for large, nation-wide purposes is demonstrated by the reactions of these Highlanders of Kentucky, Virginia, Tennessee, and the Carolinas to appeals for support of the United States Government in the World War. Considerable districts are said to have over-subscribed their quota to government loans, as well as to have responded to the draft completely and loyally (8). This is certainly not a picture that could be drawn of a population a great mass of which is technically mentally defective. Furthermore, the ancestral history of these folk, so far as it is known, in the independent and daring pioneer small farmers of western Virginia does not unqualifiedly suggest support for the hypothesis of hereditary mental defect.

INTELLIGENCE AND OCCUPATION. — It is probable that the distribution of the population amongst the professions and occupations represents a tendency of individuals to adjust themselves on the basis of intelligence levels. The most comprehensive data bearing upon this point are to be found in the records of the United States Army psychological examiners (17).

"Figure 57 * brings out the fact that there seem to be four or five occupational levels. The highest level might be termed the professional level, and is probably subdivided into two parts — those professional groups having very high educational and professional standards (median intelligence rating A) and those professional groups having slightly lower educational and professional standards (median intelligence rating B). The next lower level contains such occupational groups as clerical workers, technical workers, and probably those skilled mechanics and skilled operatives who because of high average intelligence and leadership become foremen (the median

* The figure, numbered as above, is taken from *Memoirs of the National Academy of Sciences,* Vol. XV, p. 830.

intelligence of this level is C+). In the next lower
level we have apparently a larger number of occupational groups than in any other. The bulk of these

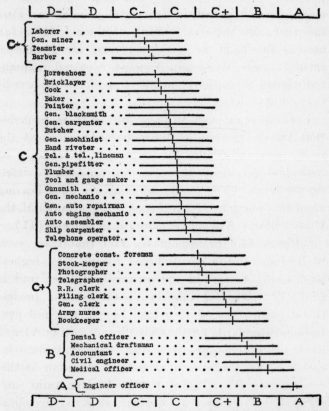

Occupational Intelligence Ratings.   Letter-grades on horizontal scale. Length of bar for each occupation is midrange of 50 per cent (distance between first and third quartiles); median point is shown by a crossline. Classification is that of Committee on Classification of Personnel

fall under the heading of skilled mechanics and skilled
operatives and the semi-skilled worker (median intelligence of this level is C). The lowest level is next

and contains those groups that may be characterized as unskilled labor (median intelligence of this level is C —)."

When we are considering the data on which the above graph is based it is extremely important — and this the army workers realized — to make allowance for the fact that in many instances, the frequency of which can hardly be estimated, highly intelligent and skilled workmen in many occupations and professions were exempted from the draft, and that the records they might have made do not enter into the calculations. Such exemptions applied to " necessary highly specialized technical or mechanical experts of necessary industrial enterprise." Undoubtedly, too, the preference given to men of family in granting exemptions has operated to leave out of the calculations, on the whole, a host of the more intelligent men. After all allowances have been made, however, as we have already said, the figures doubtless represent a tendency toward adjustment to occupations and professions within the social organization on the basis of intelligence.

Dr. Goddard, in what he calls the " deadly parallel " below, presents wage, school and intelligence data in such a manner as to suggest a correspondence of the intelligence levels amongst recruits, school grade attained and wages earned (13).

But again we must emphasize the point that it is not only on the basis of intelligence that men adapt themselves to occupational levels—intelligence whether in the sense of mental alertness, of large funds of general or of specialized information, or of any other

Wages of 100 Wage Earners	School of 100 Children	Intelligence of 1,700,000 Soldiers
9% earn $150–$200	13% leave in 4th grade, age 10	10% in "D—" group, mental age 10
12 " 250– 300	13 " 5th " 11	15 " "D" " " 11
16 " 350– 400	14 " 6th " 12	20 " "C—" " " 12
31 " 450– 600	27 " 7th & 8th grade, age 13, 14	25 " "C" " " 13, 14
68 " less than $15 per week	67 do not finish 8th grade	70 are below mental age 15
27 " $750–$1000	23 leave after 8th grade	16½ "C+" group, mental age 15
8 " 1250	10 attend high school	9 " "B" " " 16, 17
2 " over 1250	3 graduate high school	4½ "A" " " 18, 19
	1.5 college	

commonly accepted criterion. On the other hand, it is one of the commonest of phenomena to find individuals striving to make adaptation to occupational or to professional levels that, judging from their qualities of intelligence, are beyond their reach, and ultimately establishing themselves securely. This is one of many conditions that make a progressive civilization possible. The intellectual qualities of the East Indians, which McDougall recognizes, have not yet enabled them to fit into the occupations that western civilization has been carrying to their doors for upwards of a century, and the explanation of the failure lies, apparently, in those character traits, the ensemble of which are described as will. On this point we quote at length from Stoddard (27), a passage that represents a well-supported viewpoint. At the same time, it must be admitted that there are extant more hopeful views of the adaptability of the Indian people to the occupations of the west. . . . " But neither the Moslem world nor India have developed factory labor with the skill, stamina, and assiduity sufficient to undercut the industrial workers of Europe and America. In India, for example, despite a swarming and poverty-stricken population, the factories are unable to recruit an adequate or dependable labor-supply. Says M. Mitin: ' With such long hours and low wages it might be thought that Indian industry would be a formidable competitor of the west. This is not so. The reason is the bad quality of the work. The poorly paid coolies are so badly fed and so weak that it takes at least three of them to do the work of one European. Also, the Indian workers lack, not only strength

but also skill, attention, and liking for their work.
. . . An Indian of the people will do anything else in
preference to becoming a factory operative. The factories thus get only the dregs of the working class.
The workers come to the factories and mines as a
last resort; they leave as soon as they can return to
their prior occupations or find more remunerative
employment. Thus the factories can never count on
a regular labor supply. Would higher wages remedy
this? Many employers say no — as soon as the
workers get a little ahead they would quit, either
temporarily till their money was spent, or perma-
nently for some more congenial calling.' These statements are fully confirmed by an Indian economic writer,
who says: 'One of the greatest drawbacks to the
establishment of large industries in India is the scarc-
ity and inefficiency of labor. Cheap labor, where there
is no physical stamina, mental discipline, and skill
behind it, tends to be costly in the end. The Indian
laborer is mostly uneducated. He is not in touch with
his employers or with his work. The laboring population of the towns is a flitting, dilettante population.'

" Thus Indian industry, despite its very considerable growth, has not come up to early expectations.
As the Official Year Book very frankly states: ' India,
in short, is a country rich in raw materials and in
industrial possibilities, but poor in manufacturing
accomplishments.' In fact, to some observers, India's
industrial future seems far from bright. As a competent English student of Indian conditions recently
wrote: ' Some years ago it seemed possible that India
might, by a rapid assimilation of Western knowledge

and technical skill, adapt for her own conditions the methods of modern industry, and so reach an approximate economic level. Some even now threaten the Western world with a vision of the vast population of China and India rising up with skilled organization, vast resources, and comparatively cheap labor to impoverish the West. To the present writer this is a mere bogey. The peril is of a very different kind. Instead of a growing approximation he sees a growing disparity. For every step India takes toward mechanical efficiency, the West takes two. When India is beginning to use bicycles and motor-cars (not to make them), the West is perfecting the aeroplane. This is merely symbolic. The war, as we know, has speeded up mechanical invention and produced a population of mechanics; but India has stood comparatively still. It is, up to now, overwhelmingly medieval, a country of domestic industry and handicrafts. Mechanical power, even of the simplest, has not yet been applied to its chief industry — agriculture."

Because those who belong to the same occupation or profession or to closely allied occupations or professions, most clearly understand one another, a sense of unity grows up amongst them severally. We have, therefore, in the intelligence levels amongst a people, and whatever other characteristics they hold in common, one source of those lines of occupational cleavage that tend to form a partial separation of one class from another.

INTELLIGENCE AND ELIMINATION FROM SCHOOL. — Another angle of the effect of intelligence upon adaptation to the forms of our social organization is found in the statistics of elimination from school grades and in estimated correlation between intelligence (as measured in the army) and schooling:

The psychological examiners in the army report (18): "Of 100 white recruits who entered the first grade in this country, 95 remained in school till grade two, 92 till grade three, 87 till grade four, 79 till grade five, 70 till grade six, 59 till grade seven, and 45 till grade eight; 21 of them entered high school, 16 kept on till the second year, 11 till the third, and 9 of the 100 graduated from high school; 5 of these entered college, and 1 graduated from college." These figures include the foreign-born but not the negro draft, and do not include officers.

Corresponding figures for the native-born white draft alone are as follows: Of 100 who entered school 98 remained till grade two, 97 till grade three, 94 till grade four, 90.5 till grade five, 83 till grade six, 73.5 till grade seven, 63 till grade eight, and 48 graduated from the grades. Of these 23 entered high school and continued till the second year, 17 till the third year, 12 till the fourth year, and 9.5 graduated. Of these five entered college and continued till the second year, 4 till the third, 2 till the fourth and 1 graduated. These figures correspond closely to those earlier given out by Ayres (4, 5), Strayer (29) and Thorndike (30).

The coefficients of correlation between intelligence, as estimated in the army, and schooling run high. "In general it may be said of examination Alpha that in an unselected group (i.e. *including* those men who would ordinarily be considered too illiterate to take

Alpha) the correlation with the number of years óf
schooling reported approximates +0.75; in an Alpha
group (*i.e. excluding* illiterates) the correlation coefficient approximates +0.65. If Alpha were to be
given to an unselected group the dispersion of whose
scores covered the whole range of the examination,
and whose reported schooling varied from none at
all to seven years or more of college work, the correlation coefficient would doubtless be greater than any
here presented." The nearest approach to this is a
combination of companies A and B, Third Provisional
Regiment Ordnance Training Camp, and Company B,
Ordnance Supply School, with an unselected group of
1047 white English speaking recruits from nine camps.
This is the special experimental group known as
Group X. It is a composite group and is of wide
range as to schooling and also as to Alpha weighted
total.

PSYCHIC INSTABILITY AND SOCIAL MAL-ADJUST-
MENT EVIDENCED IN MENTAL DISEASE. — In the foregoing pages we have been thinking solely of peculiarities of adjustment as occasioned, apparently by levels
of intelligence. Such adjustment may be studied from
the viewpoint of psychic instability. The data in this
relation are of a less specific nature than those with
which we have been dealing, but no less important,
doubtless, perhaps more so, according to authoritative opinion. In the instable and certainly fertile
springs of mental disease, of ineffectiveness in daily
occupation, probably of much of the unrest in every
generation, and certainly of a deal of criminal behavior. In periods of stress upon the individual or

upon the group as a whole these instabilities most apparently bear upon adjustment.

The immense importance of these considerations for our viewpoint cannot be more clearly expressed than in the words of Dr. Pearce Bailey written apropos of the Great War, but before the results of psychiatric examining in the army had been brought together (6):

" The world over, insanity is rated as being approximately three times as frequent, even under peace conditions, in the army as in the civil community. Those who see nothing but evil in armies may construe this as proof that army life produces mental disease. But another explanation seems nearer the truth. It seems a more reasonable hypothesis that the army demonstrates constitutional incapacity and weakness rather than creates mental disease; that, under a service which requires a robuster mental stability than do some of the varied opportunities of civil life, slightly unbalanced persons, who might get along fairly well in a suitable civil capacity, are immediately detected as not fully fit for an army, and so are discharged from it. A large percentage of the soldiers who break down mentally have, before recruitment, already either passed through nervous episodes which required sojourns in sanitoria, or through periods of mental distraughtness which interfered for a time with the usual routine of their lives. That these interruptions in activity are symptoms of constitutional unsoundness rather than initial attacks of mental disease, is borne out by the fact that the recovery rate from insanity in soldiers is nearly twice that in civilians. Inferences drawn from statistics, to be informative, must be considered with some knowledge of the purpose for which the statistics were gathered and the way they were collected. For its own safety, a military organization must, sooner or later, identify and count its undependable persons. In civil life there is neither demand nor opportunity for such a minute survey of mental health. Civil communities count only the insane who actually require confinement, and so even in the best-surveyed states, the registered insane are well under the actual number; in those states which provide inadequately for the insane, and keep them herded in almshouses or jails classed as paupers and criminals, the insanity rate falls far below the normal rate of one insane person for every thousand of adult population. But, obviously, a rate so arrived at is untrue and misleading.

" The army rate of insanity, three to every 1,000, high as it seems, remains at that level only under peace conditions and only then when the troops stay at home. Foreign service causes it to go up, even in peace. For example, there is more insanity among our troops serving in China than those stationed at home. Under war conditions, the normal rate rises. This cannot be entirely explained by the actual hardships of war. It must be partly explained by the same emotional factors as those which upset civilians. The outbreak of war, like the occurrence of such allied catastrophes as earthquakes and conflagrations, dislocates all mental operations. To be harmonious, mental actions must be in accord with actual conditions, and during the process of a sudden and violent readjustment of new conditions the mind undergoes severe tests of its resistance. Some cannot make the adjustment to war-times at all, as is shown, at the outbreak of war, by the increased number of old persons who die, by the increase in apoplexy, and by the fact that many persons who were able to maintain their equilibrium under ordinary conditions find their way, as though called by the clarion, to asylums. In countries such as England and America, in which three years ago war seemed like some legend, war brings with it to many a collapse of moral support and a complete transmutation of ethical values. They are suddenly told to renounce their cherished belief that the world has reached a point of perfection where wars are impossible. They become much depressed, and face the alternative of making some personal adaptation to the new and ugly condition, or of going mad. Some find their relief in believing that this marks the end of all thought-out destruction; in others the early distress is replaced by a welling martial spirit as they realize the actual peril or humiliation of their own country. They thus construct for themselves psychological defenses of some kind, although few who are not actual combatants can do so completely, as is shown in the falling off in all original work not directly connected with national defense. The compensation most commonly arrived at is the sinking, for a time, of personal considerations. National interest absorbs all others. Under its stimulus, professional and social differences fade away and exclusiveness becomes less a goal. Even butlers find their long-deferred opportunity to converse. There is an emotional desire for action, to do something for the

common cause, to help at no matter what personal sacrifice. In Germany, at the outbreak of this war, the
luxurious sanitoria lost most of their wealthy patients,
and in one prison the complaints of the prisoners
diminished by half. Under the steady daily routine
of discipline and service and sacrifice, as organization
replaces enthusiasm, these emotional reactions become
less conspicuous: and as war becomes a grim business,
the whole nation settles down to its work, accepting its
hardships and sorrows more and more as a matter of
course. That people live with more temperance and
less leisure may explain the strange contradiction that
the admissions to civilian institutions for the insane,
which go up at the beginning of a war, sink below
normal finally.

" The struggle to attain a personal adaptation,
which disturbs the civil population, must also in a
measure account for the increase in insanity among
soldiers at the outbreak of war. It is greatest during
the earlier months — that is, during mobilization and
training, before the fatigue and exposure and exhaustion of continuous fighting. With the exception of
campaigns carried out in foreign countries under unusual conditions, insanity is noted most at the main
bases and diminishes with an actual approach to the
front. Under the exactions of discipline, of prompt
obedience, or giving up or doing without what he
prizes, the individual who is physically and mentally
sound usually experiences a distinct gain from the
new form of life. But such measures are not always
so successful in persons who are distinctly neuro-
pathic. They may think themselves unjustly treated,

feel they are persecuted, or may find themselves falling short of the expected, and thus be brought to a fuller realization of their own inadequacy. They become much depressed in this way and their minds become troubled, less over the present situation, perhaps, than over past problems of their own life, which in civil life, with its protection and possibilities of avoidance, they were able to compensate for. It has been noted over and over again in this war that soldiers, in their mental distress, referred less to immediate issues than to the facts in their own past conduct and relationships.

" The figures, which show a three-fold increase during the war of a disability which strikes harder at military effectiveness than any other medical disability, *are drawn from the cases of actual insanity only. They by no means express all that armies suffer by reason of mental disability.* Among other conditions which, while not classified as insanity, are allied to it, both in causation and effects, are two well-known neuroses, neurasthenia and hysteria. Of eighteen United States Army officers retired for disability in 1915, four were for neurasthenia. It is never possible to define exactly the limitations of these two neuroses, but they are generally understood as indicative of mental worry or of anxiety, or of shock; they are essentially recoverable and do not correspond to the general symptoms of insanity. They are always frequent in armies even during peace, and are more apt to arise at the front than are cases of actual insanity. By hysteria is usually understood a mental state which, more or less independently of consciousness,

arouses physical symptoms or dictates some specific
behavior for the purpose of obtaining a personal advantage or avoiding a disagreeable situation.   The
hysteric, without entirely realizing it, shams illness
for an end, under the various circumstances which
make illness an asset rather than an incubus, and which
changes the normal impulse to get well into an impulse to stay ill, until certain disagreeable conditions
are removed.   In civil life it is found in many of the
ailments of children, among plaintiffs who are suing
for damages for personal injuries, and as a classical
means for one party to a matrimonial contract to
keep the other in hand.   Armies have always had to
contend with it as the soldier's way of signifying his
unwillingness to endure longer.   It even gets into his
slang, as when he says he ' is sick of it.'   The appeal
for relief is expressed not in words, but in physical
terms of the situation itself.   Hysterical blindness is
a mute way of stating unwillingness to look any longer
at horrible sights, deafness a refusal to hear any
longer the explosions.   The paralytic refuses to stand
up or go, and the tremors, speech defects, and other
symptoms of hysteria are a way of saying, ' Don't you
see how ill or badly injured I am? ' "

An analysis of statistics of mental disease in the
State of New York made by Dr. Horatio M. Pollock
supports the preceding statement and is therefore in
line with the thought of this chapter (21).   All the
more so because it is dealing with elements in the civil
population, not in the military forces.

" It is but reasonable to suppose, however, that the
war, by increasing excitement, anxiety and grief, has

been a precipitating factor of no small importance in the causation of mental disease.

" The available facts that have a bearing on the question may be set forth under the following heads:

I. Increase of insane patients in institutions.
II. Increase in first admissions.
III. Changes in the principal clinical groups.

I. Increase of Insane in Institutions

" The statistics of the institutions for the insane in New York State are compiled by fiscal years. Prior to 1916 the fiscal year ended on September 30; since that time it has ended on June 30.

" The yearly net increase in patients in all the institutions for the insane in the state since 1911 has been as follows:

Fiscal Year	Net Increase
1911	653
1912	662
1913	1,060
1914	691
1915	939
1916 (9 mos)	918
1917	1,183
1918	937

" The net increase in patients during the four years preceding the war was 3,066; a yearly average of 767; during the 3¾ years following the outbreak of the war it was 3,977; a yearly average of 1,061. The difference between the increases in the two periods was quite remarkable, but it is accounted for in part, at least, by the accumulation in the hospitals of deportable aliens who could not be taken to their homes in Europe while the war was in progress.

" Additional light is thrown on the subject by the following tabulation showing the ratio of patients under treatment to the general population of the state from 1908 to 1918.

INSANE PATIENTS IN ALL INSTITUTIONS AT END OF FISCAL YEAR

Year	Number	Per 1,000,000 of general population of the state.
1908	30,457	349.6
1909	31,540	352.1
1910	32,658	358.3
1911	33,311	361.0
1912	33,973	363.6
1913	35,033	370.4
1914	35,724	373.2
1915	36,663	378.4
1916	37,581	383.4
1917	38,764	391.9
1918	39,701	395.7

" It is seen that the rate per 100,000 increased 11.4 points from 1908 to 1911; 12.2 points from 1911 to 1914; and 22.5 points from 1914 to 1918. The rates are based on the federal census of 1910, and the state census of 1915, and estimates made therefrom for the other years. As immigration has been greatly reduced by the war and as many men have been removed from the state for military purposes, it is probable that the estimates of population for 1917 and 1918 computed according to standard methods are too high. If this be true, the ratios of the insane to the general population for these years as given above are correspondingly low.

II. *Increase in First Admissions*

" In New York State first admissions have been
carefully distinguished from readmissions since the beginning of the fiscal year of 1909. We are therefore
able to compare the rate of first admissions during
the war period with that of the years immediately preceding the war.

FIRST ADMISSIONS TO ALL INSTITUTIONS FOR THE INSANE IN
NEW YORK STATE, 1909–1918.

Year	Number	Rate per 100,000 of general population of the state.
1909	5,784	66.4
1910	5,944	65.2
1911	6,228	67.5
1912	6,300	67.4
1913	6,650	70.3
1914	6,789	70.9
1915	6,690	69.1
1916 (9 mos)	5,269	53.8
1917	7,340	74.0
1918	7,244	72.2

" The average annual rate for the four years, 1911–
1914, was 69.0 and for the 3¾ years from 1915–1918,
71.7. For the reason stated above, it is probable that
the rates given for 1917 and 1918 are too low. . . .

III. *Changes in the Principal Clinical Groups*

" A closer view of mental disease in the state during
the war period may be obtained by examination of
the varying distribution of the principal psychoses
over the past ten years. For this purpose we take
only the first admissions to the civil state hospitals
and select the senile, paretic, alcoholic, manic-depressive, involution melancholia, dementia praecox and

psychoneurotic groups. Together these constitute about 70% of all first admissions.

FIRST ADMISSIONS WITH CERTAIN PSYCHOSES, CIVIL STATE HOSPITALS
1909–1918

Year	Senile	General paralysis	Alcoholic	Manic-depressive and allied forms	Involution melancholia	Dementia praecox and allied forms	Psycho-neuroses
1909	606	658	561	574	207	1181	44
1910	615	815	581	769	143	1015	61
1911	583	758	580	826	143	1031	66
1912	596	719	567	854	119	1129	74
1913	594	768	572	924	133	1250	105
1914	542	774	464	880	188	1445	106
1915	570	814	345	879	165	1663	73
*1916	486	640	297	846	164	1173	57
1917	585	866	594	1136	201	1786	77
1918	652	913	354	976	219	1883	83

* 9 months.

" Computing the average annual admissions for the 4 years 1911 to 1914 and for the 3¾ years 1915 to 1918, we have the following results:

	Average annual admissions 1911–1914	Average annual admissions 1915–1918	Per cent of increase or decrease
Senile..........................	579	611	5.5
General Paralysis...............	755	862	14.2
Alcoholic.......................	546	424	22.3*
Manic-depressive and allied forms.	871	1023	17.5
Involution melancholia..........	145	200	37.9
Dementia praecox and allied forms	1214	1735	42.9
Psychoneuroses.................	88	77	12.5*

* Decrease.

" Referring to the foregoing figures we note a slight increase in senile cases and a more marked increase in cases with general paralysis. The etiology in these groups is well known and it is probable that the war is not responsible for the increase to any great extent.

" In the alcoholic psychoses the decrease in cases might have been influenced by the restrictions placed on the liquor traffic during the war, but a marked decline in the influence of alcohol in causing insanity was noted the year before the outbreak of the war. The reasons for the rise in the number of cases in this group in 1917 and for the sudden drop again in 1918 are not known.

" In the manic-depressive, involution melancholia and dementia praecox groups the increase in the annual number of admissions during the war period is quite striking. In dementia praecox especially the change has been remarkable. Part of this increase may be due to modifications in diagnostic principles, but in the main the figures may be taken at their face value.

" The influence of the war in bringing the constitutional cases of mental disorder into the hospitals is a matter of conjecture. *It seems but reasonable to ascribe a part of the increase in the annual admissions in these groups to the mental conflicts arising from circumstances connected with the great war. Social and economic changes produced by the war may also have a bearing on the matter.*

" The annual rate of first admissions of the psychoneurotic group decreased during the war period.

However, as this group is so small and is subject to such marked variations no significance can be attached to the change during the war period."

PSYCHIC INSTABILITY AND UNREST. — But psychic instability finds many other avenues through which it makes its appearance when thousands together are contending to effect adaptation on their part to the conditions of daily life. They easily become followers of the isms and fads and radical movements of the day (what the conservative describe as " isms and fads and radical movements "), sustained often by a vague sense of being in the front ranks of the procession. The more brilliant among them may be sporadic local leaders at least and altogether they are an almost ready-made audience for their local leaders, " the apostles of unrest," and even for the balanced and thoughtful student who now and again proposes a program for social reconstruction. But they contribute no steadying morale; on the other hand they are sources of embarrassment to many an institution, the personnel of which may be earnestly attempting to do the best toward keeping abreast with the needs of the day.

One would be going quite too far, however, if one were to say or imply that all unrest in industry and in society generally is attributable to psychic instability — or if the implication were made it should be accompanied by the admission that in many relations such psychic conditions may be an asset rather than a liability. Certainly, at any rate, one cannot off-hand draw a line between those natures that make inconsequential apostles of unrest and their followers, and those other natures that make up in their respective times the grandly discontented Socrates, Jesus, Waldensians, Albigensians, Martin Luther, the fathers of the English Bill of Rights, and the fathers of American independence. Without such " apostles of unrest " as these we should soon become hopelessly bound up and entangled in our conventional states.

If unrest is any more prevalent in our day than heretofore it may be for the reason that the masses of men and women are thinking more than they have done in the past — and this whether they are victims of unstable natures or not. But it is for the additional reason that in our generation great masses of people have experienced profound and sudden dislocations in their social and industrial life. In other words, old established adjustments have been wrecked or severely strained and these circumstances have carried with them the urgency for new adaptations.

In the course of the World War, for illustration, hundreds of thousands of men almost literally awoke on a morning to find themselves no longer in the furrows, before the blast furnace, or behind the counters but in a military camp and over seas, thrust with breathless speed into conditions in which not even their lives were their own. Other hundreds of thousands, not in the military service, were dislocated from their accustomed occupations to fill the gaps left by those who had gone, and other gaps like them created by the extraordinary expansion of industry as an incident to the war. The new adjustments had by no means been completed when suddenly the abrupt cessation of hostilities dislocated them again and made new adaptations necessary. Those who had lately come into industrial life where they saw a possibility of realizing their wish for economic independence, for elbow to elbow association with others of their kind, and for the feeling of co-operation with others in the accomplishment of results that appeal to the senses — creating, for example, a monster gun or ship-loads of munitions — had to return to the farm and store where they were soon faced by conditions of depression. Those who had gone into the military service — particularly into its most active phases — returned to what seemed to them the unbearable monotony of farm and village and factory life where the contrast at once made them feel intensely the grip of the wish for excitement and action which war inevitably stimulates, both in those who are actually in the fight and in those who are in prospect of engaging therein, and whose imagination is continuously stimulated by contact with those who have already been at the front. Social recognition which all crave by nature, and to which the soldier probably felt he held a title by reason of his service, was undoubtedly short of expectations in the experience of hosts of men. By reason of industrial depression, actual or foreseen, employment and wages were insecure. All in all the war period and the years immediately following were times of extraordinary dislocations, that entailed indescribable strains incident to adjustment and untold disappointments of some of the deepest motives of human nature — the wishes, on the part of ambitious folk, for independence, for social recognition, for novel, exciting experience or romance.

The roots of the unrest now prevalent in India are described by Stoddard in terms that are instructive in this connection. Having referred to the Industrial Revolution in Europe he quotes a British economist, Dodwell, with respect to conditions just preceding the war (27): " But the revolution was not nearly so sweeping as that which is now in operation in India. The invention of machinery and steam-power was, in Europe, but the crowning event of a long series of years in which commerce and industry had been constantly expanding, in which capital had been largely accumulated, in which economic principles had been gradually spreading . . . No, the Indian economic revolution is vastly greater and more fundamental than our Industrial Revolution, great as it was. Railways have been built through districts where travel was almost impossible, and even roads are unknown. Factories have been built, and filled by men unused to industrial labor. Capital has been poured into the country, which was unprepared for any such development. And what are the consequences? India's social organization is being dissolved. The Brahmins are no longer priests. The ryot is no longer bound to the soil. The banya is no longer the sole purveyor of capital. The hand weaver is threatened with extinction, and the brass-worker can no longer ply his craft. Think of the dislocation which this sudden change has brought about, of the many who can no longer follow their ancestral vocations, of the commotion which a less profound change produced in Europe, and you will understand what is the chief motive-power of the political unrest. It is small wonder.

The wonder is that the unrest has been no greater than it is. Had India not been an Asiatic country, she would have been in fierce revolution long ago."

These lines were written, as has already been said, before the Great War broke over the heads of Europe. They present a picture of an unrest that differs from that which we have experienced in America since the close of the war. The difference is in the motives in which it has its roots. We must guard against that extreme simplification of a complex phenomenon that would find it growing out of but one causal relation — one human motive in this case. Yet it cannot be far from the truth that in America since the war the tap-root of social unrest is in that inner urging or wish for effecting adjustments or adaptations different from those that have already been made; these are hum-drum and there is a reaching out away from them to others that are conceived as ideal or as approximating the ideal. In India, on the other hand, before the war unrest was an expression by a people dazed by the sudden onslaughts of civilization, of a wish to be let alone; to remain upon the old tread-mills; to continue their purely domestic arts. It is another angle of an old picture: a picture of a people who have not already the dispositions acquired or native that enable them to use, even approximately, the opportunities and responsibilities that a new age or a new occasion has brought to their door. It is another case of a Francis Joseph thrusting reforms upon a people before they are able to play their part. Thrust them against a task that for them is insuperable and you have discouragement and finally rebellion. Let successive tasks be but a little beyond the level of present attainments and let each one be presented when the people are already fully habituated in what has preceded; thus conditions are made favorable for new adjustments with enthusiasm.

It is, no doubt, this wish to be let alone upon the old levels; this complacency of the masses of Indian people that has accounted for the measure of success of Ghandi's movement of non-co-operation: *i.e*, boycott of everything British including voting, the payment of taxes, the purchase of British-made goods, and the like. This is in effect a bid to solve the unrest of the day by sitting still or by returning to the old ways and standing by them. Given a leader, such a call was assured of a large response because it opened an outlet to some basic motives of the Indian people.

So in any case unrest is interpreted as a symptom of failure in adaptation: of unrealized wishes for security of wage and employment; for freedom to go about in search of contacts with novel situations, and, as a corollary to this, for release from what has become the hum-drum of commonplace tedium of the occupation at hand; for active contacts and participation in the affairs of institutions and communities; and for recognition as demonstrated by the level to which the individual has attained in the councils of his own group and class by the consent of his co-laborers, and in those of other groups and classes. These wishes may not become vocal; they may not even be definitely conscious as one consciously wishes for clearing weather in order that the morning may be suitable for hunting or fishing, but it is present none the less and is a symptom of ill-adaptation to the complex circumstances surrounding.

Among the less intelligent, unbalanced, or instable folk of any age, the sense of unfulfillment which is the vague conscious sign of inner conflict, finds expression in more or less bizarre behavior; in grasping at straws thrown out by leaders of circumscribed vision, it may be. But in the case of the more intelligent and poised, it is not so. There comes to their attention now one and now another aspect of their present situation, trade or profession, that is of sufficient interest to make the case bearable, and even more than just bearable. They soon see attractive pictures in clouds of smoke and discover an element of humor in the contacts of men in the office force. They so bide their time and occasion for making the adaptation for which their nature is pushing. The instable lack the balance needful for such compensatory behavior as this. They must break away now and realize the end of their inner urging at once. This may take the shape of fixing against all comers upon an uncompromising individualistic ideal; in other words, of an utter blindness to all considerations that arise in the minds of others, the mass of intelligent folk, who believe that ideals that are held in common are conditioned and grown out of circumstances that are common, oft-repeated experiences; and that in crises the herd must be next to unquestioningly supported in the expectation that in the long run new occasions will teach new duties to all.

One could conclude, *a priori*, that such folk, as compared at least with the general average of the population, are not lacking in native intelligence, whatever be the other aspects of their psychic quality. Were they so lacking it could be assumed that they would placidly and pliantly accept things as they are.

It is possible that many " conscientious objectors " brought to light in the period of the World War belong in the group we are considering. If so there is support in the experience of army examiners for the *a priori* conclusion mentioned in the paragraph above. The following table, for example, shows the distribution of letter grades amongst conscientious objectors of the religious and political types respectively, and, for the purpose of comparison, of the principle sample of the white draft, Groups I, II and III.

Per cent of Intelligence Ratings of Conscientious Objectors in Isolation at Fort Leavenworth Compared with that of the White Draft, Groups I, II and III.

Group	E,D—	D	C—	C	C+	B	A
Religious	5.0	5.0	20.0	20.0	15.0	25.0	10.0
Political		11.7	11.7		11.7	5.9	50.0
Total	2.7	8.3	16.4	10.8	13.5	16.4	32.6
White Draft							
Groups I, II, III . .	7.0	17.1	23.8	25.0	15.0	8.0	4.1

The late Dr. E. E. Southard was certainly one of the first amongst the psychiatrists to sense the function of his professional group in the face of the unrest that is so prevalent in the social organization, as well as to point, from the psychiatrist's angle, to fundamental causes. This he does in his discussion of the findings of the Commission on Industrial Unrest in England. That the evidences of unrest that the commission had to deal with were, in their sum total, *reactions of individuals to unfulfilled wishes* may be accepted as at least a satisfactory working hypothesis. That they are altogether indications of psychic instabilities in any but a normal, harmless sense in those individuals is quite beyond the bounds of possibility. Dr. Southard writes as follows (23):

" According to the Commission's report, there were the following four universal causes for unrest in England: (1) food prices and distribution of supplies; (2) restriction of personal freedom; (3) card system for military and industrial service; (4) inco-ordination of government papers. Certain acute, though not universal, causes of unrest were housing, drinking, and fatigue. The commission speaks also of psychological conditions and remarks that the great majority of the causes of industrial unrest specified in the (8 district) reports have their root in certain psychological conditions. Among these may be mentioned lack of confidence in the government, feeling of inequality of sacrifice in army and industry, the idea that solemn pledges were broken and turned into scraps of paper, feeling of unreliability of certain trade union officials; and feeling of the uncertainty of the whole industrial future.

" The commission was no doubt justified in laying enormous emphasis on what it calls psychological conditions. The psychiatrist and the medical men in general must feel that the blanket term ' psychological condition ' covers a good many psychiatric difficulties. Thus, whoever follows the strong trend to individualization in medicine, psychiatry, in education — both intellectual and moral — and even in the law courts, must be convinced that individualization should proceed to greater lengths in industry. There is nothing more wide spread in modern sociology than certain ideas about group action as the be all and end all of progress and failure in social developments. As one author puts it, group experience leads to group thought, group thought to group action. If we take, for example, the universal causes of unrest summarized by Barnes of England, we shall of course be convinced that food prices might well be a group experience; a poor distribution of supplies might be to a large extent a group experience. There would also be a group experience of the evils of card systems which might lead to a group thought, and unrest of mind might create tendencies to strikes; distribution of supplies would tend to follow group experience and thought as in the case of prices and service cards. When it comes, however, to a question of the restriction of personal freedom and to a question of government inco-ordination, it must be observed that these are hardly group experiences as much as individual experiences. The workman who objects to being passed automatically from one sphere of labor to another may make himself heard effectively in group thought; the victim of some inco-ordination on the part of government departments may do the same. But it certainly must be true that the effects of such restriction of freedom and of temperamental inco-ordination are, as a rule, individual. The voices of the victims, however, are raised along with the voices of general unrest concerning food prices and the service-card system.

" We cannot help thinking that the principles of social work and especially of psychiatric social work, applied to the problems of the restriction of personal freedom or of temperamental inco-ordination, will solve most of the problems. The matter of automatic transfers from certain spheres of labor is of course a war rather than a peace matter, but the item will serve as well as another to indicate that universal causes of unrest need not be the product of group experience, need not have led to group thought, and need not lead to group action unless in the presence of other more general causes of unrest. Many of these problems, possibly the majority of them, are extraordinary rather than main problems. The same holds for the acute as contrasted with the universal causes of unrest, most of which acute causes are described by the commissioners as arising locally from different problems, such as family housing, drinking, fatigue, or even such a problem as that of lack of confidence in the government, specified among the findings as lack of commercial sense. We find from the commission's report that this lack of commercial sense was especially noticeable in South Wales where there had been a break-away in faith in parliamentary representation. I do not know any single important fact relative to South Wales and its break-away from the democratic faith, but certainly there must have been a local condition which no doubt had local causes, some of which are almost certain to have been due to the operations of particular men in a group of men.

" This introduces us to the most general aspect of the unrest problem, the aspect which leads me to give my paper the somewhat cryptic title: *The Modern Specialist in Unrest.* It may be — or, as I suspect, it may not be — that group experience leads to group thought and group thought to group action as the ordinary course of events in social developments. But whether these developments are group matters or not, it remains true that most of the information we possess concerning group psychology and group psychopathy is derived from the psychology or the psychopathy of the individual. If this statement be accounted true, then I do not need to insist that the psychiatrist is rather more likely than any other expert to know how the main lines of unrest will run. Unrest on the part of the individual is the big problem of the psychiatrist; year in and year out he comes in contact with the finest, as it were, and the most brilliant examples of unrest in the shape of particular patients in his wards. If this general account of things be correct, the psychiatrist ought to have a message for industry. Psychiatric knowledge about the unrest of the individual ought to be turned to account in our analyses of group unrest. . . .

"What is unrest? The theory that group experience leads to group thought, which in turn leads to group action, may be sound theory for a portion of industrial phenomena, but the individual experience, individual thought, and even individual action are also factors in industrial situations. How far is unrest a matter of group or crowd or mass psychology? How far does mass psychology depend upon the psychology of the individual member? It will not be wise to generalize to the effect either that industrial unrest is entirely a group phenomenon or that it takes its rise entirely in the minds or in the hearts of individuals. We have seen that some of the causes of unrest in England might well be matters of group psychology, but that other causes of unrest seem almost in their nature to have been of individual origin.

" That portion of the unrest problem which depends not upon group experience, but upon individual experience, not upon group thought, but upon individual thought, and finally not upon group action, but upon individual action, is the proper topic for the psychiatrist. The psychiatrist, particularly in company with the psychiatric social worker, has always been a specialist in unrest — unrest, to be sure, confined within asylum walls. The modern psychiatrist has under more or less definite supervision large numbers of the so-called psychopathic personalities — persons who are not insane in a kind or degree to warrant their commitment to institutions, but who are psychopathic enough or in such wise as to benefit from community supervision. It is this modern contact with the psychopathic personalities, with instances of so-called psychopathic inferiority, with psychopathic states, that makes the modern psychiatrist a specialist in a kind of unrest that interests the community very deeply. These psychopathic personalities have been recognized even in the immigration laws and in the official tabulations of the army and navy under the terms constitutional psychopathic inferiority, constitutional psychopathic state, and similar designations."

Additional support for the thesis respecting the

psychic background that is manifest in unrest is
afforded by Spargo in his " The Psychology of
Bolshevism " (26):

" Their most marked peculiarity is the migratory
nature of their lives. Whether this is self-determined,
a matter of temperament and habit, or due to uncon-
trolled factors, it is largely responsible for the contempt in which they are popularly held. . . . They
rarely remain long enough in any one place to form
local attachments and ties or anything like civic
pride. They move from job to job, city to city,
state to state. . . . The absence of friends, combined with the prejudice against vagrants which
everywhere exists, subjects them to arbitrary and
high-handed injustice such as no other body of
American citizens has to endure. . . . In this manner the ' Wobbly ' becomes a veritable son of Ishmael,
his hand against the hand of nearly every man in
conventional society. In particular he becomes a
rebel by habit, hating the police and the courts as his
constant enemies.

" Doubtless the great majority of these men are
temperamentally predisposed to the unanchored,
adventurous, migratory existence which they lead.
Boys so constituted run away to sea, take jobs with
traveling circuses, or enlist as soldiers. The type is
familiar and not uncommon. Such individuals cannot be content with the prosaic, hum-drum, monoto-
nous life of regular employment."

It is another case of men of approximately *the same
temperamental equipment*, unadapted or ill-adapted to
the conventional forms of organized society, coming

together into the same current where, through mutual recognition and understanding of one another they have developed into a solid social group. In that current they remain quite apart from the rest of us, and no assimilation can be accomplished until we can know their psychology and act thereupon precisely as the unruly victim of psychoses in our hospital ward can not re-establish social relations with us, his earlier neighbors, until we have grown to understand his psychology and until we act upon our knowledge by relieving him of his tensions. It is a case that calls for alteration of conditions in such manner that those conditions may elicit behavior that will provide satisfaction for the patient and for others; and the " conditions " may imply both physical and spiritual surroundings, mental habits and even bodily health.

CRIMINAL BEHAVIOR. — Other phenomena of imperfect social adjustment are to be found in criminal behavior, and it has been and is a fruitful hypothesis that such behavior represents a failure in adjustment due to the psychic quality and intelligence level of individuals. There is no hard and fast catalogue of forms of such behavior. A given act may today be in no sense regarded as criminal, but tomorrow, owing to legislation that may have occurred in the meantime, the same act may be so described. Leaving such instances aside, however, and considering the matter in the rough, it will be satisfactory in this connection to follow Garofalo (12) in his conception of " Natural Crime " which he limits to offenses against the sentiment of pity on the one hand and on the other to offenses against the sentiment of probity.

The first category includes (a) attacks upon human life and all manner of acts that tend to produce physical harm to human beings such as the deliberate infliction of physical torture, mayhem, the maltreatment of the weak and infirm, the voluntary causing of illness, the imposition upon children of excessive labor or such work as tends to injure their health or stunt their physical development; (b) physical acts which produce suffering at once physical and moral such as the violation of personal liberty; abduction and kidnapping for ransom are types; (c) acts which directly produce moral suffering such as defamation of character and false accusation.

The second category includes: (a) attacks upon property involving violence, such as robbery, extortion, malicious mischief, arson, and the like; (b) attacks without violence but involving breach of trust: such as obtaining money under false pretences; embezzlement; fraudulent conveyance of property; bankruptcy through fraud or negligence; the revelation of professional secrets; plagiarism and all forms of counterfeiting; (c) indirect injuries to property or civil rights by false statements or entries made in a formal manner as on oath. Among these are perjury, forgery, destruction of documents, etc. There are important differences of psychic make-up amongst individuals who commit crimes of the foregoing categories, respectively.

Juvenile offenders are not classed with criminals nor their offenses with crimes for the good reason that there is a gap between the psychologic nature of juveniles and adults by reason of which the misdeeds of the former are regarded less seriously than those of the latter. But the two groups are not in wholly distinct classes. The offenses of each may be interpreted as indications of a failure in the process of adaptation of the individual to his world. The analysis of the cause of this failure is not a simple operation. There are certainly many causal factors. Among these is mental defect — feeble-mindedness. Its frequency in both juvenile and adult groups has been the subject of many debates, and estimates on the basis of mental testing have varied greatly — as to the juvenile group from 7% to more than 16%. The estimates were made upon examination of the population of juvenile reformatories and the personnel of the daily grist of cases in juvenile courts. The average has been, by competent observers, set at 45% to 50%. Some difference in frequency amongst localities occurs and should be expected owing to variations in the practices of the courts in the matter of commitment, to different methods and standards in use by examiners, to the nature of the population in the localities respectively, etc. The drift of opinion of competent students is undoubtedly toward the lower estimates. Of 1212 juvenile delinquents in Boston 7% have been reported as definitely feeble-minded (16). Even of these cases it can never be asserted positively that the mental defect is the sole cause of the failure in adjustment that is described as the delinquent act or the delinquent career. The " born criminal " and the " moral imbecile " hypotheses have no support in the facts as they have become known in recent years. What has been interpreted as a moral imbecile is but a low-grade feeble-minded person whose inhibitions are therefore weak and whose natural impulses are for that reason peculiarly lacking in restraint. Undoubtedly, too, there are other psychic defects than this in his make-up. The psychological tests themselves do not bring forward the sole criteria of diagnosis.

It is possible that feeble-mindedness is in no case, strictly speaking, even a primary cause of delinquency. By reason of it the individual is unable to map out his course so as to avoid pitfalls; he may not recognize the meaning or the consequences of an act that he is about to do; he has few interests that can serve as inhibitors and consequently he is more likely than a normal individual to act impulsively whenever an occasion may arise.

It is important to observe that special abilities and disabilities occur amongst juvenile delinquents so that the individual requires at the outset a *particular* adjustment in order that he may avoid unnecessary grating against the conditions of existence. If a youth has a high grade of musical talent and is mediocre in general the particular adjustment he requires is easily apparent. But there are highly specialized abilities in mathematics, in engineering, in drawing, in the management of men, etc. (7) One of all-round ability may fit in without irritation at any one of many points in the social organization; not so in the case of the natural specialist. A misplaced individual who possesses a highly specialized capacity may quickly become an example of unrest; and this unrest may (depending upon the nature of the total person-

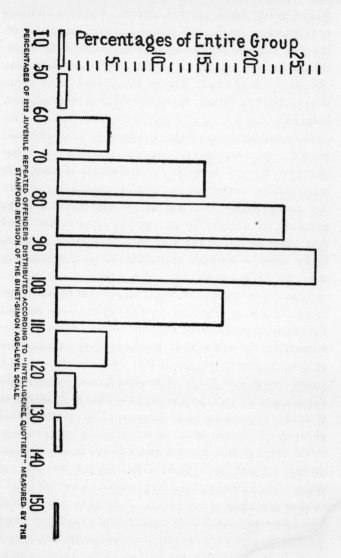

ality and circumstances surrounding) find expression in delinquent acts, in other behavior not so described, but of a character disturbing to the established course of affairs — vagrancy for example — or in minor psychoses or in frank mental disease.

However significant the proportion of 7% or 10% of feeble-minded amongst juvenile delinquents may be, other facts relating to the distribution of intelligence levels amongst them are full of meaning also. Of the 1212 in the Boston group referred to, 8% are supernormal. The whole group presents a fairly normal distribution — somewhat skewed toward the lower levels. This makes it apparent that other factors than mental level are at work — probably many others. If both the very bright and the very dull are misdoers; if many feeble-minded youths live decently and do their simple work well, there must certainly be other causes of delinquency than low intelligence level.

There is lack of balance amongst natural impulses; those qualities that express themselves in the vigorous or the lethargic use of one's endowments; personality traits such as love of adventure, revengefulness, stubbornness, etc., with their outlet in such attitudes as the grudge; habitual mental imagery with its outlet in impulsions, illustrated without doubt in the behavior of many a " model man " in the community who has " gone wrong " over night as it were, and the like.

If feeble-mindedness is minor amongst the psychic causes of delinquency in juveniles it is probably still less pronounced as a cause of criminality amongst adults. Because the practise of the psychologists in the camps in the World War has had the effect of producing relative uniformity of method and interpretation in psychologic diagnoses in civil life, investigators here and there have begun to report for the population of their institutions, respectively, a hardly larger proportion of defective intelligence than was found in the United States Army. And the intelligence of the army was probably of but little lower level than that of the population at large. Thus ". . . we have come to the rather radical conclusion that the adult prisoner in this state (New Jersey) is of average normal intelligence when compared with such standards as were obtained as a result of psychological examining in the army. To be sure, the median intelligence of prisoners is slightly inferior to the median intelligence of army recruits, but this is because among the prisoners certain factors of selection are at work which make the two groups somewhat incomparable. It is only after allowance has been made for nationality, color and occupational selection that the prisoner is seen to have approximately the same intelligence as the soldier." The characteristic repeating offender in this state is a native white of even somewhat superior intelligence (9). Practically the same conclusion (not referring to repeating offenders) has been reached in an investigation of less scope in Indiana (28) and in one of broad scope in Illinois (3).

In this connection we quote the army findings as to the relative intelligence of the principal sample of the white draft and of military prisoners convicted on serious charges by general courts-martial and con-

fined in the United States disciplinary barracks at
Fort Leavenworth (18).

	E, D—	D	C—	C	C+	B	A	Total No.
Number: Prisoners in each grade group	201	633	700	799	538	300	197	3368
Per cent	6.0	18.8	20.8	23.8	16.0	8.8	5.8	
White draft, Per cent	7.1	17.0	23.8	25.0	15.2	8.0	4.1	94004

This group of prisoners, in comparison with the
white draft " is normal or average. There is a slight
tendency to higher ratings than those obtained by the
white draft, but it is probably not significant."

The table below compares Camps Dix and McClellan
prisoners who were convicted of minor charges with
both the Fort Leavenworth and the white draft
groups:

	E, D—	D	C—	C	C+	B	A	Total No.
Dix and McClellan prisoners, per cent	20.6	25.5	21.6	18.9	8.3	3.4	2.1	1004
Leavenworth prisoners, per cent	6.0	18.8	20.8	23.8	16.0	8.8	5.8	3368
White draft, principal sampling	7.1	17.0	23.8	25.0	15.0	8.0	4.1	94004

A comparison of the two preceding tables makes
it appear that low intelligence may be a factor in the
less serious delinquencies but not in those of graver
concern.

On the whole those who had been convicted on
charges of acquisitive crimes such as larceny, robbery,
forgery, fraud, etc. — offenses against the sentiments
of probity (Garofalo, *supra*) — are of a higher intelligence level than the average. Those who were convicted of crimes of aggression (excepting those whose
aggression took the form of disloyalty), — offenses

against the sentiments of pity (Garofalo, *supra*) — were below the average intelligence level.

It appears, therefore, on the whole, that a psychologic account of those evidences of mal-adjustment that we call the crimes of adults, if the new trend be borne out by further investigation, is very likely to relegate feeble-mindedness to the negligible. A substitute for the old emphasis upon this factor is in the field of emotional and temperamental constitution which includes all those factors that we have previously referred to as psychic instabilities, and, we may add, defects of personality.

But the ill effects upon adjustment to the social organization, produced by warped human nature, are not limited to such traits as have been mentioned in the foregoing. Habit-formed traits may be no less effective. Indeed it is possible that such peculiar tendencies or readiness for reaction as have been implied in the foregoing discussion are — many of them — properly classified as habitual. Certainly we are justified in considering our mental capacities, even, in their concrete practical operation, as habituated forms of behavior. We take this position in effect each time we state the proposition that capacities can not be improved but that we can acquire the benefit of improvement by training in the art of using the capacity. It is better than a plausible hypothesis that the forests conceal many a woodsman who possesses the natural capacity that, had it been trained appropriately, would have accounted for a highly competent mathematician, scientist, or follower of a practical art. In other words, what the capacity lacks in such an instance, is the support of a complex of acquired habits. This hypothesis is supported by the data in Chapter IX, particularly by Dr. Cattell's "Statistical Study of Men of Science" in America, and by many a casual observer, who now and again finds, in the more obscure walks of life, an individual of inquiring disposition, keen observation, and originality.

This consideration prompts the thought that those who live and grow in the midst of conditions that are unfavorable; conditions, that is, that thwart the "wishes" of human nature for security of maintenance, for release from hum-drum and contact with the unfamiliar, for enlarging participation in daily work: that those who live in such thwarting conditions and react to them over and over again must develop something analogous to a professional disposition. And a disposition so developed may be merely a grudge or any other psychic twist or deformity that impedes, rather than aids, normal social adjustment, if it does not positively facilitate mal-adjustment.

Obviously it is the proper function of leaders of society not to attempt to find relief from mal-adjustments of whatever nature by forcing the ill-adjusted into ready-made modes but to look upon the conditions in which we live — both material and spiritual — as so many stimuli or situations that induce the reactions or responses that are called "unrest" and "crime" and what not; and secondly, in-so-far as possible, to alter those stimula with a view to obtaining more favorable responses.

This may or may not lead to increasing wages and

guaranteeing an income; to granting enlarged participation in the control of working conditions; to revolution of the educational system. But wheresoever it
leads, to be successful it must create and maintain a
sense of satisfaction from having relieved and from
continuous relief of the pressure of the sense of unfulfilled wishes. But this is not even an expression of
a pious hope that by manipulation of the external
conditions of life all such difficulties as we have had
in mind may be made to disappear. The best that
may be reasonably expected from such experiments in
stimulation and response is an approximation to relief
from crime and pathological unrest and the like.

CHAPTER XI

POTENTIALITY FOR DEVELOPMENT
OF CIVILIZATION

THE considerations brought forward in the last chapter raise the question whether such evidences of mal-adaptation as were cited are increasing from year to year. If so the fact would probably be accepted as evidence of the absolute or relative decadence of human nature: relative, that is, to the increasing demands that civilization places upon it. The question may be considered as preparatory to the further enquiry whether the race is able to sustain and develop the complex and exacting civilization that we ourselves have created.

QUESTIONS OF DECADENCE vs. IMPROVEMENT. — The scope of reliable information is today so narrow that the question of the increase of that restlessness that was described in the last chapter as an illustration of social mal-adaptation can be summarily dealt with. There is no reliable evidence of such increase. If restlessness is more apparent today than it was a generation ago it may be so for the reason that there are more instruments now than there were formerly for registering the varied voices of unrest: that is, there is a vast increment of periodicals, of lecture platforms, of organizations, and the like, for the expression of opinion than formerly could be found, and for these and other reasons communication is speedy today as compared with that of a half century ago and less. Furthermore, even if an increase could be demonstrated it could hardly, unqualifiedly, be interpreted as a sign either of absolute or relative progressive decay. It might, on the other hand, be attributed to an intellectual awakening to unnecessary inequalities and injustices in the social order. Certain unrest undoubtedly springs from pathological or from defective natures and is contagious amongst others of approximately the same sort to the embarrassment of the social order. But it was the unrest of individuals and their mal-adaptation to conditions as they were that led to Magna Charta and to the American and French Revolutions. That the spirit of unrest is abroad is one of the hopeful things in any generation, assuming, of course, that it is an expression of a healthy vitality and that it is guided by enlightened leaders.

Neither is there satisfactory evidence of the increase of mental defect and of mental disease over a generation. According to the reports of the United States Census Bureau the mentally diseased in the hospitals of the United States, in proportion to the population of the country has increased from 81.6 per hundred thousand in 1880, to 118.2 in 1890, to 183.6 in 1904, and to 204.2 in 1910. In the report of 1880 it was estimated that there were 101.7 insane per hundred thousand of the general population outside of institutions in this country, and in 1890 when the estimate was made on a different basis the figure was reduced. These estimates are probably very inaccurate.

In England and Wales the total number of insane per hundred thousand inside of institutions and outside of them by decades from 1859 to 1899 inclusive, and yearly from 1904 to 1908 inclusive, is as follows: 186.7, 239.3, 275.4, 296.5, 329.6, 347.1, 350.9, 353.1, 354.8, and 366.7. Other European countries show much the same increase in the reported numbers of the insane. But the increment that is suggested in these figures may be a reflection of the increase and improvement of facilities, legislative and institutional, for the care of the insane and for their discovery and diagnosis. The farther back we go the smaller is the number of insane segregated in institutions and therefore the less complete is the enumeration. The same considerations apply to the question of the increase of feeble-mindedness or mental defect. Recent legislation, grown out of general enlightenment with respect to the subject, has immensely stimulated the discovery and enumeration of the feeble-minded.

The prevalence of crime as reported in what statistics are available is no less sensitive a barometer of legislation, of economic and industrial conditions, of the state of mind of the people who compose a community, and even of orders from police headquarters. If a group of citizenry persistently insist upon the prosecution of offenders in a certain type of cases, and if the chief of police gives the appropriate orders to his force, the showing of offenses of the sort will be larger, at least temporarily, than otherwise. Furthermore, at least in America, there is no systematic and reliable body of criminal statistics of more than very limited scope. Moreover there are undoubtedly

many sociological and economic causes of crime which
are effective in co-operation with psycho-physical
causes, and, for that matter, altogether independent
of psychic or of physical defect.

An alleged decreasing death rate and an increasing
average duration of life have been accepted as support
for the proposition that the members of the race are
improving their capacity for adapting themselves to
their complex environment. This may be due, not to
an increased resistance on the part of the race but
to an accession of skill on the part of physicians and
hygienists in warding off diseases and so in prolonging
life. On the other hand Rittenhouse of the Equitable
Life Insurance Company claims that the mortality
from degenerative diseases is increasing for all ages
of life (7). He says: " In sixteen cities the mortality
rate from heart, apoplexy and kidney affections alone
has increased in thirty years from 17.94 to 34.78, or
94 per cent; during ten years (1900–1910) it increased from 29.4 to 36.78 or 18 per cent. In
New Jersey (1880–1910) it increased from 16.5
to 34.3 or 108 per cent." He shows also that
in these cities the death rate in ages over 45–54
has increased. According to the same author
this is true also of Massachusetts and New
Jersey. In these states the death rate of the total
population aged 40 and over has increased during
thirty years (1880–1910) 21.2 per cent; in sixteen
cities, 25.3 per cent, and in ten states from 1900–1910,
3 per cent. The writer concludes from such data as
these that while the average length of life has increased the extreme span has been shortened. Upon

this point Holmes urges a caution and says: ". . . the increasing mortality after middle age in this country may be largely explained by the increasing proportion of foreigners and their immediate descendants, among whom the average expectation of life is considerably lower than among the native population of native parentage. As an inspection of Glover's life tables will show, the differences in the mortality rates of the native and the foreign-born become greater with advanced ages, although they have become reduced in extreme age. That the decreasing longevity in advanced age groups is not a general characteristic of modern civilization is indicated by a comparison of the life tables of several countries of Europe. Taking the expectation of life at sixty years as an index of vitality in old age, we find in France a slight increase from 1861–1865, when it was 13.55 years, to 13.58 years in 1877–1881, and a further increase in 1898–1903 to 13.81 years. The increased expectation of life at sixty years in Germany is shown as follows:

Dates	1871–1881	1881–1890	1891–1900	1901–1910
Expected years of life	12.11	12.43	12.82	13.14

Denmark shows a steadily increasing expectation of life at sixty years from 1835–1844 to 1900, and Norway shows a general increase since 1856 and Sweden since 1861. The expectation of life at sixty years in England fell somewhat from the middle of the 19th century to 1881–1890, after which it has increased about two years. For the past thirty to forty years people of the old-age groups have been living slightly

longer on the average in Australia also. In the more
advanced ages the expected duration of life has shown
a smaller amount of increase, but in a number of
countries even the man of eighty may count on living
a little longer than he would a few decades ago."

The nature of the variations in the birth rate from
group to group in the general population is another
phenomenon that occasions misgivings as to the ability
of the race to adapt itself to the vast complexities
of modern civilization and to sustain it. Those districts that show evidence of prosperity have a low
birth rate while in poverty-stricken regions the reverse
is true. Bertillon gives the following figures relating
to the birth rate per thousand women aged 15 to 50
years in four European cities (1):

	Paris	Berlin	Vienna	London
Very poor districts	108	157	200	147
Poor	95	129	164	140
Comfortable	72	114	155	107
Very comfortable	65	96	153	107
Rich	53	63	107	87
Very rich	34	47	71	63

It has been estimated that the death rate in the
poorer districts is not sufficiently high to counter-
balance the distribution of the above figures.

Among the graduates of three American colleges
for women, the birth-rate per hundred is as follows:

Number of Children per 100

1890–99	1900–09
147	68.8
171.5*	77.4
182.3	91.2

Such data can be multiplied and from them students have drawn the disturbing conclusions that we are losing our native American stock and that those elements in our population that have achieved success financially, socially and intellectually are being lost. Other supplementary data, furthermore — namely the known fecundity of the mentally defective — lead some to fear that the average level of intelligence may become progressively lower rather than higher — a result that would necessarily make it impossible, ultimately, to sustain civilization at its present level of complexity and that would cause a progressive social decay, rather than further growth.

No data of the sort referred to thus far in this chapter afford sufficient proof of the decadence of the race, and even if extensive changes of the sort had taken place it is certain that the facts could not be established by the kind of records that have been compiled. In other words, up to this point, there are no reliable data that deny the potentiality of the race for sustaining the present level of civilization at its highest and even of lifting it to higher planes.

FACTORS AFFECTING DEVELOPMENT. — Possibly we can judge of the present trend of racial development by a study of some of the forces that are assumed to be producing changes in human nature. The most prominent of these and perhaps the most potent is urban life.

In the United States the per cent of the total population in cities of 8,000 and over has increased rapidly from 3.35 in 1790 to 38.8 in 1910. Including those who were living in towns and cities of 2,500 or more inhabitants, the per cent was 46.3 in 1910, and it is probably over 50% at the present time. It is estimated that 30.7% of the increase in urban population in this country has been produced by migration from the rural districts, so that the population of cities is increasing much more rapidly than is that of the country at large.

The crude death rate in the city is lower than in rural districts. The actual condition, however, is obscured by the fact that that portion of the population of the city that is made up of adolescents and of men and women in the prime of life is relatively large. Such people crowd into the cities on account of the opportunities afforded there for occupation and for preparation for a profession, or what not. The following figures show the age composition of the cities of Germany and the rest of the country, respectively (5):

No. per 1,000

Inhabitants	Under 16 yrs.	16–30	30–50	50–70	Over 70
In large cities............305		301	264	111	19
Outside of large cities....380		234	226	131	29

The mortality by age groups is indicated in the following (5):

Deaths per 10,000 in Germany (Mombert) 1900–1901

	In large cities	Outside large cities
Died in 1st year................2322		2134
” ” 1st to 15th yr..........1073		930
” ” 15th to 60th yr.......... 899		879
” ” 60th yr...............6861		7207

These figures show the city at a disadvantage and so do those relating to the per cent of recruits accepted in Germany in 1907 and 1908 for military service. According to Bindewald the larger the city the smaller the per cent accepted and the largest per cent of all are from the country. That this is not a reflection of the occupations of city and rural men respectively, is shown by the fact that the same condition holds within the occupations.

These considerations suggest that the city exceeds the country in the strength of its deteriorating influences, and that the enormous growth of cities at the expense of other districts imparts increased potency to them.

What these influences are may be conjectured. Crowding and poor housing afford peculiar opportunity for infection, but medical and hygienic science may be expected to keep pace, as the years go on, with this factor. Other conditions are probably more serious. The rural migrant and the immigrant from foreign countries suffer a considerable break-up of their conventional anchorages. They drift and are at once living a life to which they are not accustomed. The morals of the weaker ones suffer and the conditions are all the more favorable for deterioration. Add to these considerations the fact that the city affords innumerable stimuli of all sorts that arouse as many reactions and we have that constant state of tension or of excitement that Nordau emphasizes among the deteriorating influences of the day. It is not difficult to conceive of the condition we have in mind if we imagine the number and character of the stimuli our grandfathers experienced each day of business in the town or upon the farm and compare them with the situations we meet today in the heart of a great city. Even the journey to the city today entails responses to unknown numbers of stimuli where our grandfathers responded to but one. Compare the noisy subway or elevated with the horse and carriage. It is not to the point to urge that we become accustomed to the thousand jangles of the train and that we do not notice them. Nor is it pertinent to urge that because we have got into the way of sleeping soundly during the night, surrounded by city noises, they have no effect upon us. When we have become so accustomed and have gone to the country for a week we are usually sleepless at night for the silence of the surroundings. This is proof enough that during the nights when we are asleep in the city we are, though unconsciously, reacting to the city noises. If this is the case our muscle system must be tensed up, and the organism is not at rest. In the long run our organisms are being torn down by these conditions. This is undoubtedly a sound position. It is entirely conceivable that the conditions operate to break the health ultimately, to impair our effectiveness and even to shorten life.

But even though we assume that this is actually the case it does not afford indubitable proof that the city, in however long a run, is producing conditions that, by tearing down the quality of the race, stand in the way of the maintenance and even of increasing the complexity of our civilization. There are undoubtedly many compensating factors by dint of which conceivably, in the course of a shorter period of life, or of health, more may be accomplished than in a longer.

It is pertinent, at any rate, in this connection to make a reference to experimental work with distracting stimuli (for the multitude of stimulations that the city dweller and worker meets daily may be described as distractions). By distracting stimuli one means stimulations that tend to produce reactions that are different from those required by the work in hand. When we are writing letters at our desk and the shouts of bathers in the lake reach our ears we are receiving distracting stimuli: distracting, because they tend to arouse in us those reactions that are preparatory to swimming or bathing in the lake rather than the reactions of writing. Morgan, for instance, has shown that, when the stimulating value of a problem or task in hand, whatever it may be, is kept at high pitch, the loss in output, or decrease in work done on account of distraction is less than has been popularly supposed, notwithstanding that in such circumstances the subject works with more effort than otherwise. He required his subjects to press a key similar to that of a typewriter a certain number of times when a given symbol appeared. The behavior was probably not very different from that of typewriting. As the subject continued to make his adjustments a firebell with an eight-inch gong was sounded directly behind and eight feet away. Bells of other sorts, buzzers and phonograph records were used also. He concludes that the *initial* effect of such distractions was to retard the subject's speed in successively pressing the key . . . no doubt an . . . effect of shock. But after this initial retardation there was *an increase of speed*. During the period of distraction extra pres-

DISTRACTING STIMULI 291

sure was exerted upon the keys and there were changes in breathing and more or less verbal articulation occurred. *By means of this additional muscular effort the amount of work done per unit of time was not materially decreased* (6).

It is appropriate to the same situation that Watson says (9): " One of the most striking illustrations of this was observed in the army. In the Air Personnel office when the force was small typewriters had to be stopped when long-distance calls were answered. As the pressure of the work was increased and as the office force trebled and quadrupled, it was no uncommon sight to see a man answering a long-distance telephone call with fifteen or twenty typewriters going in his immediate neighborhood and a hundred or more going in the one large room." With respect to this sort of situation Watson says further that " while experimentation over short periods of time may show that such stimuli are without immediate effect, it still seems safest to have offices and factories arranged so that the worker is as free as possible from extraneous disturbances. The wear and tear upon the human organism is probably a positive thing even though temporary laboratory studies fail to give marked evidence of it ": a precautionary statement that may run only to the question of the duration of the period over which successful adjustment to the conditions of work may be maintained and to the duration of life itself. The statement does not necessarily apply, however, to the possibility of the individual's adjustment to the complexities of daily life in such manner that the work entailed by our civilization, and even more complex orders of life, may be done and done effectively.

Compensations for the alleged drains upon human vitality and capacity incident to the diverse pushings and pullings of a thousand varied stimuli may be effected as we go on from period to period in proportion as employers of labor and other leaders who deal with men encourage systematic studies aimed at improving the conditions in which work is done and then take advantage of the results of such studies.

For example, the results of a certain investigation bear upon the proper adjustment of periods of work and rest. The " Iron Age," quoted by Watson, describes a situation in which a group of laborers who were engaged in wheeling heavy loads in barrows up an incline were offered a premium for increased amounts of this labor, but without result. " Prompt investigation by an expert disclosed that the trouble lay in the fact that the men were working without sufficiently frequent periods of rest. Thereupon, a foreman was stationed by a clock, and every twelve minutes he blew a whistle. At the sound every barrowman stopped where he was, sat down on his barrow, and rested for three minutes. The first hour after that was done showed a remarkable change for the better in accomplishment; the second day the men all made the premium allowance by doing more than what had been too much; and on the third day the minimum compensation had to risen, on the average, 40 per cent, with no complaints from overdriving from any of the force."

Other investigations relative to the effects of quantity and quality of food and drink, narcotics, cocaine and the like upon the capacity of the organism to endure the complex strains of a modern day's work are significant in this connection. Rivers, for example, has the following to say of the effect of doses of alcohol upon the capacity to work: " In the case of muscular work, we have seen that there is a definite evidence that small doses, varying from 5 to 20 c.c. of absolute alcohol, have no effect on the amount or nature of the work performed with the ergograph, either immediately or within several hours of their administration, the results previously obtained by other workers being almost certainly due to defects of experimental method. With a larger dose of 40 c.c. there was evidence — in one case, at least — of an increase in the amount of work under the influence of the substance; but the increase was uncertain and inconstant, and the possibility cannot be excluded that it was due to disturbing factors. With larger doses than 40 c.c., we have the work of Hellsten, showing a decided falling off in the amount of work with a dose of 80 grammes " (8).

Upon the effects of caffeine Hollingworth has made comprehensive tests during a period of forty days, covering speed of movement, motor co-ordination and steadiness. There was an increase in the speed of movement which depended somewhat upon the size of the dose from 2 to 6 grains. The effect was usually noticed within an hour and lasted from 1 to 4 hours. There was no secondary depression within 72 hours. Small doses appeared to increase the efficiency of motor co-ordinations but larger doses of 4 to 6 grains decreased it. Both small and large doses appeared to occasion tremor. Caffeine doses of every size appeared to increase the efficiency of certain intellectual functions like association, and naming of colors, and the increase lasted during 3 to 7 hours. Speed at the typewriter was increased by small doses and decreased by larger ones (4).

The experimental studies of the effect of tobacco indicate that it is always a depressant. This is recognized by athletic trainers who prohibit its use by members of a team.

The point in all this discussion is that as experts study and report upon such subjects as those referred to above — and one may add dietetics to the list — knowledge will be accumulated and disseminated in the light of which such self-control may be instituted as will go a long way toward compensating for the extraordinary tensity of the conditions under which we are living. It places a responsibility upon educators and educational institutions not only to search out the truth relating to every aspect of human adaptation but to broadcast the truth in such a vitalized atmosphere that not only the leaders but the populace as well will seek it and react to it; for the ideal in these relations is attained when the restraints and impulsions by which individuals and groups make their compensations are *self-imposed*. However benevolent the motives of leaders may be they, in the long run, contribute to the unhappiness and hence to the ineffectiveness of their followers when they impose their " thou shalts " and their " thou shalt nots " from without.

Obviously it is premature to urge or conclude that human nature is incapable of sustaining so complex a civilization as ours, let alone a more complicated one, until we first shall have exhausted the possibilities that lie in the line of economizing, not wasting, our human capacities, and so compensating for the assumed destructive over-stimulation of our day. Each of us has observed individual instances, at least, in which such compensation has been actually realized. There is undoubtedly a deal of truth in the frequently quoted statement (though obviously it does not lend itself to accurate verification) that men do not use more than 25% of their muscular power nor more than 10% of their mental ability.

Those who question from time to time the capacity of the race to advance the complexity of modern life far beyond its present level or even to sustain it at its present pitch are wont to draw attention to the fact that President Lincoln never communicated by means of the telephone nor had his letters written by typewriters nor rode on an electric car and the like; and much more recent characters never sped from place to place by gasoline motor car or by airplane. The assumption is made in such connections that human nature can not stand up under such sudden and extreme transitions. But the acuteness of the readjustments implied as required of individuals whose lives have spanned the era of invention through which we have been passing is much overdrawn. If our fathers, before they had attained their majority, had never talked over a telephone, they nevertheless had talked; they had dictated their letters prior to middle age though not to a typist; they had controlled other machines before they undertook the gasoline engine;

they had been transported from place to place in a high-powered motor car before they rode in the air. The point is that, however novel the experience of a new day, some habits have already been acquired that serve as a foundation stone and so facilitate the transition. Strictly there is nothing new under the sun. Furthermore, our ancestors of a hundred years ago were wont to speak now and again of the complexities of their times — which seem to us simple almost beyond comparison with ours. Again, it has never been necessary, and it is not needful now, that an individual, even a leader, comprehend the whole of an intricate civilization — let alone, possess in his own person the capacities to sustain it *in toto*. Specializations of adjustment there have always been and they must be more and more numerous as the faces of civilization become more manifold. What is needful and more needful with the multiplying angles of social life is that men and women become better and better acquainted with the conditions that affect the psychophysical life of the organism and its capacities to react to many types of situations. As such knowledge increases we will be in progressively better position to direct ourselves and others so as to increase accomplishment without increment of energy expended.

Our present knowledge affords no measuring rod, to determine in advance the extreme possibilities of adjustment either for an individual or for a group. We have again and again been amazed to see the capacity of an individual to handle himself creditably when he has been thrust into a situation of unusual complexity entailing heavy responsibility. And the World War

similarly afforded in every warring nation illustration
of unthought-of capability for mass and co-operative
effort. As to America's part in it Le Bon says (5);
". . . Thanks to the vigor of its character, the
American people, despite its love of comfort and
independence, was able in a few months to adapt itself
to all the necessities involved in such a conflict.

"Its devotion was absolute. Accepting entirely
novel conditions of existence, it renounced all the
liberties of which it was so proud, subjected itself to
the abnormal despotism of the state, to severe privations, and above all to that obligatory military system
of which the very idea had formerly seemed intolerable
to it.

"All sorts of inconveniences were suffered without
a murmur. No taxation seemed too heavy, and in the
trenches of Europe the improvised American soldiers
acquitted themselves as valiantly as the best."

*Let there be but increased motivation and, with our
knowledge of human nature as it is, we can enormously
increase the quantity and quality of our output even
in the face of unaccustomed complexities.*

In the next place, with respect to our capacity to
sustain what we have built, there is surely an automatic control; it is hardly conceivable that the race
would build that to which it can not make a successful adjustment, any more than a manufacturer would
build a machine so complicated that men would be
unable to comprehend it and to control it.

Finally — running now to the question of the ability
of the race both to maintain what has already been
built and to build further — it is a question of our

capacity for learning; that is, our capacity for forming habits and complexes in the background of our personalities. At the same time, it is a question of maintaining sufficient pliability in human nature so that the individual may not be entirely breakable and helpless in the face of a variety of differing and changing circumstances. This is the duplex purpose of education that both now and always tries the soul of the educator, of the curriculum and of the system of education; to build individuals who will be always substantially and doggedly upon the road toward high ends, — which implies a vision to see those ends — and at the same time so pliable that he can co-operate with many others who are not entirely like himself, compromising where necessary, in order that all together they may the sooner realize their purpose.

Now it will be conceded that the building of habits and complexes is less the creation of new " pathways " in the nervous system and more the modification and the linking up of larger or smaller habits and complexes that are already a part of the organization.

These linkings together are called neurone patterns because the individual elements or units are so thoroughly knitted together and co-ordinated that they altogether function as one. They, on their part, are the products of every adjustment and partial adjustment that the organism has made in the course of its history. For it is assumed upon the basis of good evidence that has been brought to light in recent years by means of many psychiatric investigations that the effects within the organism of no single experience are ever entirely erased but that they persist and, singly and collectively, make up the substantial background of our personality. They determine the character of our dreams, our phantasy, our fears and obsessions, our prejudices and conventions, our interests and desires, our all but unconscious feelings of continuous urging toward the purposes of life, and our capacities for adjustment. These are the more or less submerged complexes of our personality. They are just as numerous as are the spontaneous and other movements of the babe and the growing child plus the reflexes and simple and complex habits, prejudices, likes and dislikes, of the youth and the adult. The number of possible combinations of these units or patterns into new complexes — the number of new habits or adjustments that are possible theoretically for an individual — could be determined only by application of the rule of permutations given the correct number of units to start with; and the permutations of even a hundred units, to say nothing of more of them, is sufficient to stagger computation.

From such theoretical considerations as this, and in view of the probability that research may teach us how to conserve our energy, it would appear to be a groundless fear that our civilization must crumble due to the frailities of human nature. They should, on the other hand, contribute to our confidence in the possibilities that lie in mankind for further building, so far, at least, as its maintenance and building depend upon developing the mechanism of human nature and upon understanding the conditions in which it may operate most effectively.

When we speak in this manner of developing a

mechanism we mean to suggest training in technique which is implied in 'technical education. As complexities are added, one after another, to the conditions of community life, technical education becomes more and more essential in order that the many phases of necessary activity in the city and state may be done successfully and in order that the whole web of civilization may be kept intact and made to grow.

No person can be adapted all along the line. If he could be, the question of this chapter might easily be answered in the affirmative: civilization can be maintained at its present level and pushed to higher levels, for in such a case, very few at most will suffer and fall from the failure of one. Each one would copy his successful neighbor on the whole line and avoid the errors of the unsuccessful. Community life, such as there would be, would run on smoothly. This is precisely the way things go in primitive pioneer life where each person, or each family is an economic unit. But, as we have said, no one individual in a complex life can be adapted all along the line. He is by necessity a specialist in considerable measure (though there must be many, too, who are not in the strict sense specialists). As a specialist the product of his work must join up smoothly with that of many another: as, for example, when one man is making the cylinder of an engine and another, miles away, the piston; or when one is making a certain drug and putting it up for use, and another is practicing medicine. In these instances and hundreds of the like training in technique, — that is, training in doing things according to rules and formulae that have been generally agreed upon is a *sine qua non* of highly civilized life. This is a point that many educators, of an older generation, whose outlook was that of a much simpler time than ours, apparently find it difficult to comprehend. Technical education must be on the increase in such a time, and in such circumstances as ours.

But at the same time, *merely* technical education (as we might say, in a " narrow " sense) defeats its own ends. A striking illustration of this point is at hand in the experience of a youth, — a ward of the juvenile court, — who, by the aid of a probation officer, found employment in the shoe section in the basement of a large department store. He had grown up in a small village and was confused by the complexity of his immediate surroundings. He was active and of normal intelligence but he " could not see the town for the houses," judging from his account of himself, and he quit his " technical training in the narrow sense " at the bottom of a long ladder that could conceivably have led him to eminence. A young girl from the country entered a training school for nurses. Her somewhat slow imagination had not yet been stirred and she did not see that her tedious training was dovetailing usefully into a vast web of interrelated social functions. She dropped training after a few months of apparently hopeless inefficiency in the training school and returned to her home. In the course of a year she began to see the larger meaning of it all, re-entered the school, completed her training with credit, and at once became successfully adapted and enthusiastic in her occupation.

The point in these illustrations is that the technical training that our day requires must be accompanied by a heavy emphasis upon a view of a broad social landscape. What do the men and women of one calling contribute to those of another? What are the capacities, habits, prejudices and likes and dislikes, in the large, of the groups and classes of people who compose the state? What is the machinery by which men and women of one group co-operate with one another? What are the indications of failure and of success in co-operation? The technical student must be led to think seriously upon such questions as these if he will be successful in the larger sense demanded by our civilization. These questions, like those of a more narrowly technical sort, must, as far as possible, be tested in the crucible of the laboratory method, — for even history can be approached from the angle of the laboratory and there is nothing compared to it as a means for developing the open and interrogative mind that guarantees both stability and pliability of nature. This is the scientific spirit, and it, quite as well as blind adherence to the doctrine of high protection, may become conventional.

The emphasis of the education of the day so far as it relates to the development of specialists, or to fitting men and women into "jobs" must be at the same time upon technique and upon broad social relationships such as will eventuate in mutual understanding or the ability to "put one's self into the other fellow's shoes." This involves some redirection of educational effort, to be sure, but at the same time it puts the broad-visioned professional or incidental teacher where he belongs. Those who dwell intellectually, for the most part, in the realm of ideas and of ideals and who are impatient and unhappy amidst the details of technical procedure in the shop, in the laboratory, and at the counter belong in a place of immense advantage for the *running of affairs* in a complicated civilization. The greater the number of specialists the larger must be the group of capable men and women who think in large outlines of the whole web of civilization.

Professor William James' figurative saying is a truism: " We learn to swim during the winter and to skate during the summer." We learn some things of utter importance about running a business so as to meet the needs of our civilization even when we are far away from the statistical laboratory and the interest tables, studying even human nature and the aspirations of groups of people, whether we find these people in the fields or in authoritative literature. These things will determine how they may unite and co-operate satisfactorily.

APPENDIX I

THE ALPHA AND BETA TESTS

At many points in the text very frequent reference has been made to the Alpha and Beta tests that were used in the United States Army in the course of the Great War and to the results of their application to the problems of race differences and intelligence levels. For those who are not already familiar with these tests this sketchy description is added. For a detailed description and account of the method of use of the tests the reader is referred to The National Academy of Sciences — Memoirs, Volume XV, 1921, Part I, Chapter 5.

The Alpha test was designed for the literate as defined in the army; that is, for those who had such a command of the English language that they could read simple directions and requests for information regarding their age, nativity, occupation, schooling and the like, and not only so but to write replies thereto. Those who satisfied the examiners on this score were admitted to the group examination Alpha.

The Beta test was made up for those who were illiterate in this sense, and for those who were unable to make use of the English language; certain recent immigrants, for example.

Each of these tests comprises a number of part tests and each part requires of the persons who are being examined from ten to forty responses or answers. One or two samples of each part test are included for the purpose of illustration.

1. The first test gets at the examinee's capacity to grasp and follow very simple verbal directions. For example: "When I say 'Go' make a cross in the space that is in the triangle but not in the square, and also make a figure '1' in the space that is in the triangle and in the square. — Go!" This is the fourth

item in the first part Test 1, — (Not over 10 seconds are allowed for this performance).

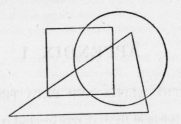

2. The second test comprises twenty arithmetical problems of various degrees of complexity as: "How many are 30 men and 7 men?" and "A commission house which has already supplied 1897 barrels of apples to a cantonment delivered the rest of its stock to 29 mess halls. Each mess hall received 54 barrels. What was the total number of barrels supplied?" Spaces are provided for answers and the recruit is asked to supply them as quickly as possible.

The number and quality of the answers in this test indicate at once, within the limits of the test, the degree of the soldier's profit from school training and his capacity to handle arithmetical concepts and his intellectual insight into arithmetical situations.

The directions are as follows: "Attention! Look at the directions at the top of the page while I read them. 'Get the answers to these examples as quickly as you can. Use the side of this page to figure on if you need to.' I will say 'Stop' at the end of five minutes. You are not expected to finish all of them but to do as many as you can in the time allowed. The two samples are already answered correctly. — Ready, — Go!"

3. Number three is a test of practical judgment. Following is the preamble or direction in the printed form: "This is a test of common sense. Below are sixteen questions. Four answers are given to each question. You are to look at the answers carefully; then make a cross in the square before the best answer to each question as in the sample: 'Why do we use stoves? Because — they look well, — they are black — , they

keep us warm —, they are made of iron.' Here the third answer is the best one and is marked with a cross. Begin with No. 1 and keep on until time is called." (Before each alternative, as in the sample, a small square is printed, and in the sample a cross is inserted before the third choice.) One minute is allowed for the test.

4. In the next test forty pairs of words are set down, some of which are opposites. The directions are as follows: "If the two words of a pair mean the same or nearly the same, draw a line under *same*. If they mean the opposite or nearly the opposite draw a line under *opposite*. If you cannot be sure, guess. The two samples are already marked as they should be. Below are reproduced the first five of the forty pairs and the samples for the examinee's guidance. One and one half minutes are allowed.

5. The fifth test consists of 24 groups of mixed words each of which will make a sentence, true or false when properly arranged. The examinee is instructed to *think* their proper arrangement — not to write them out — and to indicate the character of statement they would make by underscoring either the word "true" or the word "false." Two minutes are allowed. Below are reproduced the first and the twenty-fourth groups:

1. dogs meat eat. ...... true ...... false.

24. cardinal not cultivated virtues the be should. ...... true ...... false.

This may be interpreted as a test of general information though it is more particularly so of mental alertness as indicated by the use of words.

6. Number six is a "number series completion test." There are twenty groups, each containing five numbers. Each number has a certain relation to those that precede it. The examinee is to discover this relation and when he has done so, he is to use it in supplying a sixth number in the series. Two samples are printed on the sheet as follows: 2, 4, 6, 8, 10 — (here the sixth, obviously is 12 and it, in the sample, has been printed in heavy type in the space provided for it.) 11, 12, 14, 15, 17, — (here the sixth number of the series should be 18 and in the sample that number is printed in heavy type in its proper place.) Two minutes are allowed.

7. The ninth is an analogies test. The directions to the examinee are approximately as follows: "In each of the lines below, the first two words have a certain relation. Notice that relation and draw a line under the *one* word in the parenthesis which has that particular relation to the third word. Begin with No. 1 and mark as many sets as you can before time is called." There are forty sets. Three samples, properly marked, are as follows: Sky — blue; grass — (grow, green cut, dead). Fish — swims: Man — (boy, woman, walks, girl). Day — night: white — (red, black, clear, pure). Three minutes are allowed.

8. This is a general information test, samples of which are as follows: "The anvil is used in — blacksmithing, — carpentry — , typewriting, — bookkeeping." "Jess Willard is a — fortune-teller, — labor-leader — , pugilist, — singer." "Bile is made in the — liver, — kidneys, — spleen, — stomach."

The test includes forty such arrangements as these. In each, there are four choices and the examinee is asked to underscore the word that, with the fore part of the arrangement, makes the truest sentence. There is but one correct underscoring in each case.

The test as a whole affords a standard by which to assist the examiner in forming an estimate of the soldier's mental alertness and interest in a very wide range of subjects. Three minutes are allowed for this performance.

This completes the Alpha test, (Form 7). Other forms vary more or less from this. A definite time is allowed for each part, and it is so brief that one must work very rapidly to cover the whole. In fact, few can complete any test before time is called. Taken together, the responses afford a good outlook over a wide range of capacities and as well, an index of one's alertness.

The Beta test for illiterates comprises (in its final form) seven part tests. Neither reading nor writing is involved in making answer.

1. In the first test are five mazes or labyrinths, simple and complex. The examinee can pass his pencil through from entrance to exit, following of alleys, so to speak, formed here by vertical and there by horizontal lines. He can do so without

touching a line, and this is his problem. There are many blind alleys to be avoided.

This may be described as a test of the speed of visual perception of a complex situation, and of hand-eye coordination. A sample, the fifth maze, is reproduced below.

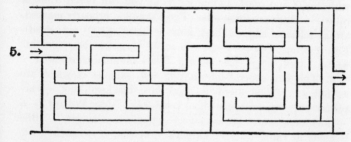

2. The second test is for ability at cube analysis. Sixteen piles of small cubes are illustrated. Not all are visible in the drawing. The examiner has solid models at hand, by the aid of which he suggests to the examinees that each drawing represents a solid body. They are then to estimate the number of small cubes in the group, and write the number in a space provided therefor. Below are samples:

Test 2

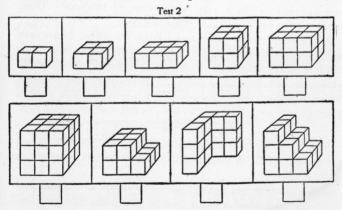

3. The third is the "x-o" test. It is somewhat analogous to the number completion test in Alpha. A more or less com-

plex scheme of repetitions of x and 0 is set forth on the sheet.
The examinee must find by insight what the scheme is in twelve
instances and carry it on through several spaces. The samples
below will be understandable:

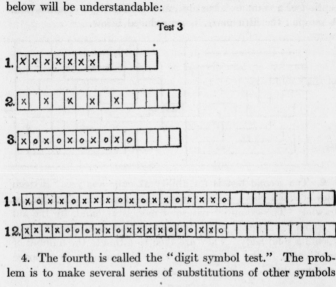

Test 3

1. | X | X | X | X | X | X | X | | | | |

2. | X | | X | | X | | X | | X | | | | | |

3. | X | o | X | o | X | o | X | o | X | o | | | |

11. | X | o | X | X | o | X | X | X | o | X | o | X | X | o | X | X | X | o | | | | | | | |

12. | X | X | X | X | o | o | o | o | X | X | o | X | X | X | X | X | o | o | o | o | X | X | o | | | | | | | | | | |

4. The fourth is called the "digit symbol test." The problem is to make several series of substitutions of other symbols

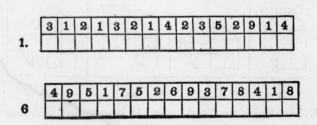

Test 4

1	2	3	4	5	6	7	8	9
−	И	Ↄ	L	∪	0	∧	X	=

1. | 3 | 1 | 2 | 1 | 3 | 2 | 1 | 4 | 2 | 3 | 5 | 2 | 9 | 1 | 4 |
| | | | | | | | | | | | | | | |

6 | 4 | 9 | 5 | 1 | 7 | 5 | 2 | 6 | 9 | 3 | 7 | 8 | 4 | 1 | 8 |
| | | | | | | | | | | | | | | |

for digits. Thus the digit "1," wherever it occurs in a series, is always to be substituted for by a dash (—): the digit "8" by a cross (x) etc.

5. In the fifth test the examinee is required to place a cross between two numbers that are alike and to leave vacant the space between unlike numbers. There are fifty pairs of numbers before him and they vary in length from three to eleven digits. The pairs are equally divided as to the likeness and unlikeness of their numbers.

Test 5

650	 650		10243586	 10243586
041	 044		659012534	 6590211354
2579	 2579		388172902	 381872902
3281	 3281		631027594	 631027594
55190	 55102		2499901354	 2499901534

6. The sixth is a picture completion test. Twenty drawings are on the sheet and each one is incomplete in some one detail; the pistol, e.g., lacks a trigger, the violin lacks strings, the tennis court with players upon it in action has no net. The missing parts are to be supplied. This requires a quick insight, not into the relations of ideas, but into objects.

Test 6

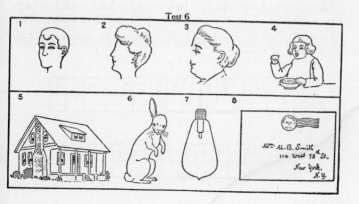

7. The last in this series of tests in on "geometrical construction." There are ten parts, each of which contains the drawing of a square, and, in addition, two or three other geometric figures. The examinee's problem is to show by lines drawn within the square that the other objects will just fill it.

Test 7

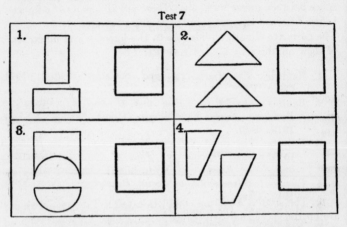

All together, the Beta tests are assumed to afford an indication of an individual's untrained ability to understand and to execute orders, to perceive quickly the nature of an objective situation, and the like.

A method of scoring was devised and used in connection with these tests by the aid of which letter grades were assigned for various degrees of excellence in performance in connection with each series of tests.

APPENDIX II

REFERENCES AND EXERCISES

CHAPTER I

1. Baldwin: *The Individual and Society;* Boston, 1911, Chap. VII.
2. Bentley: *Studies in Social and General Psychology:* A Preface to Social Psychology. Psych. Monog. XXI, 4, 1916, 6–25.
3. Editors: The Field of Social Psychology and its Relation to Abnormal Psychology. *Jour. of Abnormal Psychology and Social Psychology*, XVI, 1, 3–7, April, 1921.
4. Ellwood: *Introduction to Social Psychology.* New York, 1917, Chap. I.
5. McDougall: *The Group Mind.* New York, 1921, Chap. I.
6. McDougall: *Introduction to Social Psychology*, 13th ed. Boston, 1918, Chap. I.
7. Ross: *Social Psychology.* New York, 1918, Chap. I.
8. Tourtoulon: *Philosophy in the Development of Law* (translated by Martha McC. Read), New York, 1922, Chap. V.
9. Urwick: *Philosophy of Social Progress.* London, 1912, Chaps. IV and V.
10. Wallas: *The Great Society.* New York, 1914, Chap. II.
11. Woodworth: *Dynamic Psychology.* New York, 1918, Chap. VIII.

CHAPTER II

1. Davis: *Psychological Interpretations of Society.* New York, 1909, Chaps. XI and XII.
2. Ellwood: *Introduction to Social Psychology.* New York, 1917, Chaps. IV, V, VI.
3. Ellwood: *Sociology in its Psychological Aspects.* New York. 1912, pp. 143–152, 182–197.

4. Giddings: *The Principles of Sociology.* New York, 1896.
5. Gumplowicz: The Outlines of Sociology (English translation by Frederick W. Moore, of *Grundriss der Sociologie.* Wien, 1895). Bulletin of the American Academy of Political and Social Science, No. 253. Philadelphia, 1899, pp. 145–150. See also L. Gumplowicz, Le rôle des luttes sociales dans l'evolution de l'humanite. Annales de l'institut international de sociologie, XI, 1907, pp. 131–143.
6. McDougall: *The Group Mind.* Cambridge, 1920, Chaps. VI, VII, VIII, XI.
7. Stoddard: *The New World of Islam.* New York, 1921, Chap. V.
8. Tourtoulon: *Philosophy in the Development of Law.* New York, 1922, Chap. V, f.
9. Urwick: *A Philosophy of Social Progress.* London, 1912.

1. Write out a description of your feelings when you were tempted to participate in a form of conduct that is disapproved by your family and neighbors with whom you have lived until now, and that you yourself have until now more or less conventionally disapproved.

2. Write a statement of the means that you would adopt to develop a sense of unity in a football team, school, church, and club.

Chapter III

1. Ayres: Instinct and Capacity. *Jour. of Philos.,* XVIII, 1921, pp. 561–566.
2. Conradi: Song and Call Notes of English Sparrows when Reared by Canaries. *Amer. Jour. of Psych.,* XVI, 1905, 190–198.
3. Dewey: *Human Nature and Conduct.* New York, 1922.
4. Dunlap: The Identity of Instinct and Habit. *Jour. of Philos.,* XIX, 1922, pp. 85–94.
5. Dunlap: Are there any Instincts? *Jour. of Abnor. Psych.,* XIV, 1919, pp. 307–311.
6. Ellwood: *Introduction to Social Psychology.* New York, 1917, Chaps. III, IX, X, XI.
7. Gross: *Criminal Psychology.* Modern Criminal Science Series, Boston, 1911.

8. Kuo: Giving up Instincts in Psychology. *Jour. of Philos.* XVIII, 1921, pp. 645–664.

9. Mackenzie: *A Manual of Ethics* (pp. 37–38).

10. McDougall: *Introduction to Social Psychology*, 13th ed. Boston, 1918.

11. Muirhead: *Elements of Ethics* (p. 56).

12. O'Higgins: *The Secret Springs.* A Popular Treatment of Psycho-analysis. New York, 1922.

13. Prince: *The Unconscious.* New York, 1914.

14. Patrick: *The Psychology of Social Reconstruction.* New York, 1920.

15. Putnam: *Human Motives.* Boston, 1915.

16. Salleilles: *Individualization of Punishment.* The Modern Criminal Science Series. Boston, 1911, p. 240.

17. Scott: Data on Song in Birds: Observations on the Song of Baltimore Orioles in Captivity. *Science*, N. S. XIV, 1901, pp. 522–526.

18. Scott: Data on Song in Birds: The Acquisition of New Songs. *Science*, N. S. XV, 1902, pp. 178–181.

19. Scott: The Inheritance of Song: *Science*, N. S. XIX, 1904, pp. 154 and 957–959.

20. Scott: The Inheritance of Song. *Science*, N. S. XX, 1904, pp. 282–283.

21. Stocks: Motives. *Mind*, N. S. XX, 1911, pp. 54–66.

22. Tarde: *The Laws of Imitation.* Translated from the 2d French edition by Elsie Clews Parsons. New York, 1903.

23. Thorndike: *The Original Nature of Man.* New York, 1913.

24. Tolman: Instinct and Purpose. *Psych. Rev.* XXVII, 3, 1920, 217–233.

25. Trotter: *Instincts of the Herd in Peace and War.* London, 1916.

26. Watson: *Psychology from the Standpoint of a Behaviorist.* New York, 1919. Chaps. VII and VIII.

27. Woodworth: *Dynamic Psychology.* New York, 1918.

1. What are the traditional distinctions of instincts, reflexes, and habits?

2. Discuss the implications of *instinct* and *instincts*.

3. Describe as completely as possible two different instinctive acts you have performed within the last twenty-four hours and point out as accurately as possible their differences as well as their likenesses.

4. What is the meaning of the terms *complex* and *conflict* and why should a discussion of them enter into a chapter in Social Psychology?

5. What is the significance of the Freudian wish for the student of Social Psychology?

6. Write a short paper to show the bearing of this chapter upon industrial life.

7. An adult tendency or propensity may be simply an unmodified instinct, or it may be derived from instinct by combination, etc. Try to identify each of the following as an instinct, or to analyze it into two or more instincts:

> (*a*) Love for adventure.
> (*b*) Patriotism.
> (*c*) A father's pride in his children.
> (*d*) Love for travel.
> (*e*) Insubordination.
> (*f*) Love for dancing.

8. What so-called instincts are most concerned in making people work?

9. What so-called instincts find outlet in (*a*) dress, (*b*) automobiling, (*c*) athletics, (*d*) conversation?

CHAPTER IV

1. Bailey and Haber: Mental Deficiency: its Frequency and Characteristics in the United States as Determined by the Examination of Recruits. *Ment. Hyg.* IV, 3, 1920, 564–596.

2. Danielson and Davenport: The Nam Family. *Mem. Eugen. Rec. Off.* 2, 1912.

3. Danielson and Davenport: The Hill Folk. *Mem. Eugen. Rec. Off.*, I, 1912.

4. Davenport and Love: Defects Found in Drafted Men. *Sci. Mo.* X, 1, 1920, 5–26.

5. Dugdale: *The Jukes.* New York, 1877.

6. Estabrook: *The Jukes in 1915.* Washington, 1916.

7. Goddard: *The Kallikak Family.* New York, 1912.

8. Goddard: *Feeble-Mindedness, Its Causes and Consequences,* New York, 1914.

9. Holmes: *The Trend of the Race*. New York, 1921.
10. Kuhlmann: Distribution of the Feeble-Minded in Society. *Jour. of Crim. Law and Criminol.* VII, 2, 1916, 205–218.
11. *Memoirs of the National Academy of Sciences*, XV, Part III, Chaps. VIII, XI, XIII, 1921.
12. *Report of the Minister of Public Instruction for the Year 1911–1912.* Melbourne, 1913.
13. *Report of the Royal Commission on the Care and Control of the Feeble-Minded.* London, 1908.
14. Smith: Immigration and Defectives. *Canadian Jour. of Ment. Hyg.* II, 1, 1920, 73 ff.
15. White: *Principles of Mental Hygiene.* New York, 1917.

1. What methods are extant in your community (a) for discovering and encouraging those of high intellectual level? (b) for discovering those of low level and helping them to find themselves? (c) What methods would you recommend?

2. Write an appraisal of our methods of discovering the intellectual level of a group. What do you mean by "intellectual?"

CHAPTER V

1. Boas: *Mind of Primitive Man.* New York, 1911.
2. Boas: Human Faculty as Determined by Race. *Proceedings of the American Association for the Advancement of Science*, XLIII, 1894, 301–327.
3. Faris: Mental Capacity of Savages, *Amer. Jour. Sociol.* XXIII, 5, 603–619.
4. Ferguson, Jr.: The Psychology of the Negro. *Archives of Psychology*, XXV, 36, New York, 1916.
5. Fishberg: *The Jews. A Study of Race and Environment.* London and New York. 1911.
6. Garth: Proceedings of the Meeting of the American Psychological Association. *Psychol. Bul.*, 1921.
7. Gulick: *The American Japanese Problem.* A Study of the Racial Relations of the East and the West. New York, 1914.
8. Hunter: Proceedings of the American Psychological Association, *Psychol. Bul.*, 1921.
9. Le Bon: *Psychology of Peoples.* New York, 1899.
10. Le Bon: *The World in Revolt.* New York, 1921.

11. Mayo: Mental Capacity of the American Negro. *Archives of Psychology*, XXII, 28, 1913.

12. McDougall: *Is America Safe for Democracy?* New York, 1921, pp. 69, 70.

13. Memoirs of the National Academy of Sciences, XV, 1921. Part III, Chaps. 8 and 10.

14. Odum: Negro Children in the Public Schools of Philadelphia. *Amer. Acad. Pol. & Soc. Sci.*, XLIX, 86-208.

15. Park: Social Contacts and Race Conflict. (Introduction to Steiner, *The Japanese Invasion*, Chicago, 1917.)

16. Park: Racial Assimilation in Secondary Groups. Publications of the American Sociological Society, VIII (1913), 75-82.

17. Pyle: The Mentality of the Negro Compared with the Whites. *Psych. Bul.*, XII, 71, XIII, 82-83.

18. Pressey and Teter: A Comparison of Colored and White Children by Means of a Group Scale of Intelligence. *Jour. of App. Psychol.*, 1919.

19. Radosavljevich: The Psychology of the Slav. *The Russian Review*, III, 3, July, 1917.

20. Ross: Race Fibre of the Chinese. *Pop. Sci. Mo.*, LXXIX.

21. Stevenson: *Socio-Anthropometry: An Inter-Racial Critique.* Boston, 1916.

22. Stoddard: *The New World of Islam.* New York, 1921.

23. Stone: Is Race Friction between Blacks and Whites in the United States Growing and Inevitable? *American Jour. Sociol.*, XIII, 1907-1908, 677-698.

24. Strong: Three Hundred and Fifty White and Colored Children Measured by the Binet-Simon Scale of Intelligence. *Ped. Sem.*, XX, 1913, 485-515.

25. Thorndike: *Educational Psychology*, New York, 1913, Vol. II, 33.

26. Tourtoulon: *Philosophy in the Development of Law*, New York, 1922, Book II, Chapter III.

27. Waugh: Comparison of Oriental and American Student Intelligence. Proceedings of the American Psychological Association. 1920.

28. Weale: *The Conflict of Color.* New York, 1910.

29. Weatherly: The Racial Element in Social Assimilation. Publications of the American Sociological Society, V, 57-76.

30. Woodworth: Racial Differences in Mental Traits. *Science*, N. S. XXI, 1910, 171-186.

1. Interpret the phrase: "Man is not born human."
2. To what extent are racial differences natural and acquired, respectively?
3. In what way do racial temperament and tradition determine national characteristics? To what extent is the religious behavior of the negro determined (a) by temperament, (b) by imitation of white culture? How do you explain Scotch economy, Irish participation in politics, the intellectuality of the Jew, etc.?
4. What is the distinction between racial traits and individual differences?
5. What significance for social psychology is to be found (a) in Boas' anthropometric studies of immigrants and their descendants and (b) in Stevenson's Socio-Anthropometry?
6. Write a critical analysis of Ferguson, Mayo, Odum and Pyle with respect to the subject of racial differences.

Chapter VI

1. Bunnerman: Ueber Pschogene Schmerzen. *Monatschr. f. Psychat. w. Neur.*, XXXIV, 1913, 142–171.
2. Cooley: *Human Nature and the Social Order.* New York, 1902, Chap. II.
3. Jaffa: *Beitrage zur Psychologie der Aussage*, B.I., H.I., p. 79.
4. McDougall: *Introduction to Social Psychology*, 13th ed., Boston, 1918, Chapter XV.
5. Munsterberg: *Psychotherapy.* New York, 1909, Chapter V.
6. Otto: Testimony and Human Nature. *Journal of Criminal Law and Criminology*, IX, 1, 98–104.
7. Pfungst: *Clever Hans* (The Horse of Mr. Von Osten). New York, 1911.
8. Ross: *Social Psychology.* New York, 1913, Chap. II. Also 13th Annual Report of the Bureau of Ethnology, p. 917.
9. Sidis: *The Psychology of Suggestion.* New York, 1898, pp. 88–89.
10. Starbuck: A study of Conversion. *American Journal of Psychology*, VIII, 268–308.
11. Stoll: *Suggestion w. Hypnotismus in der Völkerpsychologie.* Zweite Auflage, Leipzig, 1904, pp. 6, 41.
12. Thomas: *Sex and Society*, Chicago, 1907, p. 311.

13. Titchener: *A Textbook of Psychology*, New York, 1910.
14. van Langenhove: *The Growth of a Legend*, New York, 1916.
15. Varendonc: Les temoinages d'enfants dans un proces retentissant. *Arch. de Psychol.*, XI, 1911, pp. 129, 171.
16. von Gennep: *La Formation des legendes*. Paris, 1910.
17. Washburn: *Animal Mind*. 2d ed., New York, 1917, pp. 257–312.
18. Watson & Raynor: Conditioned Emotional Reactions. *Journal of Educational Psychology*, III, 1920, pp. 1–14.

1. Explain the deadliness of the innuendo.

2. How is it that with faint praise one can damn a rival more than with downright depreciation?

3. Show why, in exchange or diplomacy, the one who best dissembles his estimate of the thing he has and of the thing the other man has is likely to get the better of the bargain.

4. Account for the fact that the best way to get the offer of a coveted position is to affect an indifference to it.

5. Explain why, in coping with men, boldness is so often justified by the outcome.

6. What is the point of the saying, "He doth protest too much?"

7. Assume that the succession of hero types in the development of the boy into the man corresponds to the succession of folk heroes in the rise of a people from barbarism to civilization, account for the correspondence on the ground of the psychology of suggestion and suggestibility?

8. Show why education, custom, tradition and religion displace force in the government of a people.

9. How do you distinguish suggestion from other forms of stimulus?

10. What is meant by the saying that historical figures embody in themselves the emotions and desires of the masses?

11. What are the criteria by which you distinguish so-called imitation responses from responses to suggestion?

CHAPTER VII

1. Aria: Fashion, Its Survivals and Revivals, *Fortnightly Review*, CIV, (1915), 930–937.
2. Clark: The Crowd, *University of Illinois Studies: Psychol. Monog.*, No. 92, XXI, 26–36.
3. Conway: *The Crowd in Peace and War.* New York, 1915.
4. Down: The Rush to the Klondike, *Cornhill Magazine* IV, 1898, 33–43.
5. Ellwood: *Introduction to Social Psychology*, New York, 1917, pp. 237–239.
6. Ellwood: *Introduction to Social Psychology*, New York, 1917, pp. 235–237.
7. Ellwood: *Introduction to Social Psychology*, New York, 1917, pp. 155–157.
8. James: *Principles of Psychology*, New York, 1907, Chap. X.
9. Kroeber: On the Principle of Order in Civilization as Exemplified by Changes of Fashion. *American Anthropologist*, U.S., XXI, 1919, 235–263.
10. Le Bon: *The Crowd.* London, 1897.
11. Martin: *The Behavior of Crowds.* New York, 1920.
12. McDougall: *The Group Mind.* New York, 1920, pp. 264 and 270 and Chap. II.
13. Patrick: The Psychology of Crazes. *Pop. Sci. Monthly*, LVII, (1900), 285–294.
14. Ross: *Social Psychology.* New York, 1913. Chaps. II, IV, V, VI, XVIII and XXII.
15. Shaler: The Law of Fashion. *Atlantic Monthly*, LXI, 386–398.
16. Simmel: The Attraction of Fashion, *International Quarterly*, X, 130–155.
17. Tarde: *The Laws of Imitation*, Translated from the 2d French Ed. by Elsie Clews Parsons. Chap. VII, pp. 244–365.
18. Tawney: The Nature of Crowds. *Psychol. Bull.*, II, 329–333.
19. Wallas: *The Great Society.* New York, 1914, Chap. VIII.
20. Woolbert: The Audience. *Psychol. Monog.*, No. 92, XXI, 1915, 36–54.

1. Why, from the psychologic angle, does the popular orator find it useful in haranguing his audience to:
    (a) Seem to agree with it at the outset?
    (b) Make each one in the audience imagine that he himself is being addressed personally?
    (c) Cut out statistics and formal proof?
    (d) Be an actor.
    (e) Make frequent use of such phrases as "home," "the church," "the fathers," "our country," "our cause," etc.?

2. Distinguish open-mindedness and suggestibility.

3. Does cultural difference or class difference present the greater obstacle to the sweep of an idea or emotion? Why?

4. How do financial and familial responsibilities affect one's responsiveness to the crowd and the mob and their leaders? Why?

5. Does mental epidemic show itself more in the United States in rural or in urban populations? Why?

6. What can be said for and against the guidance of public opinion by the "better classes" and by experts?

7. Distinguish public opinion, advertising and propaganda as means of social control.

8. What is the relation of news to social control?

Chapter VIII

1. Addams: *Democracy and Social Ethics.* 257–258.
2. Baldwin: *Mental Development in the Child and the Race. Methods and Processes.* pp. 308–319. New York, 1895.
3. Chesterton: *Heretics.* 302–303 (Quoted by Ross: Social Psychology, 118–119.)
4. Commons: *Races and Immigrants in America.* Chap. IX, pp. 198–238. New York, 1920.
5. Hall: Morale in War and After. *Psy. Bul.,* Vol. XV, No. 11, Nov. 1918, 361–426.
6. Hall and Allin: The Psychology of Tickling, Laughing, and the Comic. *Amer. Jour. Psychol.,* IX, 1, Oct. 1897, 1–41.
7. James: *Principles of Psychology.* New York, 1907.
8. Koch: *Books and the War,* New York, 1919.
9. Mayo-Smith: Theories of Mixture of Races and Nationalities, *Yale Review,* III, 166–186.

10. Park: Racial Assimilation in Secondary Groups with Particular Reference to the Negro. *Am. Jour. of Sociol.*, XIX, (1913–1914), 606–623.

11. Pillsbury: *Psychology of Nationality and Internationalism.* New York, 1919.

12. Prince: A World Consciousness and Future Peace, *Jour. of Abnor. Psychol.*, XI, 287–304.

13. Ross: *Social Psychology*, New York, 1913, 118–119.

14. Tarde: *The Laws of Imitation*, Translated from the 2d French ed. by Elsie Clews Parsons. New York, 1903.

15. Warren: Social Forces and International Ethics. *International Journal of Ethics*, XXVII, 350–356.

16. Weatherby: The Racial Element in Social Assimilation. *Publications of the American Sociological Society*, V, 57–76.

1. Name three wide-spread conventionalities and describe the psychological roots of each of them.

2. Explain the following: "Social institutions are not founded in similarities any more than they are founded in differences; but in relations, and in the mutual interdependence of the parts."

3. Give an illustration of transition from "morale" to "convention."

4. (*a*) Describe what methods are now in use in a particular relation, in a community with which you are familiar, to develop morale. (*b*) What is the evidence of success, if any?

5. Criticize Pillsbury's views, as quoted in this chapter, concerning the conditions that facilitate the assimilation of immigrants.

CHAPTER IX

1. Allport and Allport: Personality Traits: Their Classification and Measurement. *Jour. of Abnor. Psych. and Social Psych.*, XVI, 1921, 6–40.

2. Aschaffenburg: *Crime and its Repression.* Modern Criminal Science Series, Boston, 1913, pp. 149, ff.

3. Baldwin, J. M.: *Social and Ethical Interpretations in Mental Development*, Chap. XIV, pp. 537–550. New York, 1906.

4. Baldwin, B. T., and Stecher: Mental Growth Curve of Normal and Superior Children. Studied by means of

Consecutive Intelligence Examinations. *Univ. of Iowa Studies in Child Welfare*, II, 1, 1922, pp. 61.

5. Bosanquet: The Psychology of Social Progress. *Internat. Jour. of Ethics*, VII, 1896, 265–281.

6. Bronner: *The Psychology of Special Abilities and Disabilities.* Boston, 1916.

7. Cattell: Families of American Men of Science, *Pop. Sci. Mo.*, 86, 1915, pp. 504–515.

8. Cattell: A Statistical Study of Eminent Men. *Pop. Sci. Mo.*, 74, 1903.

9. Cattell: *The Biographical Dictionary of American Men of Science.*

10. Cattell: A Statistical Study of American Men of Science, III. *Science*, XXIV; also XXXII, 623, 633, 672, 1906 and 1910.

11. Cooley: *The Social Process.* Chap. XXVII, pp. 309–328, New York, 1918.

12. Dewey; Progress. *Internat. Jour. of Ethics*, 26: 1916, 312–318.

13. Dolbear: Precocious Children. *Ped. Sem.*, 19: 1912, 461–491.

14. Downes: Seven Years with Unusually Gifted Pupils. *Psych. Clinic.*, 6: 1912, 13–17.

15. Ellis: *A Study of British Genius.* 1904.

16. Eltinge: *Psychology of War.* Fort Leavenworth, 1918.

17. Galton, et al.: Eugenics, Its Scope and Aims. *Amer. Jour. of Sociol.*, X, 1904.

18. Galton: *Hereditary Genius*, London, 1914.

19. Galton: *English Men of Science.* London, 1874.

20. Harley: Physical Status of the Special Class for Bright Children at the University of Pennsylvania, Summer Session, 1912. *Psych. Clinic.*, 7: March, 1913, 20–23.

21. Ireland: *The Blot upon the Brain: Studies in History and Psychology.* Second Edition, Edinburgh, 1893.

22. Ross: *Social Psychology.* New York, 1913, pp. 300–302.

23. Sakaki: Some Studies on So-called Abnormally Intelligent Pupils. *Psy. Clinic.*, Vol. VI, 1, pp. 18–26.

24. Sterb: The Supernormal Child. *J. Educ. Psych.* 2: 1911, 143–148 and 181–190.

25. Terman: The Intelligence Quotient of Sir Francis Galton. *Amer. Jour. Psych.*, Vol. XXVIII, Apr. 1917, pp. 209–215.

26. Terman: *The Intelligence of School Children*, Chap. X. New York, 1919.

27. Terman: Genius and Stupidity. *Ped. Sem.* 13, 1906, 307–373.

28. Terman: A Preliminary Study of the Psychology and Pedagogy of Leadership. *Ped. Sem.*, XI, 1094, 413–451.

29. Thorndike: Exceptional Children. *Educational Psychology*, Chap. XII, New York, 1903.

30. Todd: *Theories of Social Progress.* New York, 1918.

31. Whipple: *Classes for Gifted Children:* School and Home Education Monographs, No. 1, Bloomington, Ill., 1919.

32. Whipple: The Supernormal Child. *J. Educ. Psych.* 2: 1911, 164, 287.

33. Whipple: *Supernormal Children*, in Cyclop. of Educ., 1913.

34. Woods: *Mental and Moral Heredity in Royalty.* New York, 1906. p. 312.

35. Woods: *The Influence of Monarchs.* Steps in a New Science of History. New York, 1913.

36. Yoder: The Study of the Boyhood of Great Men. *Ped. Sem.* 3: 1894, 134–156.

1. (a) Define what may be called the eugenic, the psychological and the social concepts of progress, respectively.

   (b) Name a leading representative of each conception.

   (c) Are their views mutually inconsistent? Explain.

2. How can progress be controlled under each of the foregoing conceptions?

3. How is our instinctive nature related to progress?

4. Discuss thoroughly the value of illustrating the progress of a race by submitting tables of statistics showing the race's economic improvement.

5. Describe, from as many angles as possible, two mature leaders in a community with which you are familiar.

6. Select four students who are recognized as leaders and four who are not so recognized. Have four persons, independently, rate each of the eight according to their personality traits. Put results into convenient graphic or tabular form and compare. (See Allport and Allport, *Jour. of Abnor. Psych. and Soc. Psych.*, XVI, 1921, 6–40.)

CHAPTER X

1. Abbott: Crime and the War. *Jour. of Crim. Law and Criminol.*, X, 1, May, 1918, 1–32.
2. Adler: Unemployment and Personality — A Study of Psychopathic Cases. *Mental Hygiene*, I, 1917, 16–24.
3. Adler: Publications of the Department of Public Welfare, Springfield, Illinois, 1922.
4. Ayres: *Laggards in Our Schools*, New York, 1909.
5. Ayres: *Cleveland Education Survey*, Vol. 3; Cleveland, 1917.
6. Bailey: Psychiatry in the Army. *Harper's Magazine*, No. 806, July, 1917, 251–257.
7. Bronner: *Special Abilities and Disabilities*. Boston, 1917.
8. Campbell: *The Southern Highlander and His Homeland*, Chap. VI. New York, 1921.
9. Doll: Criminal Psychology: *The Training School Bulletin*, April, 1921, 1–10.
10. Doll: A Classification of Defective Delinquents. *Jour. of Crim. Law and Criminol.*, XII, 3, 1921, 360–368.
11. Doll: The Comparative Intelligence of Prisoners. *Jour. of Crim. Law and Criminol.*, XI, 2, 1920, 191–197.
12. Garofalo: *Criminology:* The Modern Criminal Science Series, Part I, Chap. I. Translated from the First Italian and the Fifth French editions by Robert Wyness Millar; Boston, 1914.
13. Goddard: *Human Efficiency and Levels of Intelligence.* Princeton University Press, 1920.
14. Gross: *Criminal Psychology.* The Modern Criminal Science Series. Translated from the Fourth German edition by Dr. Horace M. Kallen. Boston, 1909.
15. Healy: *The Individual Delinquent*, Boston, 1915.
16. Healy: *The Practical Value of Scientific Study of Juvenile Delinquents.* Children's Bureau Publication, No. 96, Washington, 1922.
17. *Memoirs of the National Academy of Sciences*, Vol. XV, Part III, Chap. XV; 1921.
18. *Memoirs of the National Academy of Sciences*, Vol. XV, Part III, Chap. IX; 1921.
19. *Memoirs of the National Academy of Sciences*, Vol. XV, Part III, Chap. XII; 1921.
20. Parker: *The Casual Laborer and Other Essays*, New York, 1920.

21. Pollock: Mental Diseases in New York State during the War Period. *Mental Hygiene*, III, 2, April, 1919, 253–257.

22. Salmon: Some New Problems for Psychiatric Research in Delinquency. *Jour. of Crim. Law and Criminol.*, X, 3, 1919, 375–384.

23. Southard: The Modern Specialist in Unrest: A Place for the Psychiatrist in Industry. *Mental Hygiene*, IV, 3. 550–563.

24. Southard: The Mental Hygiene of Industry. *Bul. of the Mass. Dept. of Ment. Diseases*, V, 1, Jan. 1921, 57–77.

25. Southard: Trade Unionism and Temperament: The Psychiatric Point of View in Industry. *Bul. of the Mass. Dept. of Mental Diseases*, V, 1, Jan. 1921, 78–93.

26. Spargo: *The Psychology of Bolshevism.* New York, 1919.

27. Stoddard: *The New World of Islam*, Chap. VII, New York, 1921.

28. Stone: A Comparative Study of 399 Inmates of the Indiana Reformatory and 653 Men of the United States Army. *Jour. of Crim. Law and Criminol.*, XII, 2, 1921, 238–257.

29. Strayer: *Age and Grade Census of Schools and Colleges*, U.S. Bur. of Ed. Bul., 1911, No. 5.

30. Thorndike: *The Elimination of Pupils from School.* U.S. Bur. of Ed. Bul., 1907, No. 4.

1. Recall a particular instance of failure in social adaptation — an individual with whom you have been acquainted who has been eliminated from school, become delinquent or criminal, or pronouncedly at unrest with respect to his occupation — to see if you can find in it any indication of one or more of the factors referred to in the text.

2. What does the psychology of play suggest as to means of preventing the mal-adjustments referred to in this chapter?

3. Describe as fully as you can your own or others' behavior in the face of "baulked disposition" or an unfulfilled wish in the sense of this chapter.

4. Describe the possible consequences to society of the doctrine that all criminals are feeble-minded or insane — assuming such a doctrine.

5. Account in as much detail as possible for the great variation between present-day estimates of the frequency of feeble-

mindedness among criminals and those that were extant prior to 1917.

6. Describe one or more reconstructions in any department of human activity that in your judgment would relieve, somewhat, that irritation of individuals that is assumed to facilitate mal-adjustment of any form.

Chapter XI

1. Bertillon: Birth Rates in European Cities. *Bull. Inst. Internat. Stat.*, 11, 1899, 163–176. (Holmes, P. 132–133.)
2. Fosdick: *Our Machine Civilization.* Privately printed, 1922.
3. Gillette: *Constructive Rural Sociology.* 2d ed., New York, 1916.
4. Hollingworth: *The Influence of Caffeine on Mental and Motor Efficiency.* New York, 1912.
5. Holmes: *The Trend of the Race.* Chaps. VII, XIV, XVI. New York, 1921.
6. Morgan: See Watson. *Psychology from the Standpoint of the Behaviorist*, p. 380.
7. Rittenhouse: The Increasing Mortality from Degenerative Diseases. *Pop. Sci. Mo.*, 82, 1913, 376–380.
8. Rivers: *The Influence of Alcohol and other Drugs on Fatigue.* London, 1908.
9. Watson: *Psychology from the Standpoint of the Behaviorist.* New York, 1919, Chap. X.

INDEX

329

INDEX

Sense of Social Unity, 13–26; unity, 48, 50; unity dependent upon activity, 46

Sex factors in suggestibility, race and, 134–136

Sidis, describing a mob erroneously called an audience, 163–165; on suggestibility 127, 128

Similarity in bodily form, 20

Slavic immigrants, 89

Smith, on proportion of feeble-mindedness, 67

Social, continuity, 22–23; life, Instincts and their rôle in, 36–43; mind, 17, 206; mind an unnecessary concept, 25–26; Mal-Adjustment evidenced in mental disease, 243–255; motives, 27–64; progress, 202–232; relations, 11; unity, 10, 11, 52; unity, sense of, 13–26; not intellectualistic, 23

Solidarity, 13

Southard, on industrial unrest in England, 262–269

Spargo, on Bolshevism, 268

Spirit of the age, 185–187

Stanford-Binet examinations, 72

Starbuck, on suggestibility of women, 135

Statistical studies of men of science, 221–227

Statistics, 12

Stevenson, on the Teutonic, Mediterranean and Alpine races, 101, 102

Stimulus-Response, 15

Stoddard, on status of oriental women as affecting the education of the youth, 104, 105; on the adaptability of the Indian people to occupations, 239–241

Stoll, on the witch trial at Zug, 129

Strong, on the intelligence of the negro, 90, 91

Stuart, Gilbert, 7

Suggestibility, acquired disposition and, 138–142; as dissociation, 127, 128; due to superstitious nature, 128–130; of the American Indian, *Ross* on, 134; of women, *Starbuck* on, 135; race and sex factors in, 134–136; *Sidis* on, 127, 128; suggestion and, 12–154; suspicion and, 136–138

Suggestible disposition, testimony of adults illustrating the, 131–134; nature, testimony of children illustrating the, 130, 131

Suggestion, and Suggestibility, 122–154; definition of by *Bunnerman,* 123, 124; definition of by *Titchener,* 122, 123, 124; factors limiting the play of, 153; mass effects of, 142–154

Super-consciousness, 11

Superior children, 227–232; Professor *Terman's* summary of the nature of, 231

Superstitious nature, suggestibility due to, 128–130

Suspicion and Suggestibility, 136–138

Swift, on the reflex eye-wink, 39

Technical education, 300, 301

Terman, 228, 229

Terman's summary of the nature of superior children, 231

Testimony, experiment in Professor *von Liszt's* School of Criminology, 132–134; of